SEQUOIA National Park

From the book...

Between the western foothills at the edge of the San Joaquin Valley and the high desert of Owens Valley to the east, the southern Sierra sprawls across California, reaching a zenith in altitude and in spectacular scenery.

Discouraged by the rugged landscape, Europeans knew little about the area until settlers in the San Joaquin Valley began to venture into the mountains in the mid-1850s.

While much of nearby Yosemite sees a more vehicle-oriented tourist crowd, the main way to see the incredible sights in and around Sequoia and Kings Canyon is by foot or by horseback.

Parts of two of the most famous long-distance trails are found within the region, the John Muir and the High Sierra, exposing backpackers to some of the most stupendous scenery in the range.

Ordinary small mammals one might expect to encounter include deer mouse, pocket gopher, vole, shrew, broad-handed mole, pika, chipmunk, chickaree, Belding ground squirrel, golden-mantled ground squirrel, northern flying squirrel, mountain beaver, white-tailed jackrabbit, and yellow-bellied marmot.

SEQUOIA
National Park

A COMPLETE
HIKER'S GUIDE

MIKE WHITE

 WILDERNESS PRESS · BERKELEY, CA

Sequoia National Park: A Complete Hiker's Guide

1st EDITION January 2004

Copyright © 2004 by Mike White

Front cover photo © 2004 by Larry Ulrich
Back cover photo © 2004 by Mike White
Interior photos, except where noted, by Mike White
Maps: Mike White and Fineline Maps
Illustrations: Danny Woodward
Cover and book design: Larry B. Van Dyke

ISBN 0-89997-327-2
UPC 7-19609-97327-0

Manufactured in the United States of America

Published by: **Wilderness Press**
               1200 5th Street
               Berkeley, CA 94710
               (800) 443-7227; FAX (510) 558-1696
               info@wildernesspress.com
               www.wildernesspress.com

Visit our website for a complete listing of our books and for ordering information.

Cover photos: Mountain dogwood and giant sequoias at Giant Forest *(front)*;
                  On the Mt. Whitney Trail *(back)*
Frontispiece: Founders Group, on the Circle Meadow Trail

Dedication

True friendship is a priceless treasure. For over 30 years my wife and I have been abundantly rewarded with the tremendous fortune of knowing our dearest friends, Tic and Terrie Long. Together the four of us have shared dreams and heartaches, laughs and tears, adventures and mishaps, and triumphs and struggles. May God in His grace fill the rest of our days with many more moments together and an even deeper friendship.

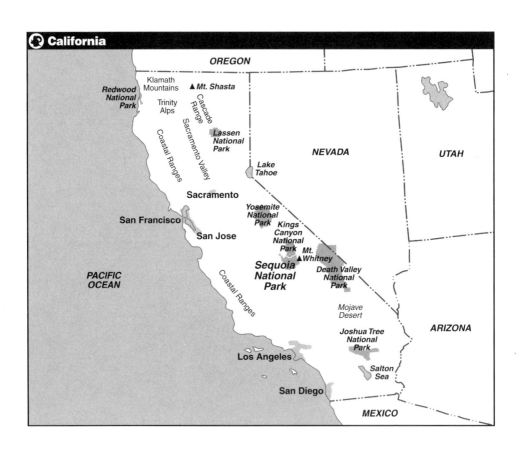

California

OREGON

Redwood National Park

Klamath Mountains

Trinity Alps

▲ Mt. Shasta

Cascade Range

Sacramento Valley

Coastal Ranges

Lassen National Park

Lake Tahoe

NEVADA

UTAH

Sacramento

San Francisco

Yosemite National Park

San Jose

Kings Canyon National Park

Mt. ▲ Whitney

Sequoia National Park

Death Valley National Park

PACIFIC OCEAN

Coastal Ranges

Mojave Desert

ARIZONA

Joshua Tree National Park

Los Angeles

Salton Sea

San Diego

MEXICO

Contents

Emerald Lake, on the Lakes Trail

Acknowledgments

First of all, I extend my thanks to the Creator for the majesty of His creation and for granting me the privilege of experiencing much of the best parts first hand. Secondly, none of my projects would ever realize fruition if not for the never-ending support of my wife Robin, who believes in me even when I'm not very believable.

Then, there's the staff at Wilderness Press, including Mike Jones, Jannie Dresser, Elaine Merrill, and Roslyn Bullas, with whom I worked most directly on this project, and all the support staff that somehow fashioned my manuscript, photographs and maps into a real book. Thanks also to David Disbrow for his photograph of Trail Camp. I extend a special thanks to Tom Winnett, the founder and patriarch of Wilderness Press, who, with his usual care and expert eye, performed the editing.

Although I spent many a lonely night in campgrounds and backcountry campsites, there was a group of friends who blessed me with their presence on several of the many outings necessary for completion of the fieldwork. Among them are Robin White, Stephen White, Carmel Bang, Tic Long, Andy Montessoro, Bob Redding, Chris Taylor, Dal and Candy Hunter, Lisa Kafchinski, Art Barkley, Joe Tavares, Kim Small, Darrin Munson, and the youth group from RCF. Thanks for keeping me somewhat sane in the midst of so much isolation.

Several National Park and Forest Service rangers and personnel were very helpful in providing information during the course of this project. Although most of them remain anonymous, they were always courteous and informative. Special thanks are extended to Kris Fister, former Public Information Officer for Sequoia and Kings Canyon national parks, and Chief Park Interpreter, Ranger Bill Tweed, who were invaluable in providing needed help on a variety of items.

Preface

A couple of years ago, I had a conversation with Caroline Winnett concerning my next guidebook project for Wilderness Press. At the time, Caroline was charting the course of the company for her recently retired father and Wilderness Press founder, Tom Winnett. Simultaneously, we came up with the same possibility: creating a comprehensive guide to Kings Canyon and Sequoia national parks that would be roughly similar to the highly popular *Yosemite National Park*, written by Jeff Schaffer. When summer rolled around, I began fieldwork, undertaking several hikes and backpacks, initially on the east side of the Sierra. During the next two seasons, I explored the remaining areas of the parks and surrounding wilderness areas on countless day hikes and extended backpacks.

Once I had hiked the last mile of trail, I shifted my focus to completing the manuscript, which I submitted for editing. After wading through the resulting bulky tome, the staff at Wilderness Press debated the pros and cons of publishing the guide in a single volume versus restructuring the text to create two separate books. After careful consideration, they decided to make two guides, one for the region in and around Sequoia National Park and a companion volume for the territory in and around Kings Canyon National Park.

The Park Service completed years of restoration work at Giant Forest shortly before *Sequoia National Park: A Complete Hiker's Guide* went to press. The last of the unnecessary structures have been removed, and finishing touches were put on the Giant Forest Museum and the refurbished trails and parking lots nearby. By the beginning of tourist season in 2003, Giant Forest was ready for visitors, with a new parking area and trailhead for the General Sherman Tree in the works. A revitalized shuttle-bus system serving the most popular destinations is due in 2005.

Most likely, you will not have the privilege of hiking all 62 of the trips described herein, as I had the blessed good fortune of doing, but my hope is that whichever trails you undertake, they will be as rewarding for you as they were for me.

—Mike White
August 2003

Foxtail pine at Little Claire Lake, Soda Creek Trail

CHAPTER 1

Introduction

Although this guide and the companion volume, *Kings Canyon National Park: A Complete Hiker's Guide*, correspond to the federal designation of the area as two separate parks, Sequoia and adjoining Kings Canyon national parks are managed as one entity. Encompassing 402,108 and 459,995 acres respectively, Sequoia and Kings Canyon national parks, along with the surrounding national forest lands, contain the bulk of the southern Sierra Nevada. The overwhelming majority of this area is managed by the National Park Service and the U.S. Forest Service as wilderness, providing hikers, backpackers, equestrians, and mountaineers with a virtually unlimited number of possibilities for enjoyment.

Sequoia and Kings Canyon national parks and the surrounding region are marked by extremes. Mt. Whitney, along the eastern fringe of Sequoia, is the highest mountain in the continental United States, at 14,494 feet. The 10,760 feet between the summit and the town of Lone Pine is the greatest relief between mountaintop and base in the lower 48 states. Just west of the confluence of the South and Middle Forks of the Kings River, the canyon becomes one of the deepest gorges in North America, measured at over 8000 feet from river level to the top of Spanish Mountain. Giant Forest, in western Sequoia, is home to the largest living tree on earth, the General Sherman tree, a giant sequoia with a volume of more than 52,500 cubic feet.

The entire Sierra Nevada range is some 450 miles long, between 50 and 80 miles in width, and contains 13 peaks over 14,000 feet high. In addition to its extreme physical features, the Sequoia and Kings Canyon region includes some of the most sublime country in the Sierra Nevada. Between the western foothills at the edge of the San Joaquin Valley and the high desert of Owens Valley to the east, the southern Sierra sprawls across California, reaching a zenith in altitude and in spectacular scenery. Besides Mt. Whitney, the rugged Sierra crest of Kings Canyon and Sequoia offers a dozen other peaks over 14,000 feet and scads more 12,000- and 13,000-foot mountains of equally impressive beauty.

Kings Canyon—the gorge of the South Fork Kings River from Lewis Creek upstream to Bubbs Creek—isn't the only deep canyon in the region; the major rivers of the Kern, North, and Middle Fork Kings, and Kaweah all flow down other canyons that are also thousands of feet deep. In the high country, these streams tumble down characteristic U-shaped canyons that have been carved over time through rugged granite. As they near the foothills, during peak season these rivers become rushing torrents of water, careening through deep V-shaped gorges of multi-hued metamorphic rock.

**SEQUOIA & KINGS CANYON:
LAND OF EXTREMES**

Highest mountain in 48 states:
Mt. Whitney, 14,494 feet

Greatest relief in 48 states:
Lone Pine to Mt. Whitney,
10,760 feet

**One of the deepest gorges
in North America:**
Kings River, 8000+ feet

Largest living tree:
General Sherman sequoia,
52,000+ cubic feet

Major rivers in the Sequoia area include the South Fork San Joaquin; North, Middle, and South Fork Kings River; North, Marble, Middle, and East Fork Kaweah River.

The only place on the entire globe where the giant sequoia (*Sequoiadendron giganteum*) occurs naturally is the western side of the Sierra Nevada, between 5000 and 8200 feet. Of the 75 giant sequoia groves in the Sierra, only eight are located outside of the region, north of the Kings River. Most of the largest trees are found within the Sequoia and Kings Canyon area, including the top five, General Sherman, Washington, General Grant, President, and Lincoln. Several of the most impressive groves and largest individual sequoias within the parks are easily accessible to both tourists and hikers.

Along with high peaks, deep canyons, and huge trees, the Sequoia and Kings Canyon landscape hosts a diverse cross-section of outstanding terrain. The foothills region in the extreme southwest corner of Sequoia is a protected pocket of oak woodland and chaparral, a habitat that is often subject to urban development in other areas of California. Lush woodlands of mixed conifers carpet the western slope of the Sierra, above the foothills. Here are the famed giant sequoia groves, and stands of old-growth forest, wildflower-covered meadows, and gurgling streams. Above the forest belt, high mountain lakes, towering granite peaks, sharp ridges, and sweeping meadows crown the range. The southern Sierra truly offers some of the most magnificent scenery in North America.

Only a handful of roads penetrate the fringes of the Sequoia and Kings Canyon region on both the west and the east; the overwhelming majority of the area is roadless. Thanks to an extensive area of rugged terrain, no major highways cross the Sierra between the seasonally open Tioga Pass Road in Yosemite and the all-weather route of Highway 178 well south of the parks. Of the nearly 900,000 acres of land within the two parks, over 90% is managed as wilderness. Combined with the acreage from the surrounding John Muir, Golden Trout, Jennie Lakes, and Monarch wilderness areas, these protected lands create a vast, unbroken chain of exquisite backcountry. More than 800 miles of trail lure sightseers, hikers, and backpackers away from the roads and into the picturesque terrain of the parks.

The Sequoia and Kings Canyon region is a hiker's and backpacker's paradise. While much of nearby Yosemite sees a more vehicle-oriented tourist crowd, the main way to see the incredible sights in and around Sequoia and Kings Canyon is by foot or by horseback. An extensive network of short trails provides day hikers with a wide range of opportunities to explore diverse environments, from foothill canyons to giant sequoia groves to alpine lakes.

WORLD'S LARGEST SEQUOIAS:

1. **General Sherman**, 52,508 cubic feet

2. **Washington**, 47,850 cubic feet

3. **General Grant**, 46,608 cubic feet

4. **President**, 45,148 cubic feet

5. **Lincoln**, 44,471 cubic feet

However, the ultimate experience is to backpack through the mountainous terrain on some of the High Sierra's most excellent backcountry trails. Parts of two of the most famous long-distance trails are found within the region, the John Muir and the High Sierra, exposing backpackers to some of the most stupendous scenery in the range. An abundance of lesser-known routes leads travelers through deep canyons, over high divides, around spectacular meadows, and past picturesque lakes. This vast backcountry of the southern Sierra is one of the nation's most treasured resources.

Monarch butterfly

Human History

Native Americans and Early Settlement

The Native Americans who lived in the Sequoia and Kings Canyon region were divided into four separate tribes—the Monache, Tubatulabal, Owens Valley Paiute, and Yokut. These groups traveled extensively within the area, hunting, trading, and establishing summer camps. Several sites within the parks give evidence of some of these settlements; Hospital Rock is perhaps the most visited by modern-day tourists.

Early explorers, such as Jedediah Smith and John C. Fremont, avoided the difficult terrain and high mountains characteristic of the Sequoia/Kings Canyon region in favor of easier traverses across the Sierra to the north and the south. Discouraged by the rugged landscape, Europeans knew little about the area until settlers in the San Joaquin Valley began to venture into the mountains in the mid-1850s.

Hale D. Tharp, who established a ranch near the future site of Three Rivers, was perhaps the first Anglo to see the Giant Forest. In 1856 he headed east into the hills at the invitation of some friendly Potwishas to see the rumored Big Trees and scout a summer range for his livestock. He followed the Middle Fork Kaweah River to Moro Rock and then climbed up to Log Meadow in Giant Forest. A couple of years later, Tharp retraced his route to Giant Forest, continued into the Kings River area, and returned to his ranch via the East and South Forks of the Kaweah. Eventually, he grazed his cattle each summer in Log Meadow, using a fallen and burned out sequoia as a makeshift cabin.

Increased settlement in the San Joaquin Valley spelled doom for the Native Americans, as exposure to various illnesses devastated their population. Surviving members of the four tribes either crossed the Sierra to the less desired eastern desert or attempted

Columbine Lake, Sawtooth Pass Trail

to adapt to the growing culture of the white man on the west side.

As time wore on, Europeans came to Sequoia and Kings Canyon in increasing numbers, encouraged by gold discoveries to the north, the prospect of an unending supply of lumber, and the San Joaquin Valley's fertile ranchland.

Exploitation of Resources

Mining proved to be a disappointment to the hordes of miners who sought their fortune in the southern Sierra. Mineral King, perhaps the best known mineral site in the region, was imagined to be the Sutter's Mill of the south, but it never managed to produce a significant amount of minerals, and has only been commercially viable as a recreation area in the 20th and 21st centuries. The passage of time proved that the southern Sierra did not contain the mineral wealth that had sparked the gold and silver rushes in the north.

Lumbermen turned out to be equally as disappointed as the miners. The discovery of giant sequoias in the southern Sierra seemed to bode well for entrepreneurs who anticipated enormous profits from the lumber. But despite the positive speculation, the wood proved to be too brittle for most construction purposes. With the immense effort required to fell the Big Trees, logging the sequoias became a commercially nonviable enterprise. The mills that were built never made much of a profit—some even lost money—and most of the wood ended up being used for fence posts or shakes. Unfortunately, most lumber companies did not realize the poor quality of sequoia lumber until it was too late for a number of groves. Converse Basin, perhaps at one time the finest stand of the big trees in the Sierra, saw the destruction of every sequoia in the basin except for one lone survivor— the Boole Tree—which turned out to be the eighth largest giant sequoia in the world.

Cattle and sheep grazing prospered in the San Joaquin Valley, which then led to growing competition for rangeland. In order to feed their herds and flocks adequately, cattle ranchers and sheepherders went farther afield in search of green summer pasture, eventually inflicting severe environmental destruction on the western Sierra. Fires, set to clear forest debris to make easier passage for stock, ran unchecked throughout the range. In addition, thousands of hooves trampled sensitive meadows each season. The resulting erosion from the fires and the animals produced inevitable watershed degradation.

California Geographical Survey

About the same time miners and loggers were exploiting the area's natural resources, the California Geological Survey began exploration of the High Sierra under the leadership of Josiah D. Whitney. The survey's plan was to ascend high peaks and obtain measurements that would allow accurate mapping of the as yet unmapped High Sierra. As part of the 1864 survey, William H. Brewer led Clarence King, Richard D. Cotter, James T. Gardiner, and Charles F. Hoffman from Visalia to a base camp at Big Meadow. From there the party proceeded eastward into the Sierra, climbing and naming Mt. Silliman along the Silliman Crest and Mt. Brewer on the Great Western Divide.

From a campsite near Mt. Brewer, King and Cotter left the rest of the party to make a multi-day attempt on Mt. Whitney. Although they failed to reach the range's highest peak, they did manage to scale Mt. Tyndall (14,018′), a mere 6 miles northwest of Mt. Whitney. After the climb, the party reunited near Mt. Brewer before returning to Big Meadow.

Undeterred by the failed attempt to reach Mt. Whitney, King tried again, leading a small party from Three Rivers up the recently built Hockett Trail to the Kern River. They followed the Kern north for several miles before veering away toward the mountain, where their summit bid fell short by 300–400 vertical feet.

Following his second unsuccessful attempt on Whitney, King joined the resupplied and expanded survey party at Big Meadow to explore the Kings River region, which the party would compare favorably with Yosemite Valley. After explorations of the South and Middle forks and the Monarch Divide separating the two gorges, the party traveled eastward through the heart of Kings Canyon country by way of Bubbs Creek, crossing the crest at Kearsarge Pass and descending to the town of Fort Independence.

From Independence, the group journeyed north up the Owens Valley, recrossing the Sierra crest at Mono Pass (in the south) before establishing a base camp on the west side of the range at Vermilion Valley (current site of Lake Edison). The exact route is undetermined, but the survey headed south toward the LeConte Divide, from where Cotter, along with a soldier named Spratt, made a 36-hour assault on Mt. Goddard, turning back approximately 300 feet below the summit. After yet another failed summit bid, the party returned to Vermilion Valley and headed north to Wawona, concluding their survey for the year.

The Brewer Party was the first group to develop a significant understanding of the topography, botany, and geology of the High Sierra. In addition to the scientific findings, the survey named several significant features, including Mt. Whitney, the highest peak in the range and in the continental United States. The California Geological Survey made a more limited expedition along the east side of the range in 1870 before being disbanded in 1874.

Seeds of Preservation

Over his lifetime, John Muir made nine separate excursions into the backcountry of Sequoia and Kings Canyon, ultimately increasing public awareness of the beauty and majesty of the region as a whole and of the giant sequoias in particular. An increasing number of concerned citizens joined

Muir to champion the cause of protecting the unique character of the region, including George W. Stewart, the youthful city editor of one of Visalia's newspapers. Eventually national and international figures lent their voices to the idea of setting aside this area as parkland.

As ranching and farming increased in the San Joaquin Valley, so did the demand for irrigation. Watershed degradation brought on by logging, grazing, and mining in the southern Sierra conflicted with the agricultural needs of the ranchers and farmers downstream. Concern over water issues combined with a developing preservationist ethic to create growing opposition to unmitigated consumption of the region's natural resources and the destruction of recreational areas.

The first official step towards the establishment of a national park in the region occurred in 1880, when Theodore Wagner, United States Surveyor General for California, suspended 4 square miles of Grant Grove, prohibiting anyone from filing a land claim. Unfortunately, a 160-acre claim had already been filed adjacent to the grove. Wilsonia remains in private hands to this day. Although little progress was made in subsequent years, the seeds of a grand idea had been planted.

The Kaweah Colony

A group of socialist utopians from San Francisco created one of the most colorful chapters in the history of the region. Armed with a big dream, a heady dose of gumption, and a limited supply of capital, thirty-some members of the Cooperative Land and Colonization Association filed claims on nearly 6000 acres of prime timberland in Giant Forest. As a way to fund their utopian society, the colonists planned to build a road from near Three Rivers to a mill site in the vicinity of their timber claims, where they would harvest the timber and mill it for sale.

A certain amount of controversy swirled around the legality of the colonists'

land claims, which became an ongoing dilemma. Despite the brewing controversy, by the end of the summer of 1886 nearly 160 colonists were camped along the North Fork Kaweah River, ready to begin construction on their wagon road. Idealism and optimism reigned within the colony as the road was built over the next 4 years. Despite the sole use of hand tools, the construction and grade of the road were quite remarkable. The colonists coaxed a steam tractor they named Ajax to a saddle at the end of the road and erected a portable sawmill in an attempt to turn logs into lumber. However, a variety of complications prohibited the colonists from fully realizing their dream, including inexperience, internal squabbles, insufficient funds, and inability to secure full title to their land claims. By 1892, their dream had ended and the remaining trustees officially dissolved the colony.

A creeklet of snow melt flows down from Alta Peak

Although the utopian dream of the Kaweah Colony was short-lived, their road had a much longer life. Eventually extended by the U.S. Army from Colony Mill into Giant Forest, the road opened to one-way traffic in 1903 and served as the principal access to Sequoia for the next few decades.

Creation of Sequoia and General Grant National Parks

While the Kaweah colonists were busy building their road, political winds had shifted in Washington D.C. as a more development-oriented Department of Interior took over. The General Land Office reopened several townships west of Mineral King for private sale in 1889, which alarmed Stewart and others sympathetic toward preserving these resources. The tract included the Garfield Grove, one of the finest giant sequoia stands in the southern Sierra, and expansive Hockett Meadows. In response to this threat, Stewart vigorously courted public opinion and maneuvered through political channels to pass a bill on September 25, 1890, that set aside 76 square miles of Sierra forest as a public park.

Mystery surrounds the next step toward the creation of Sequoia and Kings Canyon national parks. Unbeknownst to Stewart and his group, another bill came before Congress to establish a national park for Yosemite, a mere six days following the passage of the original bill for Sequoia. Attached to the Yosemite measure was the addition of five townships to Sequoia, including the area around Giant Forest, and four sections surrounding Grant Grove. No one seems to know for certain who was behind this bill, or how the size of the land increased by 500% from the original proposal; however, on October 1, 1890, Yosemite National Park and General Grant National Park were born, and Sequoia National Park was greatly enlarged. Speculation pointed toward Daniel K. Zumwalt, an agent of the Southern Pacific Railroad, as being behind the bill, but the motivation remains unclear.

Management of the new parks became problematic the following spring. Captain Joseph H. Dorst and the Fourth Cavalry had the unenviable task of protecting the area, although the mission of the new national parks was not clearly defined. Most of the first summer was spent dealing with the Kaweah colonists, who had rather unjustly been denied their claims in Giant Forest. A smaller contingent resurfaced near Mineral King to log sequoias at the leased Atwell Mill. The government initially took issue with the practice, but after harassing the colonists for much of the summer, it decided that the mill was located on private land and was a perfectly legal operation. However, the colonists proved to be inexperienced and failed to turn a profit. By the time the lease on Atwell Mill came up for renewal the following year, the colony had disbanded. During the remainder of the summer and into the fall, Dorst and his troops explored the parks, dealing with problems of logging, grazing, and squatting.

Stewart, Muir, and others continued their push to put more land under federal protection. As a result, in 1893, President Harrison signed a presidential proclamation creating the Sierra Forest Reserve, which withdrew most of the central and southern Sierra from private sale. The Sierra Forest Reserve was reclassified as Sequoia National Forest in 1905 and placed under the jurisdiction of the Department of Agriculture, which was more concerned with resource management (grazing, mining, and logging) than preservation. During the first part of the 20th century, the idea of a large national park for the southern Sierra was still alive, but very little progress was made toward its creation.

With limited success, the military continued to protect the parks until 1914, when Walter Fry became the first civilian superintendent of General Grant and Sequoia national parks. By then the Colony

Mill Road had been extended into Giant Forest and the Mt. Whitney Power Company had constructed several hydro-electric power plants on branches of the Kaweah River. Aside from those improvements, the area was still virtually undeveloped. Cattle grazing, private inholdings, lack of access, and poor facilities plagued the region.

The Reign of the National Park Service

In 1916 Congress created the National Park Service and Californian Stephen T. Mather was appointed the first director. Mather was quite familiar with the Sequoia region, having organized an expedition of notable figures to traverse the range in 1915. Armed with first-hand knowledge of the area and a Park Service mandate for conservation and enjoyment of the national parks, Mather ushered in a new era in park management.

Two of the most important directives from the Park Service regarding the Sequoia area were the acquisition of private lands within the existing park and the expansion of the park boundaries to include the High Sierra and Kings Canyon. Acquiring private lands was a fairly easy proposition compared to that of park enlargement, which drew opposition from cattlemen, hunters, and Mineral King property owners. Other opponents included the Los Angeles Bureau of Power and Light, which wanted to construct hydroelectric dams at Cedar Grove and in Tehipite Valley; the San Joaquin Light and Power Company, with similar aspirations; and the Forest Service, which was reluctant to give up lands that had mineral, timber, and grazing potential. A scaled-down proposal was passed in 1926, which expanded the park eastward over the Sierra crest, but excluded Mineral King and Kings Canyon.

By 1926, the Generals Highway had opened from Ash Mountain to Giant Forest, replacing the old Colony Mill Road. Nine years later the road was extended to

Grant Grove. Easier public access into Sequoia led to a dramatic rise in park visitation and a need for additional development of park infrastructure, including water, sewage, and trash systems. In addition to improving the roads and utilities, an extensive network of trails was built (including parts of the John Muir and High Sierra trails), campgrounds were improved, a variety of government and public structures were erected, and a concessionaire monopoly was created to cater to the increased tourist trade. Completion of the highway from Grant Grove to Kings Canyon accelerated development of campgrounds along the South Fork Kings River, but more intensive projects were held in abeyance until the issue of dams along the Kings River was settled.

Initially, the park improvements seemed a good and necessary way to accommodate growing numbers of tourists. However, as visitation and development continued to increase, traffic jams, congestion, and overcrowding began to characterize Giant Forest and to a lesser extent Grant Grove during the height of summer. A meteoric rise in visitors coupled with runaway development threatened the long-term health of the sequoia groves.

Additional threats to the parks surfaced in the form of vegetation and wildlife management. Fire suppression was the rule of the day, allowing a buildup of fuel for potentially disastrous future fires. The policy that prohibited cattle grazing within the parks was reversed, opening the door for inevitable damage to resources. Wildlife management suffered similar setbacks. In the 1920s, the last grizzly bear in California was shot and killed at Horse Corral Meadows, near the northwest fringe of Sequoia National Park. Increased conflicts between humans and black bears put "problem" bears at risk. The evening garbage feast at Bear Hill, where marauding bears put on a show for tourists at Sequoia's garbage dump, seemed emblematic of the times.

Colonel John R. White, superintendent of Sequoia National Park from 1920 to 1938 and 1941 to 1947, initiated a philosophical shift that was reflected in efforts to reduce visitation impact at Giant Forest. He placed limits on future development and moved many of the government structures to other areas, but he largely failed to limit the presence of concessionaires. One of his most fortuitous accomplishments in backcountry preservation was the defeat of several proposed roads, including two trans-Sierra links, one from Cedar Grove to Independence and another between Porterville and Lone Pine. Col. White also squelched the Sierra Way, a mountain highway planned to connect Yosemite and Sequoia, with a link between Giant Forest and Mineral King via Redwood Meadow.

The Creation of Kings Canyon National Park

While Sequoia National Park confronted rampant problems at Giant Forest, the fight to preserve Kings Canyon escalated. Interior Secretary Harold Ickes put forth a proposal in 1935 to create Kings Canyon National Park and manage it primarily as wilderness. Opposition came from four distinct groups. San Joaquin Valley businessmen saw extensive commercial potential in Kings Canyon, which creation of a national park would prohibit. The Forest Service favored a multiple-use approach and was reluctant to give up control of the area. Central Valley ranchers were concerned about how the park would affect steady irrigation supplies. Finally, both the Los Angeles Bureau of Power and Light and the San Joaquin Light and Power Corporation were competing for water supplies and hydroelectric-power generating sites.

Compromises were eventually made to secure passage of the bill, the potentially most significant one being the exclusion of Cedar Grove and Tehipite Valley from the park, leaving the door open for future dams on the South and Middle Forks of the Kings River. Ranchers were assuaged by the promise to construct the Pine Flat Reservoir, and commercial interests were assured of some development in Kings Canyon. After some political intrigue between two local congressmen, Franklin D. Roosevelt signed the bill that established Kings Canyon National Park on March 4, 1940, creating a vast area of protected wilderness. Included within the new park were the old General Grant National Park and Redwood Mountain. In 1965, Kings Canyon and Tehipite Valley were officially added to Kings Canyon National Park, removing the threat of hydroelectric dams on the Kings River system.

The Battle for Mineral King

After the establishment of Kings Canyon National Park, controversy began to swirl to the south. Responding to demands from the public for additional recreational facilities, in 1949 the multiple-use-oriented Forest Service began seeking proposals from private developers for a ski resort at Mineral King. A suitable developer with the necessary capital wasn't found until 1966, when the Walt Disney Company was awarded a temporary permit. Disney proposed a large-scale Swiss-style village, with 2 hotels, 14 ski lifts and parking for 3600 vehicles. The Sierra Club deemed the small subalpine valley unsuitable for such a huge project and began a series of legal battles to stop the project, acquiring a restraining order in 1969.

The Sierra Club effectively tied up the Disney Company in the courts long enough to win over public opinion. In another strike against Disney, California withdrew the proposal to build a new state highway from Three Rivers to Mineral King, which would have required that the developer come up with several million dollars for road construction and obtain all the necessary approvals for a route across state and federal lands. As environmental awareness increased among the public and within the Federal government, Disney began to lose the public-relations battle, and the concept

Tamarack Lake from the Lone Pine Creek Trail

of a Mineral King ski resort was in serious jeopardy. On November 10, 1978, President Jimmy Carter signed into law the Omnibus Parks Bill, part of which added Mineral King to the surrounding Sequoia National Park.

Recent History

The post-World War II era in the parks was characterized by an increase in visitation, improvements to park infrastructure, and the advancement of scientific research for the purpose of designing management policies. At Giant Forest, the park took steps to reduce the impact of development on the giant sequoias. By 1972 it had moved campsites, picnic areas, and most park structures to less sensitive areas. The visitor center was moved to Lodgepole and the gas station and maintenance facilities were relocated to Red Fir.

Nearly 25 more years passed before the park finally resolved the problem of commercialism at Giant Forest. After the 1996 season, the park permanently closed the historic Giant Forest Lodge complex near Round Meadow and started construction

on new facilities at Wuksachi. Two years later, most of the commercial buildings had been closed and removed, with four exceptions. The old market was restored and remodeled into the Giant Forest Museum, which opened in 2001. Additional modifications at Giant Forest included trail improvements, interpretive displays, and improved parking lots. Nearby at General Sherman, the park continues construction on a new parking area and a trail and shuttle system due to open by the summer of 2004.

The recent construction of John Muir Lodge increased the number of overnight accommodations at Grant Grove, an area that had not been nearly as overdeveloped as Giant Forest. In 1978, a lodge at Cedar Grove with 18 motel rooms, a snack bar, and a grocery store was a small-scale fulfillment of the San Joaquin Valley businessmen's vision so many years before.

Wilderness and Backcountry Issues

Since 1984, nearly 90% of Sequoia and Kings Canyon National Parks have been managed as wilderness. Combined with the

Hiker on the Mt. Whitney Trail

surrounding John Muir, Golden Trout, Jennie Lakes and Monarch wildernesses, a vast stretch of the southern Sierra Nevada is wild.

After decades of neglect, the park developed backcountry regulations and policies to prevent overuse and restore environmental health. By 1972, backcountry permits and quotas were being used to forestall the crush of backpackers in the more popular areas of the parks. In addition, the Park Service and the Forest Service began a campaign to educate backcountry users on wilderness ethics. They put into place camping bans and stay limits in areas of severe overuse, and enforced campfire restrictions above certain altitudes and in sensitive areas. More recently, both the Park Service and the Forest Service began requiring the use of bear lockers and canisters in heavily used areas and strongly suggesting their use in others.

Postscript

Sequoia and Kings Canyon national parks have faced many challenges and undoubtedly await more trials. As more and more tourists seek temporary escape from the perils of urbanization, increased park visitation remains a management problem. Pollution from urban areas and the San Joaquin Valley is a perpetual threat to air quality and plant life, reducing visibility, threatening sequoia seedlings and other plants, and producing acid rain. Although backpacking numbers are down from their mid-1970s high point, fragile subalpine and alpine environments must still be protected. Stock use has come under increased scrutiny, but the current management plan is still flawed. The age-old question for the Park Service still remains — how does the agency manage the competing goals of park preservation and public enjoyment?

Flora and Fauna

Encompassing the change in elevation from the San Joaquin Valley floor to Mt. Whitney, the Sequoia and Kings Canyon region supports a diverse cross-section of plant and animal life and several distinct plant communities. The following divisions are general and should not be viewed as definitive descriptions. The bibliography at the end of this book suggests additional sources for information on plants and animals in the Sierra Nevada.

The Foothills

Plant life: The western fringe of Sequoia National Park includes the Sierra foothills, a low-elevation area that extends from the floor of the San Joaquin Valley eastward to roughly 4500–5000 feet. The foothill plant community is characterized by the Mediterranean climate of mild temperatures, winter rain, and dry summers. Average rainfall

Deer foraging on the lush grasses in Hockett Meadow

varies from as little as 10 inches per year in the lowlands to 40 inches at the upper elevations. Much of the vegetation appears parched and dry for a large part of the year, but after winter rains, early spring bursts forth, covering the hills with a vibrant carpet of green, decorated with brilliant wildflower displays.

Grasslands cover low slopes of the foothills, as they rise from the plain of the Central Valley. Non-native grasses have overtaken most of the native species. Periods of drought coupled with severe overgrazing in previous centuries have favored the invasive European annual grasses.

Diverse woodlands alternate with chaparral on higher slopes east of the grasslands. Generally, woodland occupies shady areas where the soil is damp, while chaparral grows on dry and sunny slopes. Foothills woodland is characterized by a savanna-like growth of trees and grasses, including a variety of oaks (blue oak, live oak, valley oak and canyon oak), and California buckeye, laurel, and redbud.

Dry, rocky slopes in the foothills are typically carpeted with a tangle of shrubs known as chaparral. Common plants include chamise (greasewood), manzanita, ceanothus, buckeye, flowering ash, mountain mahogany, and California coffeeberry. Fire plays an important role in chaparral communities, regularly burning areas every 10 to 40 years.

Although the foothills zone is generally considered to be a dry environment, several rivers, streams, and creeks pass through the area carrying water from the melting snows of the Sierra to the thirsty valley below. A varied plant community thrives along these watercourses, thanks to plentiful moisture. Cottonwood, willow, alder, oak, laurel, and sycamore are common streamside companions.

Poison oak is associated with both the foothills woodland and the chaparral communities. As the saying goes, "Leaves of three, leave it be." Leaves typically grow in groups of three; they are bronze and shiny in spring, green in summer, scarlet in autumn, and fall off prior to winter. Berries are white. Poison oak may grow as a creeping plant, an erect shrub, or even as a small tree under the right conditions. All parts of the plant (branches, stems, leaves, and roots) contain the oil urushiol, which causes some people to break out in a skin rash. Even a microscopic drop of urushiol is enough to trigger itching or a severe rash, and penetration of the skin by the toxin requires less than a 10-minute exposure time. If you do come into contact with poison oak, immediate washing or attempting to absorb the oil with dirt are recommended. Touching clothing that has brushed against the plant is just as potent as touching the plant itself, so wash clothes in soap and hot water as soon as possible. If a rash develops, treat with hydrocortisone cream. For severe reactions, consult a physician.

Animal life: The mild climate of the foothills region is hospitable to a wide variety of creatures. Common woodland amphibians include three varieties of salamander and the California newt, an amphibian whose interesting mating ritual begins in mid-winter and continues into spring. Several varieties of lizards often scurry across dry and rocky slopes. Snakes are quite common to the region as well, the western rattlesnake receiving the most interest from humans.

Several rodents find a home in this zone, including brush rabbit, black-tailed jackrabbit, Audubon's cottontail, gray squirrel, dusky-footed wood rat, and deer mouse. Bats can often be seen patrolling the skies at dusk in search of insects. Medium-sized mammals such as raccoon, ringtail, gray fox, skunk, and coyote are familiar residents. Larger mammals in the foothills include mule deer and the seldom seen bobcat and mountain lion.

Numerous birds reside in the foothills —far too many to list even all of the most common species here. Some familiar raptors are red-tailed hawk, golden eagle, American kestrel, and great horned owl. California quail is the most common game bird, although hunting is not allowed within the parks. The turkey vulture, the ubiquitous "buzzard" in California skies, is also common here.

Montane Forest

Plant Life: Above the foothills region, a zone of mixed coniferous forest, composed of conifers and deciduous trees, extends across the west slope of the Sierra between roughly 4500 and 7500 feet. The two most prevalent conifers in this zone are ponderosa pine and white fir. Generally, ponderosa pine is found in relatively dry areas, while white fir occupies soils with more moisture. At higher elevations of the montane forest, Jeffrey pine replaces ponderosa pine. Closely related to the ponderosa, and also with needles in clusters of three, Jeffrey pine is better able to tolerate the colder temperatures and increased snowfall at higher altitudes. A host of other evergreens intermixes with these conifers, most often including sugar pine and incense cedar. Some of the most common deciduous trees in the montane forest are dogwood and black oak.

On the east side of the range, in the rain shadow of the Sierra crest, the montane forest is found between elevations of 7000 and 9000 feet. Stands are typically less dense than their western counterparts and are much less diverse. The forest is composed primarily of Jeffrey pine and white fir, although widely scattered examples of

PONDEROSA PINE
(Pinus ponderosa)

The three-needled ponderosa pine is the most common and widespread conifer in the western montane forest. The trees reach heights between 60 and 130 feet.

other conifers intermixed with them are not uncommon.

As expected, streamside environments within the montane forest harbor many more species of trees, shrubs, and plants. On the west side, a number of deciduous trees line the banks of streams and rivers, including quaking aspen, black cottonwood, bigleaf maple, nutmeg, laurel, Oregon ash, and numerous varieties of willow. Eastside riparian zones are home to quaking aspen, Fremont cottonwood, black cottonwood, and water birch.

Animal Life: The ensantina salamander, western toad, and Pacific tree frog are the three amphibians typically found in the montane forest. Reptiles include a variety of lizards and snakes, including the western rattlesnake which is common up to around 6000 feet.

Like the foothills, the montane forest is home to many rodents, including the broad-handed mole, Trowbridge shrew, deer mouse, pocket gopher, gray squirrel, northern flying squirrel, California ground squirrel, chipmunk, and dusky-footed wood rat. Bats also frequent the evening montane forest skies. In addition to the medium and large mammals that live in the

BLACK BEAR
(Ursus americanus)

Weighing up to 300 pounds, the black bear is the largest mammal in the Sierra, and is usually cinnamon or black in color. A female typically gives birth to two cubs every other winter. She cares for them through the summer and following winter, and forces them to fend for themselves the next spring. Male bears do not participate in raising the cubs, and would possibly kill and eat them if the mother did not fiercely protect them.

foothill zone, the porcupine, long-tailed weasel, and black bear also reside in the montane forest.

A wide assortment of birds lives in this zone including songbirds, woodpeckers, and several types of raptors.

Giant Sequoia Groves

Plant Life: The giant sequoia sets the Sierra Nevada apart from the rest of the world's forests. When Europeans first reported having seen trees of such stature, their claims were largely discounted by virtually all who had not seen a specimen first hand—even some who had couldn't believe their own eyes. A few trees were chopped down, cut into pieces, and sent to expositions where they were carefully reassembled, only to be viewed as hoaxes by the disbelieving public. Few humans could comprehend that a living tree could attain such size. Unfortunately, when lumbermen realized the size of the trees, they turned a lustful gaze toward the stately monarchs. Only after hundreds of sequoias met their doom, did they find that the brittle lumber of the giant sequoias was not commercially viable, and could be used for nothing more than mere fence posts and shakes. After an arduous battle that lasted many decades, the giant sequoia received appropriate protection. Today, the Big Trees are safe and secure in three national parks, a national monument, and a handful of state parks.

Not only is *Sequoiadendron giganteum* the largest tree by volume on the planet, in California the statuesque specimen only grows in 75 groves, on the west side of the Sierra Nevada. All but eight of the groves are found within the greater Sequoia/Kings Canyon region. The largest groves are Redwood Mountain in Kings Canyon and Giant Forest in Sequoia. Most of the largest individual specimens also occur within this region, with General Sherman receiving top honors, followed by Washington, General Grant, President, and Lincoln—all five within park boundaries. The largest trees by volume on the planet, giant sequoias

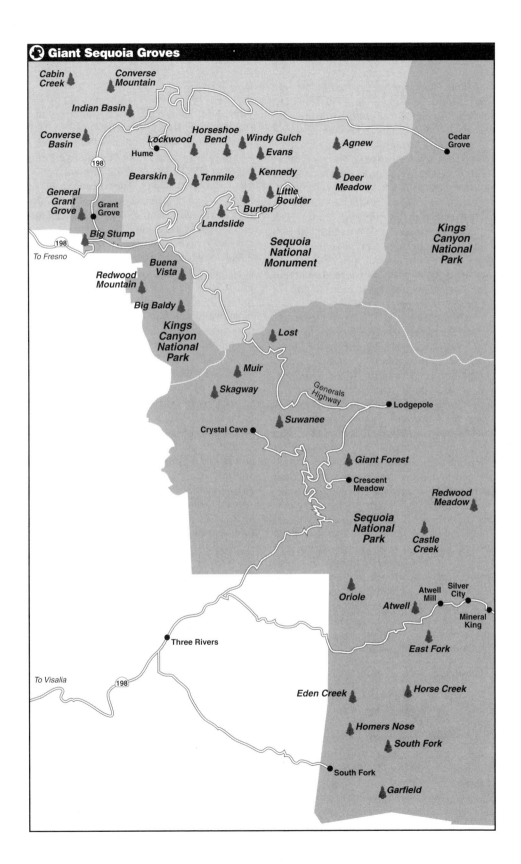

Giant Sequoia Groves

reach heights between 150 and 300 feet, and widths between 5 and 30 feet. The bark is cinnamon red with deep furrows; cones are 2 to 3 inches and oblong in shape.

The giant sequoia grows in mixed coniferous forests of white fir, sugar pine, incense cedar, and dogwood rather than in pure stands. Somewhat less drought resistant than other Sierra conifers, the big trees are found only in areas of moist soil, between elevations of 4500 and 8400 feet. Typical precipitation in sequoia groves varies from 45 to 60 inches per year, but the soil's ability to hold moisture throughout dry summers is perhaps a more important element to sequoia survival.

Although the sequoia has an extensive root system, their roots are generally shallow in relation to their immense size. Most trees meet their eventual demise by simply toppling over, rather than by succumbing to the more common tree maladies of disease, infestation, or forest fire. The characteristically thick sequoia bark makes the trees highly resistant to both insects and fire. Fire rarely does more than leave a black scar on the trunk.

Forest fires are in fact beneficial to giant sequoias. Their small cones require extreme heat in order to open and release the oatmeal-sized seeds. In addition, fire clears away debris on the forest floor and small plants that compete with sequoia saplings for light and moisture. Although fire suppression was the rule of the past, nowadays the Park Service intentionally sets fires in sequoia groves and elsewhere in the park to restore this natural process and to reduce the accumulation of forest fuels that feed unnaturally intense wildfires.

Animal Life: Same as montane forest zone.

Beaver

Red Fir Forest

Plant Life: Unlike the mixture of trees in the montane forest, the stately red fir is often the sole species of the climax forest on the west side of the Sierra. Growing to between 60 and 180 feet, red fir is susceptible to lightning strikes. The trees are generally 2 to 4 feet in width, and their bark is maroon-brown with red furrows. Cones are 6 to 8 inches long. The tall trees can form such dense cover that competitors and many understory plants cannot survive—any plant that does survive must be shade tolerant. Where the red fir is less dense, lodgepole pine, western white pine, Jeffrey pine, western juniper, and quaking aspen may join the forest. (One small stand of mountain hemlock occurs in this zone within the park.) White fir may intermingle along the lower edge of the zone. White and red firs are similar in appearance; the easiest way to differentiate between them is by examining the bark—maroon-brown on red fir and grayish on white fir.

Red fir prefers deep, well-drained soil, and is found in the southern Sierra between approximately 7000 and 9000 feet in elevations, from Kern County northward. The species thrives in areas of the range that receive the highest amounts of precipitation, particularly in the form of winter snowfall.

Animal Life: Inhabitants of the higher elevations of the upper forest zones must adapt to more severe weather conditions and periodically scarce food supplies. Common amphibians are limited to two varieties each of salamander, frog, and toad. Reptiles include garter snake and three varieties of lizard.

Ordinary small mammals one might expect to encounter include deer mouse, pocket gopher, vole, shrew, broad-handed mole, pika, chipmunk, chickaree, Belding ground squirrel, golden-mantled ground squirrel, northern flying squirrel, mountain beaver, white-tailed jackrabbit, and yellow-bellied marmot. Bats are quite common around lakeshores and meadows. Medium-

MULE DEER
(Odocoileus hemionus)

Mule deer are numerous in the southern Sierra, since their main predators, the grizzly bear and wolf, are now extinct in the region. Mountain lions are their most common predators today. Starvation and disease are other causes of death for mule deer. Mature males may exceed 200 pounds. Each March, males shed their antlers and start to grow them again in April.

sized animals in the upper forests include red fox, porcupine, coyote, long-tailed weasel, fisher, ermine, wolverine, badger, and pine marten. Black bear and mule deer are frequently seen larger mammals. The Sierra bighorn sheep lives in the zone but tends to be very reclusive.

Although not as numerous as in the lower zones, a vast number of birds find a home in the upper forest belt. Among some of the more interesting species are the blue grouse, the dipper, and the mountain bluebird. The most common (and occasionally obnoxious) bird known to backpackers in this zone is the Steller's jay, whose bold exploits around humans are often rewarded by a beak full of gorp.

Lodgepole Pine Forest

Plant Life: Perhaps no tree is more closely associated with the High Sierra than the lodgepole pine. The versatile lodgepole is found between 8000 and 11,000 feet in the southern Sierra, flourishing in soils where red fir struggles—either too wet or too dry. In stark contrast to red fir, which is almost exclusively Californian, the two-needled lodgepole pine is one of the most widespread trees in the American West. It is commonly found in exclusive stands, as is red fir, but intermingles with western white pine and a few whitebark pines in higher elevations, and with red fir in lower elevations. In areas of high groundwater, quaking aspen and lodgepole grow together. On the east side of the range, lodgepoles are quite common between 9000 and 11,000 feet, where western white pine is the most familiar neighbor.

Animal Life: Similar to red fir zone.

Subalpine Zone

Plant Life: Occurring between roughly 9500 and 12,000 feet, the subalpine zone straddles the Sierra crest and bridges the gap between the mighty forests of the lower altitudes and the austere realm above timberline.

The most dominant conifer in this zone is the interesting foxtail pine, with its characteristic pendulous branches. This five-needled pine is similar in appearance to the bristlecone pine. It occurs only in Inyo and Tulare counties in the southern Sierra, and in the Klamath Mountains of northern California. Trees grow to between 20 and 45 feet, and their cones are purplish and prickly, 2 to 5 inches long. The foxtail pine occasionally appears in pure stands along the eastern fringe of Sequoia National Park and along the Kern River. Its most common associate is the majestic whitebark pine.

LODGEPOLE PINE
*(Pinus contorta,
var. murrayana)*

Tall and thin, lodgepoles are two-needled pines that reach heights of 50 to 100 feet. Their bark is pale gray and their cones are 1 to 2 inches long.

This multi-trunked tree grows in harsh conditions just below timberline, and often resembles a windblown shrub. Less common associates include western white pine, lodgepole pine, and limber pine.

Forests are only one part of the diverse subalpine region. Mountain lakes, craggy peaks, and granite boulders and slabs are other common features of the landscape. Numerous subalpine meadows harbor a vast array of wildflowers and a remarkably varied selection of grasses and sedges.

Animal Life: Similar to red fir zone.

Alpine Zone

Plant Life: The alpine zone occurs at the highest elevations of the Sierra, where the growing season is measured in weeks rather than months. Harsh conditions characterize the alpine zone, and lower temperatures and cloudier skies mean that snow lingers in here, although the alpine zone receives less snowfall than lower regions. At altitudes above 12,000 feet, frost can occur at any time during the summer and cool temperatures, nearly constant winds, and a significant lack of precipitation produce desert-like conditions. Generally poor soil, mostly granitic, further limits the number of species able to adapt to this climate.

Most alpine plants have adapted to their environment by developing a low-growing, compact, and drought-tolerant demeanor. This allows the plants to avoid the strongest winds, grow closer to the warmth of the soil and survive on small amounts of moisture. In addition, most alpine plants are perennial as opposed to annual, which means they don't have to reproduce an entire new plant each year. Vegetation in this zone can be divided into two classifications: alpine meadow and alpine rock.

Alpine meadows are common in the upper realm of the Sierra where a sufficient layer of moist soil is present. Meadows are composed principally of sedges, with alpine sedge and common sedge the most usual,

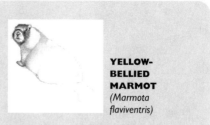

YELLOW-BELLIED MARMOT
(Marmota flaviventris)

The most common mammal in the alpine zone, marmots are often seen sunbathing on rocks. They are gray or brown on the back, dull yellow on the underside, with white around the eyes, and a dark band above the nose. Marmots utter a sharp whistle when alarmed, which accounts for the common name of "whistle pig."

and a limited number of grasses. A wide array of wildflowers put on a showy display during the brief summer, capitalizing on the greater amount of available moisture. Among them is the Sierra primrose, an alpine wildflower that prefers moist rocky soils and has reddish blossoms on a 1- to 4-inch stem. A limited variety of shrubs is found in small groupings in the alpine community. Among them are alpine and snow willows, laurel, and heather.

Vegetation grows in small patches in alpine rock communities, unlike the large swaths of foliage that are common in alpine meadows. Open gravel flats and scree areas produce a smattering of alpine plants. The protected micro-climates of boulder fields often are more suitable to the survival of a diverse group of plants; wildflowers are the most common, but a few shrubs grow in the rock community as well.

Animal Life: Aside from insects and invertebrates, there are few animals that find a home in the rarified alpine zone, where food and shelter are extremely limited. The only common residents are the heather vole, yellow-bellied marmot, and pika.

Although many different types of birds frequent the alpine zone, only the rosy finch is as common in the alpine zone as in the upper forest zones. Sierra bighorn sheep may venture to these heights during the summer, but generally prefer areas at or below timberline. Black bears that have become unnaturally accustomed to the food of backpackers may also ascend to this zone in search of treats.

Pinyon-Juniper Woodland

Plant Life: On the east side of the Sierra, between roughly 6000 and 9000 feet, lies the pinyon-juniper woodland. In the rain shadow on the east side of the Sierra crest, this zone receives little precipitation, a mere 5 to 15 inches per year. Most of the moisture falls as winter snow, with a random thunderstorm the only possibility of breaking up the usual long, dry summer. This zone is composed primarily of widely scattered, singleleaf pinyon pine, with Sierra juniper and curl-leaf mountain mahogany the two most common associates. Trees often grow in the form of large shrubs. Sagebrush, rabbitbrush, and bitterbrush commonly grow in the understory.

Spring and early summer may bring a colorful display of wildflowers to pinyon-

SINGLELEAF PINYON PINE
(Pinus monophylla)

The only single-needled pine in the Sierra, the singleleaf pinyon pine reaches between 20 and 25 feet in height; their spherical-shaped cones are 1.5 to 2 inches in length. The Piutes ate the seeds of the pinyon pine as a staple of their diet. Pine nuts, as we know them, are a gourmet food item in modern-day grocery stores.

COYOTE
(Canas latrans)

Highly adaptable and intelligent mammals, coyotes are commonly associated with the American West, but have extended their native range beyond its former borders. Although they may take a weak or sick deer on occasion, coyotes subsist as omnivores on a wide-ranging diet. Their whelps and howls are commonly heard after sundown.

juniper woodlands, including lupine, phlox, paintbrush and mule ears.

Along eastern Sierra streams at this elevation, a thick display of wildflowers, shrubs, and trees grow in stark contrast to the area immediately beyond the riparian zone. Quaking aspen, cottonwood, willow, oak, birch, and ash are common streamside trees, which may intermix with conifers from the forest zones above. Currant, wild rose, and a variety of willows are typical shrubs.

Animal Life: A wide variety of amphibians, reptiles, birds, and insects are at home in the pinyon-juniper woodland, as are a vast number of mammals. Small mammals, including a number of different species of mice, squirrel, vole, rabbit, shrew, and chipmunk, are very common. Larger mammals include coyote, skunk, badger and mule deer. Birds, including the sage grouse and red-tailed hawk, are plentiful as well.

Sagebrush scrub

Plant Life: Fortunately, only a few east side trails pass through the sagebrush scrub zone, which is often unbearably hot and dry during the usual hiking and backpacking season. This zone usually receives less than 12 inches of precipitation a year, most of which falls during the winter months. A welcome thunderstorm may water the parched ground during the summer, releasing the unforgettably pungent aroma from wet sagebrush.

At first glance, the grayish-green sagebrush creates a seemingly unbroken carpet of vegetation on the foothills above Owens Valley. A closer inspection reveals a mixture of bitterbrush, rabbitbrush, desert peach, and spiny hopsage interspersed with the sagebrush. Before overgrazing in the west replaced native perennial grasses with invasive annuals, the sagebrush zone was filled with a healthy mixture of the native bunchgrasses. Following wet winters and springs, the high desert produces a vivid display of wildflowers in late spring and early summer.

Animal Life: Similar to pinyon-juniper zone.

Geology

Although the origins of the Sequoia and Kings Canyon region may be rather speculative, as we have no human witness to the process, at least geologists can tell us with certainty the composition of the rock that forms the region's soaring peaks and deep canyons.

Even a cursory examination by the untrained eye reveals that the Sierra is overwhelmingly composed of granitic rocks. These light-colored, salt-and-pepper speckled, and coarse-grained rocks include granite, granodiorite, and tonalite (formerly called quartz diorite). They also contain varying degrees of minerals, such as quartz, feldspar, biotite and hornblende. The Sierra Nevada Batholith, as geologists commonly refer to this large mass of granitic rock, was formed when molten magma below the earth's surface cooled and crystallized. The batholith, over 300 miles long and more than 50 miles wide at some points, was subsequently uplifted and exposed. Today, the characteristic granite of the Sierra Nevada is evident across the range.

Meadow along the Lone Pine Creek Trail

Geologic Types	Example	Location	Access
Granitic Rocks	Moro Rock	Giant Forest	road
	Great Western Divide	Panoramic Point—Grant Grove	road/trail
	Mt. Whitney Area	Sequoia N.P.	road/trail
Metamorphic Rocks	Kaweah Peaks Ridge	Sequoia N.P.	trail
	Mineral King Peaks	Mineral King	road/trail
	Crystal Cave	West of Giant Forest	road
	Boyden Cave Sequoia N.P.	Kings Canyon, Hwy. 180	road
Volcanic Rocks	Big Pine Volcanic Field	South of Big Pine, West of US 395	road
Water-sculpted canyons	South Fork Kings River	Kings Canyon, Hwy. 180	road
	Middle Fork Kings River	North of Kings Canyon	trail
	Middle Fork Kaweah River	Ash Mountain/Foothills Area	road
Glacier-sculpted canyons	Tokopah Valley	Lodgepole	road/trail
	Kern Canyon	Sequoia N.P.—SE quadrant	trail
	LeConte Canyon/Evolution Valley	Kings Canyon N.P.—John Muir Trail	road/trail
Glaciers	Palisade Glacier	Palisades—N. Fork Big Pine Creek	trail
	Middle Palisade Glacier	Palisades—S. Fork Big Pine Creek	trail
	Goethe Glacier	Glacier Divide—Humphreys Basin	trail

A much smaller proportion of the rock in the Sierra Nevada is metamorphic. Dark in color and variegated in appearance, metamorphic rocks are older than granitic rocks. Remnants of these rocks are scattered across the Sequoia and Kings Canyon region, and four distinct metamorphic terranes have been identified in the area. A number of caves, including Crystal Cave near Giant Forest and Boyden Cave near Kings Canyon, have been discovered in concentrations of marble, a type of metamorphic rock.

An even smaller percentage of the region's geologic composition includes volcanic rock. Within the park boundaries it's almost nonexistent, the lone exception being a very old intrusion occurring near Windy Peak along the Middle Fork of the Kings River. Smatterings of additional vol-canic activity are evident in small pockets west of Kings Canyon and southeast of Sequoia near Golden Trout Creek. The most noticeable evidence of volcanism in the region occurs east of Kings Canyon in the Big Pine Volcanic Field, where passing motorists on Highway 395 can see cinder cones and lava flows.

The Sequoia and Kings Canyon area is home to some of the most impressive canyons in North America. Modern conclusions recognize the importance of both stream erosion and glaciation in the formation of these canyons. At lower elevations, the erosive power of water is clearly evident in V-shaped canyons such as the South and Middle Forks of the Kings River. At the higher elevations of Sequoia and Kings Canyon, the characteristically U-shaped canyons reflect the role of glaciation.

Speculation on the function of glaciers in the sculpting of the Sierra Nevada is as old as John Muir himself. Whatever their importance in the past, the glaciers that exist today occupy a very small percentage of territory in the uppermost realms of the High Sierra, usually above 12,000 feet on the north and east faces of the highest peaks. Despite their lack of volume, these glaciers add touches of alpine beauty to the rocky summits and dramatic faces of the range's tallest mountains. The largest glacier in the Sierra is the Palisade Glacier, a pocket of ice less than 1 square mile in size, but significant enough to qualify the surrounding Palisade peaks as part of the foremost alpine climbing area in the Sierra, luring alpinists from all over the world.

Climate

Compared to other North American mountain ranges, the Sierra Nevada is blessed with an abundance of mild, dry, and sunny weather. Summer is particularly fine, as 95% of the yearly precipitation falls between November and March. Summer thunderstorms account for the remainder, but are much more sporadic than those in other ranges, the Rocky Mountains, for instance. Summertime temperatures are generally mild, although they vary considerably from the lowlands to the alpine heights.

Because of its relatively low elevation, the foothills region provides excellent off-season hiking opportunities. Spring is perhaps the best time of year to visit, when the High Sierra is covered with the winter snowpack; grasses are green after winter rains, wildflowers are blooming, and the oak trees are leafing out. Fall is also a pleas-

Ranger Meadow, Deadman Canyon Trail

ant hiking season, when the summer heat has abated, and even winter in the foothills allows for hiking, since there are a few trails that stay snow-free all year. However, summer can be uncomfortably hot. Hikers are recommended to get an early start or plan on taking a dip in the cool waters of one of the rivers and streams during the heat of the day.

Above the foothills, snow-free hiking opportunities don't present themselves until May, when the road into Kings Canyon is opened and trails in Grant Grove and Giant Forest start to shake their winter mantle. Once the spring thaw is underway, the snow line steadily marches up the mountainsides, opening more trails along the way. By June, most west side paths are accessible into the frontcountry of Sequoia and Kings Canyon, but the High Sierra usually remains snow-covered until mid-July.

When the snow has mostly melted in the highest parts of the Sierra, backpacking season begins in earnest. Although summers in the Sierra usually bring dry, sunny days, thunderstorms are not uncommon, and backpackers should be prepared for changeable conditions, including the rare summer storm system. Afternoon highs in the summer often creep into the sixties and low seventies at the upper elevations, and if the day is sunny, the temperature will feel even warmer, thanks to the effects of increased solar radiation.

Warm weather usually persists in the High Sierra from July into September. Pleasant Indian summer conditions generally continue for another month or so, but the reliably good weather usually comes to an end at upper elevations by the end of October. Autumn is a fine time to enjoy the trails and footpaths the parks' western edge. By November of most years, the Sierra has seen the first snowfall of the season and recreationists customarily turn their attention to winter pursuits. However, some years the first snow doesn't arrive until January.

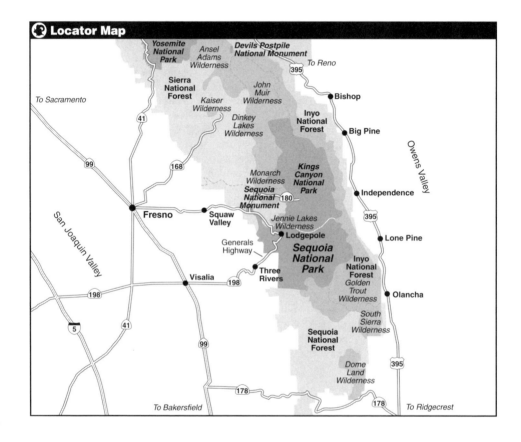

Traveling the Backcountry

Although this book focuses on Sequoia National Park and surrounding wilderness areas, the National Park Service manages Sequoia and adjoining Kings Canyon National Park as a single entity. The information in this chapter regarding fees, facilities, regulations, maps, and permits, applies to both parks. Because of the proximity of the parks to each other, locations of visitor centers, ranger stations, and campgrounds in Kings Canyon may be of use to visitors to Sequoia National Park.

Alta Peak area from the Timber Gap Trail

Fees

Since Sequoia and Kings Canyon national parks are managed as a unit, visitors pay a single fee to enter both parks. Fees are collected at the Ash Mountain Entrance Station where Highway 198 becomes the Generals Highway, the Lookout Point Entrance Station on Mineral King Highway, and the Big Stump Entrance on Highway 180. If you enter at a station that is not staffed, be prepared to pay the fee upon exiting.

Type of Pass	Fee	Duration	Terms
Standard Pass	$10 per vehicle $5 on foot, motorcycle, bicycle or bus	7 days	Access to Sequoia/Kings Canyon
Annual Pass	$20	1 year	Access to Sequoia/Kings Canyon
National Parks Pass	$50	1 year	Access to all national parks
Golden Eagle Pass	$65	1 year	Access to all national parks, monuments, recreation areas, historic sites & wildlife refuges
Golden Age Passport	$10 (U.S. citizens or residents 62 or over)	Lifetime	Access to all national parks
Golden Access Pass	Free (U.S. citizens or residents who are blind or permanently disabled)	Lifetime	Access to all national parks, monuments, recreation areas, historic sites & wildlife refuges

About Sequoia National Park and Surrounding Forest Service Lands

Tourist-related facilities in Sequoia and Kings Canyon national parks aren't as developed or as concentrated as those in Yosemite National Park, the more famous and more frequently visited neighbor to the north. Even so, the two southern Sierra parks offer visitors a wide range of services. Most hikers and backpackers may find they prefer the more sedate atmosphere of Sequoia and Kings Canyon to the typical summertime zoo at Yosemite.

Information

Sequoia and Kings Canyon national parks:

(559) 565-3341 *(24 hours)*
www.nps.gov/seki.com

USFS Headquarters:

Sequoia National Forest
900 West Grand Avenue
Porterville, CA 93257
(559) 784-1500
(559) 565-3341
www.fs.fed.us/r5/sequoia

Sierra National Forest
1600 Tollhouse Road
Clovis, CA 93612
(559) 297-0706
www.fs.fed.us/r5/sierra/

Inyo National Forest
873 North Main Street
Bishop, CA 93514
(760) 873-2400
www.fs.fed.us/r5/inyo/

Park Service Ranger Stations and Visitor Centers:

Mineral King Ranger Station
Open daily 7 A.M. – 3:30 P.M.,
June to mid-September
Maps, books, bear canisters, first aid, wilderness permits

Ash Mountain Visitor Center
Open daily 8 A.M. – 5 P.M., summer;
8 A.M. – 4:30 P.M., winter
(559) 565-3135
Exhibits, maps, books, bear canisters, first aid, wilderness permits

Giant Forest Museum
Open daily 8 A.M. – 6 P.M., summer;
9 A.M. – 4:30 P.M., winter;
9 A.M. – 5 P.M., spring and fall
(559) 565-4480

Lodgepole Visitor Center
Open daily 8 A.M. – 6 P.M., early spring
to late fall; weekends only in winter
(559) 565-4436
Exhibits, maps, books, first aid

Lodgepole Wilderness Office
Open daily 7 A.M. – 4 P.M.,
May through September
(559) 565-3341
Wilderness permits, bear canisters, maps

Grant Grove Visitor Center
Open daily 8 A.M. – 6 P.M., summer;
9 A.M. – 4:30 P.M., spring and fall;
9:30 A.M. – 4:30 P.M., winter
(559) 565-4307
Exhibits, maps, books, bear canisters, first aid, wilderness permits

Cedar Grove Visitor Center
Open daily 9 A.M. – 5 P.M.,
May through October
(559) 565-3793
Maps, books, first aid

Roads End
Open daily 7 A.M. – 4 P.M.,
late May through September
Wilderness permits, bear canisters, maps

Forest Service District Ranger Stations

West Side	East Side
Sierra National Forest:	**Inyo National Forest:**
Pineridge Ranger District	**Mt. Whitney Ranger District**
PO Box 559	PO Box 8
Prather, CA 93651	Lone Pine, CA 93545
(559) 855-5360	(760) 876-6200
Sequoia National Forest:	**Inyo National Forest:**
Hume Lake Ranger District	**White Mountain Ranger District**
35860 Kings Canyon Road (Hwy. 180)	798 N. Main
Dunlap, CA 93621	Bishop, CA 93514
(559) 338-2251	(760) 873-2500

Lodging

A wide variety of overnight accommodations are available inside the park. Advance reservations are strongly recommended during peak season, as occupancy rates are high. A few of the park's lodges remain open all year. Communities surrounding the parks, such as Fresno, Visalia, and Three Rivers on the west side and Lone Pine, Independence, Big Pine, and Bishop on the east side, offer additional lodging options.

Sequoia National Park—Mineral King:

Silver City Resort
(Open late May to November)
(559) 561-3223 *(summer)*
(805) 528-2730 *(winter)*
www.silvercityresort.com

Sequoia National Park—Lodgepole Area:

Wuksachi Village (DNPS)
(Open all year)
(888) 252-5757
www.visitsequoia.com

Backcountry Lodges:

Bearpaw Meadow Camp (DNPS)
(Open mid-June to mid-September)
(888) 252-5757 *(reservations required)*
www.visitsequoia.com

Pear Lake Ski Hut (SNHA)
(Open December to April)
(559) 565-3759
www.sequoiahistory.org

Campgrounds

Both parks offer an extensive array of campgrounds, and the surrounding national forests have many additional campgrounds.

Reservations (National Park Service)
(800) 365-2267 *(4 a.m. – 4 p.m. PST)*
www.reservations.nps.gov

Reservations (USFS)
(877) 444-6777
www.reserveusa.com

West Side

Sequoia National Park

Mineral King:
Atwell Mill
Cold Springs
Foothills:
Potwisha
Buckeye Flat
South Fork
Lodgepole Area:
Lodgepole
Dorst

Kings Canyon National Park

Grant Grove:
Azalea
Crystal Springs
Sunset
Cedar Grove:
Sentinel
Sheep Creek
Canyon View
Moraine

Giant Sequoia National Monument (USFS)

Hume Lake Area:
Princess
Hume Lake
Tenmile
Landslide
Big Meadows Road/Stony Creek Area:
Stony Creek
Upper Stony
Horse Camp
Buck Rock
Big Meadows

East Side

Mt. Whitney Ranger District (USFS)

Cottonwood Pass
Golden Trout
Lone Pine
Whitney Portal
Whitney Trailhead
Upper Grays Meadow
Lower Grays Meadow
Onion Valley

White Mountain Ranger District (USFS)

Sage Flat
Upper Sage Flat
Big Pine Creek
Palisade Glacier
Clyde Glacier
Big Trees
Forks
Four Jeffrey
Intake 2
Bishop Park
Sabrina
Willow
North Lake

Pack Trips

A number of private individuals and companies provide pack service for trips into the parks and the surrounding terrain. Each outfit operates with a permit from the Park Service or Forest Service agency that governs the area. It is a good idea to check with the governing agency about an outfitter's current status, as permitees may change from year to year.

West Side

Mineral King Pack Station (SNP)
(559) 561-3039 *(summer)*
(520) 855-5885 *(off season)*

Wolverton (SNP)
(559) 565-3039 *(summer)*
(520) 855-5885 *(off season)*

Horse Corral (GSNM)
(559) 565-3404 *(summer)*
(559) 564-6429 *(off season)*

Grant Grove (KCNP)
(559) 335-9292 *(summer)*
(559) 337-2314 *(off season)*

Cedar Grove (KCNP)
(559) 565-3464 *(summer)*
(559) 337-2314 *(off season)*

East Side

Mt. Whitney Pack Trains
PO Box 248
Bishop, CA 93515
(760) 872-8331
www.rockcreekpackstation.com

Cottonwood Pack Station
Star Route 1, Box 81-A
Independence, CA 93526
(760) 878-2015

Sequoia Kings Pack Trains
PO Box 209
Independence, CA 93526
(760) 387-2797 or (800) 962-0775
www.395.com/berners/

Bishop Pack Outfitters
247 Cataract Road
Bishop, CA 93514
(760) 873-8877

Glacier Pack Train
PO Box 321
Big Pine, CA 93513
(760) 938-2538

Pine Creek Pack Station
PO Box 968
Bishop, CA 93515
(800) 962-0775

Rainbow Pack Station
600 S. Main St.
Bishop, CA 93514
(760) 873-8877

Rock Creek Pack Station
PO Box 248
Bishop, CA 93515
(760) 935-4493 *(summer)*
(760) 872-8331 *(off season)*
www.rockcreekpackstation.com

Additional Park Facilities

Post Offices: Lodgepole, Grant Grove

Showers and Laundry: Lodgepole, Grant Grove, Cedar Grove

Groceries & Supplies: Lodgepole, Grant Grove, Cedar Grove

Snack Bar/Deli: Lodgepole, Grant Grove, Cedar Grove

Restaurants: Wuksachi, Grant Grove

Gasoline: To reduce environmental concerns, gasoline is no longer available within the parks, except for emergencies. Motorists approaching Sequoia or Kings Canyon from the west should fill up in Visalia or Fresno, where prices are reasonable. Closer to the parks, the cost rises considerably. Those in desperate need will find gas just outside the parks at Three Rivers, Hume Lake, Clingan's Junction, and Kings Canyon Lodge.

Eastside travelers will not find any bargain prices at gas stations in the smaller communities along U.S. 395. (You'll get charged the least in Bishop.)

View west from the Mt. Whitney Trail

Wilderness Ethics and Trail Courtesy

The essence of American wilderness evokes notions of wild and undeveloped places where humans are simply visitors who leave no trace of their presence. The "Leave only footprints, take only photographs" motto of the back-to-earth 1970s embodies such a principle. The goal of every visitor, hiker, backpacker, and equestrian alike, should be to leave a wilderness area as it was found, if not better. The following backcountry guidelines should help keep the wild in wilderness.

Camping

- Camp a minimum of 100 feet from any water source.
- Choose a campsite away from trails.
- Never build improvements (fireplaces, rock walls, drainage swales etc.).
- Camp on exposed dirt or rock surfaces, not on vegetation.
- Use only downed wood for fires; never cut trees (dead or alive).
- Use only existing fire rings.
- Never leave a fire unattended.
- Fully extinguish all campfires by thoroughly soaking with water.

Sanitation

- Bury waste 6 inches deep, a minimum of 100 feet from trails, and 500 feet from water sources.
- Pack out toilet paper, or burn in areas where fires are permissible.
- Cook only the amount of food you can eat to avoid disposing of leftovers.
- Wash and rinse dishes, clothes, and yourself a minimum of 100 feet away

Lake 3—Cottonwood Lakes Basin

from water sources; never wash in lakes or streams.

- Pack out all trash—do not attempt to burn plastic or foil packaging.
- Filter, boil, or purify all drinking water.

On the Trail

- Stay on the trail—don't cut switchbacks.
- Preserve the serenity of the backcountry —avoid making loud noises.
- Yield the right-of-way to uphill hikers.
- Yield the right-of-way to equestrians— step off the trail, downhill.
- Avoid traveling in large groups.
- Because trails can change, either from natural or human causes, hikers should check with NPS visitor centers for updates before starting a hike.

Regulations for Kings Canyon and Sequoia National Parks

- Group size is limited to 15 people (10 in Redwood Canyon).
- Pets, weapons, wheeled vehicles and motorized equipment are prohibited.
- Maximum number of stock is 20.
- No pets allowed on trails.
- Campfires are restricted in many areas of the parks.
- Food must be stored so that it is completely inaccessible to bears.
- No camping within 100 feet (33 meters) of lakes or streams.
- No hunting.

Maps

USGS Topographic Maps: A number of recreational maps are available for hikers and backpackers in the popular Sequoia and Kings Canyon region, including the maps provided in this guide. The 7.5-minute quadrangles published by the United States Geological Survey are the most accurate and usable maps available. The USGS maps, $4 per sheet in 2002, are available directly from the USGS or from private retailers. Park Service and Forest Service ranger stations generally sell the maps that correspond to areas within their districts. Long-distance hikers may favor maps at a larger scale, since the 1:24,000 scale of the 7.5-minute quads requires carrying numerous maps for extended backpacks.

Thanks to the advancement of computer software, programs are also available for PC users that utilize the USGS quads as a base and have numerous features for the customization of personal maps. The only disadvantage of the software versus the actual USGS maps is the inability of most computer printers to match the 22″ x 29″ size of the 7.5-minute maps. Recently, some outdoor retailers have installed kiosks where recreationists can select and print comparable maps onsite.

Government cutbacks may curtail or ultimately doom the services of the USGS, but until such a time recreationists can order maps and procure information from the following addresses:

USGS Information Services
Box 25286
Boulder, CO 80225
(888) ASK-USGS
www.usgs.gov/

The Map Center
1995 University Avenue
Berkeley, CA 94704
(510) 841-MAPS

USGS Map Name	Trip Numbers
1. Dennison Peak	1, 2, 3
2. Moses Mtn.	1, 2, 3
3. Silver City	4, 5, 6
4. Mineral King	7, 8, 9, 10, 11, 12, 13, 14, 15, 16, 17
5. Chagoopa Falls	13, 33
6. Johnson Peak	54, 57, 58
7. Cirque Peak	53, 54, 55, 56, 57, 58
8. Shadequarter Mtn.	23, 24
9. Giant Forest	18, 19, 20, 21, 22, 24, 25, 26, 27, 28, 29, 30, 31, 34, 35, 36, 37, 38, 39, 40, 49
10. Lodgepole	17, 30, 31, 32, 33, 38, 39, 40, 41, 42, 43, 44, 45, 46, 47, 48
11. Triple Divide Peak	17, 32, 33, 47
12. Mt. Kaweah	33
13. Mount Whitney	33, 54, 58, 59, 62
14. Mt. Langley	33, 56, 58, 60
15. Muir Grove	50, 51, 52
16. Mt. Silliman	46, 47
17. Sphinx Lakes	47
18. Mt. Brewer	61, 62
19. Mt. Williamson	61, 62
20. Mt. Clarence King	62

15-minute Topographic Maps: Before the 7.5-minute maps became the USGS standard, 15-minute maps (1:62,500) were available to the general public for recreational use. Wilderness Press still offers one 15-minute quad in the Sequoia and Kings Canyon area, *Mt. Pinchot*, which is printed on plastic and covers the same scope as four 7.5-minute maps: *Mt. Pinchot, Aberdeen, Mt. Clarence King, Kearsarge Peak*.

The 15-minute *Mt. Pinchot* map may be purchased from:

Wilderness Press
1200 5th Street
Berkeley, CA 94710
(800) 443-7227
www.wildernesspress.com

Forest Service Maps:

John Muir Wilderness, Sequoia and Kings Canyon Wilderness. ($10, 1:63,360) The USFS publishes a 3-sheet set of topographic maps at 1 inch = 1 mile that backcountry travelers may find useful for trip planning or trail use. These three large maps cover nearly all of the trails described in this book and its companion guide to Kings Canyon, with the exception of the Grant Grove and Redwood Mountain regions of Kings Canyon.

A Guide to the Monarch Wilderness & Jennie Lakes Wilderness ($6, 1:36,180) A 1 inch = .5 mile topographic map of the two wilderness areas on the southwest of Kings Canyon National Park.

Golden Trout Wilderness, South Sierra Wilderness ($6, 1:63,360) A 1 inch = 1 mile topographic map of the wilderness areas south of Sequoia National Park.

Inyo National Forest ($6, 1:126,720) A .5 inch = 1 mile map of the forest lands east of Sequoia and Kings Canyon national parks.

Sequoia National Forest ($6, 1:126,720) A .5 inch = 1 mile map of forest lands west of Sequoia and Kings Canyon national parks.

Sierra National Forest ($6, 1:126,720) A .5 inch = 1 mile map of lands west of Kings Canyon National Park.

Sequoia Natural History Association Maps:

The SNHA publishes a set of small foldout maps with concise descriptions of dayhikes for popular areas of the parks, including Mineral King, Giant Forest, Lodgepole, Grant Grove and Cedar Grove. These maps, available from park visitor centers and stores, at the time of writing were selling for $2.50 apiece.

Tom Harrison Maps:

Tom's maps are some of the best recreational maps available from the private sector. Maps pertaining to the Sequoia and Kings Canyon region include *Bishop Pass* ($8.95, 1:47,520), *John Muir Trail Pack* ($18.95. 1:63,360), *Kings Canyon High Country* ($8.95, 1:63,360), *Mt. Whitney High Country* ($8.95, 1:63,360), *Mt. Whitney Zone* ($8.95, 1: 31,680), *Sequoia & Kings Canyon National Parks* ($8.95, 1:125,000). Maps for the Golden Trout Wilderness, Sierra National Forest, and Sequoia National Forest are in the works. Check out the website at www.tomharrisonmaps.com/.

Wilderness Permits

Day Hikers

Hikers do not need a permit to enter the national parks or the surrounding wilderness areas for one-day excursions, with the exception of the Mt. Whitney Zone, a roughly 5 x 2.5 mile area surrounding the peak. Hikers who start at Whitney Portal and pass Lone Pine Lake on the Mt. Whitney Trail must obtain a permit to enter the Whitney Zone (see below). Note: the cross-country route beyond Lower Boy Scout Lake to Iceberg Lake and the east face of Mt. Whitney is also a part of the Mt. Whitney Zone.

Overnight Backpackers

Sequoia and Kings Canyon National Parks

All overnight users entering the backcountry must obtain a valid wilderness permit from the ranger station closest to the trailhead.

Reserved Permits: Approximately 75% of the daily trailhead quota is set aside for reserved permits. Starting March 1, you can reserve a permit up to 3 weeks prior to departure. At the time of writing, permits cost $15. Reserved permits can be picked up after 1 P.M. on the day before you begin your trip and will be held until 9 A.M. the morning of your trip. If you know you will be delayed past 9 A.M., call the ranger station to hold your permit.

Walk-in Permits: The remaining 25% of the daily trailhead quota is available for walk-in permits. You can get a walk-in permit after 1 P.M. the day before you begin your trip. More permits may become available after 9 A.M. the morning of the trip if there are any unclaimed reserved permits. As a rule, permits are not written late in the afternoon, since it takes several hours of hiking to reach most campgrounds. Walk-in permits are free (as of 2002), but the

Park Service may start charging in the near future.

Wilderness Permit Reservations
Sequoia and Kings Canyon
  national parks
HCR 89 Box 60
Three Rivers, CA 93271
(559) 565-3708
Fax: (559) 565-4239

Inyo National Forest— East Side Entry for John Muir and Golden Trout Wildernesses

Wilderness permits are required throughout the year for all overnight visits. All trails entering the wilderness have quotas in effect between May 1 and November 1, except for the Cottonwood Pass Trail, which has a quota period from the last Friday in June to September 15. Outside the quota period, backpackers may self-issue a wilderness permit at Inyo National Forest ranger stations or visitor centers.

Reserved Permits: Approximately 60% of the trailhead quota is available through advance reservations for a fee of $5 per person. Remaining permits are available on a walk-in basis. You can request a reservation by mail, phone, or fax 6 months prior to the date of departure. (Email reservations may be accepted in the near future.) You will receive a confirmation letter upon acceptance of the reservation, which you must show when you pick up your permit at a ranger station near the trailhead. Advance reservations can be made up to 2 days before the date of the trip.

Walk-in Permits: Walk-in permits are available starting at 11 A.M. the day before a trip. Unclaimed reservations become available for walk-in permits at 10 A.M. on the day of a trip.

Whitney Zone: Unlike every other trail in the system, all permits for entry into the Mt. Whitney Zone (130 hikers and 60 backpackers per day) can be reserved in advance. Lottery applications are available from the Inyo National Forest by pick-up, phone, mail, or internet. You must submit the completed application with appropriate fees by mail or fax on February 1 (earlier submissions will be discarded). On February 15, the Forest Service begins random selection of the applications. Applications arriving after that date will be added to the lottery until the end of February or until all permits are reserved. The lucky ones receive confirmation by March 31. Any remaining permits can be obtained by phone beginning on May 1. Free walk-in permits are available after 11 A.M. the day before departure for any remaining or unclaimed permits.

Inyo National Forest
Wilderness Permit Office
873 North Main Street
Bishop, CA 93514
(760) 873-2483
Fax: (760) 873-2484
www.fs.fed.us/r5/inyo/passespermits/
    index/html

Wilderness Regulations

The following acts are prohibited in Inyo N.F.:

• Leaving any debris, garbage or refuse within the wilderness.
• Camping within 100 feet of lakes, streams or trails, terrain permitting, and never less than 25 feet.
• Washing and/or discharging soap wastes within 100 feet of lakes, streams, campsites or trails.
• Depositing bodily wastes within 100 feet of lakes, streams, campsites or trails.
• Possessing or storing food, toiletries or refuse in a manner that allows access to bears or other animals.
• Discharging a firearm, except for emergencies and the taking of game as permitted by state game laws.
• Possessing or using any wheeled or mechanical device (bicycle, motorcycle, cart, etc.).

• Shortcutting a switchback on any forest trail.
• Entering or using the wilderness in a group larger than 15 persons.
• Entering or using the wilderness with more than 25 head of pack or saddle stock.
• Hitching, tethering or tying pack or saddle stock within 100 feet of lakes, streams, trails, or campsites except while loading or unloading.

Winter in the Sequoia Area

Hiking and Backpacking

Although Sequoia National Park and the surrounding area don't provide many off-season hiking and backpacking opportunities, a few possibilities do exist. A handful of trails in the foothills region on the southwest side of Sequoia offer year-round, snow-free recreation. Hiking is possible all year on Trips 1, 18–22, and the initial segments of 23 and 24. At least one of the nearby campgrounds remains open year round, and lodging is available within the park at Wuksachi and outside the park in the town of Three Rivers.

Snowshoeing and Cross-Country Skiing

During years of average snowfall, snowshoers and cross-country skiers can enjoy Sequoia National Park from December through March. Marked trails in the Giant Forest/Lodgepole area of Sequoia lure snow lovers each winter. Motorists must carry chains, as they may be required at any time. Anyone wishing to spend a night or more in the backcountry is required to secure a wilderness permit from one of the visitor centers. Be sure to check with park officials about camping restrictions, as some areas are off limits to overnighters.

In Sequoia, the Generals Highway is kept open from the Ash Mountain Entrance through Giant Forest to Wolverton, Lodgepole, and Wuksachi Village. Year-round lodging is available at Wuksachi, and Lodgepole campground is open throughout the year. Snowshoe and ski rentals are available at Wuksachi Village and at Lodgepole. A number of marked routes in the Giant Forest/Lodgepole area offer a wide range of options for snowshoers and skiers of all skill levels. The most challenging marked route is the trip to the Pear Lake ski hut, where overnighters must have advanced reservations — (559) 565-3759 or www.sequoiahistory.org.

The Generals Highway between Grant Grove and Wuksachi Village is subject to closures during and after snowstorms. The Park Service does not routinely plow this section of highway, so winter visitors should not expect to travel between Sequoia and Kings Canyon unless conditions are favorable.

CHAPTER 3

About this Guide

This guide is designed for hikers in search of dayhiking opportunities in and around Sequoia National Park, and for backpackers looking to explore the majesty of the Sierra on short weekend trips, multi-week excursions, and anything in between. Some aspects of the evaluations of the following trails are subjective, but every effort was made to insure that the descriptions are meaningful to the average hiker and backpacker.

The 62 trips in this guide are divided into two sections. West Side Trips includes 52 hikes or backpacks in 6 regions. East Side Trips covers 10 trips in the Mt. Whitney area. A brief introduction to each region will familiarize you with the featured area. You'll find information about access, services, campground locations and facilities, and the nearest ranger station, and helpful tips specific to the area.

Individual trip descriptions follow the regional introductions.

SYMBOLS: Each description begins with a display of symbols, denoting the following characteristics:

Trip difficulty

E = easy

M = moderate

MS = moderately strenuous

S = strenuous

Type of trip

↗ = out and back

↗ = point to point (shuttle required)

◯ = loop

◯ = semiloop

Duration

DH = dayhike (single-day outing)

BP = backpack (overnight or long weekend backpack)

BPx = extended backpack (backpack longer than 3 days)

X = cross-country route (backpack requiring some cross-country travel)

WC = wheelchair access

DISTANCE: Distances are given in miles. Mileages for out-and-back trips are one-way. Point-to-point, loop and semi-loop trips give total mileage.

ELEVATION: Elevations are given in feet. The first set of numbers represents the starting elevation, followed by significant high and low points.

The second set of numbers represents the total elevation gain and loss. Again, the elevations listed are one-way for out-and-back trips, and total for point-to-point, loop and semi-loop trips. (To convert feet to meters, multiply by 0.3048.)

SEASON: Conditions vary from year to year; this entry gives the general period when the trail should be open and also mostly free of snow.

USE: This entry gives you an idea of the trail's popularity (light, moderate, or heavy).

MAP: This entry lists the USGS 7.5-minute quadrangles that cover the trip. Occasionally, supplemental maps are recommended.

THE MAIN BODY of the trip description includes an introduction, directions to the trailhead, and a detailed guide to the trail.

In the margins beside the main text, you'll find quick-reference icons indicating various features found along the trip route:

⛺ = campgrounds

🌲 = giant sequoias

〰 = swimming areas

👁 = noteworthy views

✤ = seasonal wildflowers

Additional entries accompany the main description:

[O] **OPTIONS** for extending or varying your trip, sidetrips, additional cross-country routes, and peaks to climb in the vicinity.

[R] **REGULATORY INFORMATION** concerning permits, quotas, and any specific restrictions.

Map Legend

Trail Maps

— Trail

⊤ Trailhead

P Parking

⚠ Campground

⌂ Ranger Station

❓ Information

$ Fee Collection Gate

▲ Mountain

Regional and Trailhead Maps

⊤ Trailhead

P Parking

⚠ Campground

⌂ Ranger Station

❓ Information

$ Fee Collection Gate

▲ Mountain

🌲 Giant Sequoia Grove

National Park

National Monument;
Wilderness Area

National Forest

5 Interstate

395 US Highway

41 State Highway

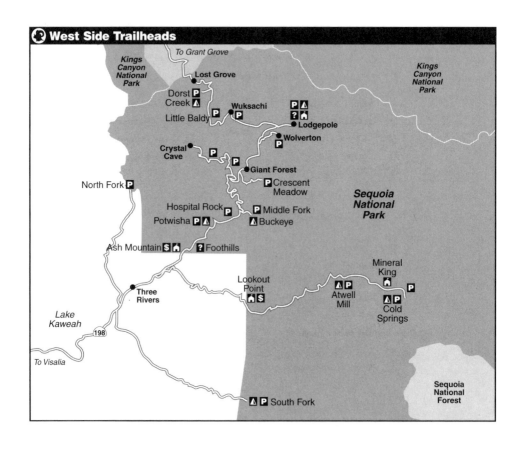

West Side Trailheads

Kings Canyon National Park

To Grant Grove

Lost Grove

Dorst Creek

Little Baldy

Wuksachi

Lodgepole

Wolverton

Crystal Cave

Giant Forest

Crescent Meadow

North Fork

Hospital Rock

Potwisha

Middle Fork

Buckeye

Ash Mountain

Foothills

Kings Canyon National Park

Sequoia National Park

Mineral King

Lookout Point

Atwell Mill

Cold Springs

Three Rivers

Lake Kaweah

198

To Visalia

Sequoia National Forest

South Fork

CHAPTER 4

West Side Trips

The west side of the Sierra Nevada rises steadily from the plain of the San Joaquin Valley toward the protected lands of Sequoia National Park. As you head east, the verdant agricultural land of the San Joaquin gives way to the grasslands and chaparral of the foothills zone, followed by the dense timber of the mid-elevation forests. A few roads penetrate into these areas of towering conifers and isolated groves of giant sequoias, but auto-bound visitors to the park must stop well below the granite cirques and jagged peaks that are associated with the High Sierra. Steadily rising, roadless terrain continues through the red fir and lodgepole pine forests into the subalpine and alpine zones, eventually culminating at the Sierra Crest, along the extreme eastern border of the park.

Recreationists entering Sequoia National Park from the west will experience a wide range of topography, flora, and fauna. The foothills region of Sequoia National Park offers year-round hiking along the South and Middle Fork Kaweah River. Once Mineral King Road is open and Giant Forest is snow free, hikers are blessed with splendid opportunities to stand beneath a majestic giant sequoia, stroll along a tumbling stream, or gaze across a verdant, flower-filled meadow. Mid-summer, the height of the season, lures backpackers with the siren call of the magnificent backcountry found within Sequoia National Park.

Giant sequoias in Garfield Grove

Introduction to South Fork

Situated in the extreme southwest part of Sequoia National Park, the South Fork trailhead provides access to some of the low-elevation trails of the foothills, in a plant community composed mainly of oak woodland and chaparral. As opposed to the typical Sierra granite of the higher elevations, much of the foothills region is covered with crumbling metamorphic rock, primarily marble, schist and slate. Steep, brush-filled canyons sliced by turbulent rivers and creeks characterize the topography.

Due to the milder climes of these altitudes, recreationists have opportunities for off-season trails that see light use, making fall, winter and spring ideal for hiking. Nor should the normally high temperatures of summer deter use of these paths, as traveling in the early morning or evening hours can help hikers beat the heat. During the summer season, backpackers can use the Garfield-Hockett Trail as a gateway into the mid-elevation forests and meadows of

Campgrounds

Campground	Fee	Elevation	Season	Restrooms	Running Water	Bear Boxes	Phone
SOUTH FORK (12 miles from Hwy 198)	No	3600′	Open all year	Pit Toilets	No	Yes	No

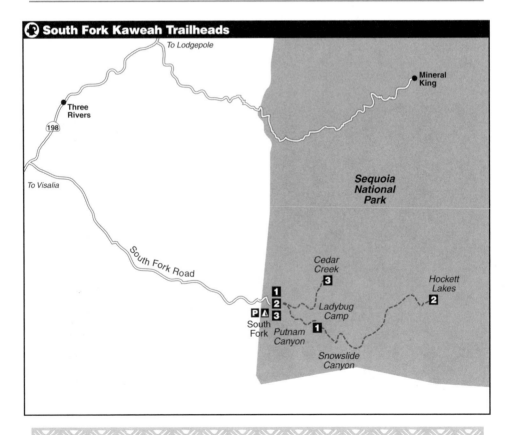

South Fork Kaweah Trailheads

the remote Hockett Plateau and regions beyond.

In the past, a fine network of trails crisscrossed the southwest region of Sequoia, but many of those paths are now overgrown, although short stretches may still be visible. Unmaintained trails should currently be considered as difficult bushwhacks. The Ladybug Trail follows a section of the historic Hockett Trail, constructed during the Civil War for travel through the Sierra between Visalia and silver mines east of Owens Valley.

ACCESS: (Open all year) South Fork Road leaves Three Rivers near the fire station and dead ends at the South Fork Campground 12 miles from State Highway 198.

AMENITIES: Three Rivers, a tourism-driven community 37 miles east of Visalia, offers a wide range of services, including motels, restaurants, gas stations and general stores. No services are available beyond Three Rivers along the South Fork Road.

RANGER STATION: The nearest ranger station is the Foothills Visitor Center. Unless the policy has changed recently, wilderness permits are available either from the South Fork Campground host in summer or by self-registration at the trailhead the rest of the year. The South Fork Ranger Station is no longer being staffed.

GOOD TO KNOW BEFORE YOU GO:

1. At these lower elevations, hikers and backpackers should be on the lookout for ticks, rattlesnakes and poison oak.

2. Mountain lions inhabit the foothills zone, but they have not presented any problems for hikers or backpackers recently. However, don't allow small children to stray from the group—good advice in any region, but particularly appropriate in cougar country. The Park Service does not recommend hiking alone in areas frequented by mountain lions.

SOUTH FORK KAWEAH TRAILHEAD

TRIP **1**

Putnam and Snowslide Canyons

Ⓜ ↗ DH

DISTANCE: 2.1 miles one way to Putnam Canyon; 3.4 miles one way to Snowslide Canyon

ELEVATION: 3260/5125, +1830'/-230' to Putnam Canyon 3260/5800, +2690'/-460' to Snowslide Canyon

SEASON: All year to Putnam Canyon; March to December to Snowslide Canyon

USE: Light

MAPS: *Dennison Peak, Moses Mountain*

INTRODUCTION: While most Sierra hikers eagerly await the snow-free months of summer, a few resourceful souls enjoy the year-round pleasures of the foothills in southwestern Sequoia National Park. The 2-mile hike to Putnam Canyon and the 3.25 mile hike to Snowslide Canyon on the Garfield-Hockett Trail provide opportunities for early-and-late-season forays into the mountains while the majority of trails in the park are buried beneath snow. This hike passes through foothill woodland for the first 2 miles to Putnam Canyon; those bound for Snowslide Canyon continue through a mixed coniferous forest that includes a smattering of giant sequoias. Fine views of Homers Nose and Dennison Mountain provide visual delight along the way.

DIRECTIONS TO THE TRAILHEAD: Take State Highway 198 to the town of Three Rivers and turn east onto South Fork Road approximately 7 miles southwest from the Ash Mountain Entrance. Follow South

Fork Road for about 9 miles to the end of the pavement and continue another 3 miles on a narrow, dirt road to the South Fork Campground (pit toilets, no water, no fee). Proceed through the campground to a small, oak-shaded parking area.

DESCRIPTION: The signed Garfield-Hockett Trail begins from the campground access road, a short distance before the parking area. You proceed up the trail on a moderate, winding climb up an oak-studded hillside. Lush trailside vegetation includes a quite healthy population of poison oak, and spring wildflowers add splashes of color. Approximately 1 mile from the trailhead, you enter a side canyon and step across the first of many small drainages you will encounter on your way across the slopes below Dennison Mountain. The moisture in these diminutive nooks creates a dramatic change in vegetation as ferns,

SNOWSLIDE CANYON

The boulder-strewn declivity known as Snowslide Canyon is aptly named: in 1867 snow-soaked debris from heavy rains and accelerated snowmelt produced a major slide that temporarily dammed the South Fork Kaweah River. Eventually the raging river breached the dam, sending a destructive flood downstream to the farmlands below.

thimbleberry, maples, nutmegs, alders, dogwoods, and cedars line the shady stream banks.

You continue on a steady climb through oak woodland to Putnam Canyon (5230′±), 2.1 miles from the trailhead. The sound of rushing water below the trail, coursing

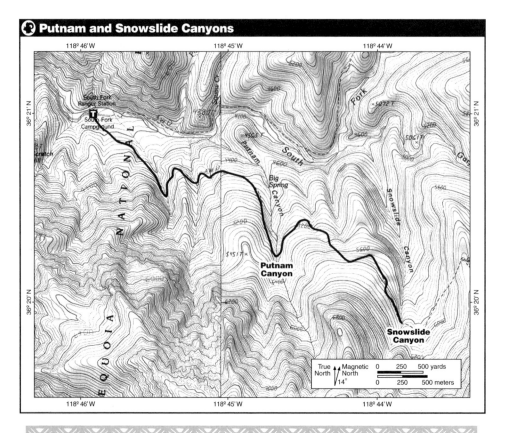

Putnam and Snowslide Canyons

down Putnam Canyon from Big Spring, should be quite noticeable, but chances are the creek will be dry after snowmelt where the trail crosses the streambed. The steep, narrow canyon is filled with boulders and low shrubs, permitting a fine view across the South Fork canyon to the bulbous granite dome of Homers Nose that protrudes from the opposite ridge.

Beyond Putnam Canyon, the steady climb continues as a smattering of ponderosa pines, white firs, and incense cedars begin to intermix with the deciduous forest. Fortunately, the arrival of the conifers coincides with the welcome departure of the poison oak, although the innocuous flowers and plants from the lush understory below start to disappear as well. A mile from Putnam Canyon, you bid farewell to oak woodland as the trail bends southeast into a canyon at the western fringe of Garfield Grove. Farther up the trail, a dozen or so giant sequoias dwarf smaller conifers before you reach the crossing of the vigorous creek that runs through Snowslide Canyon (5830´±), 3.4 miles from the trailhead.

For hikers, Snowslide Canyon makes a fine early-season goal, as the winter snowpack generally covers the trail beyond this point.

SOUTH FORK KAWEAH TRAILHEAD

TRIP **2**

Garfield-Hockett Trail: Garfield Grove and Hockett Lakes

Ⓜ ╱ DH / BP

DISTANCE: 5 miles one way to Garfield Creek; 9.8 miles one way to Hockett Lakes

ELEVATION: 3260/7700, +4150´/-200´ 3260/8585, +5880´/-935´

SEASON: Late May to mid-October

USE: Light

MAPS: *Dennison Peak, Moses Mountain*

TRAIL LOG:

3.25	Snowslide Canyon
5.0	Garfield Creek
9.25	South Fork Crossing
10.0	Hockett Lakes

INTRODUCTION: Tucked quietly away into the southwest corner of Sequoia National Park, Garfield Grove and the contiguous Dillonwood Grove make up one of the largest clusters of giant sequoias in the Sierra. The grove was named in 1926 to honor James A. Garfield, the 20th president of the United States. While hordes of tourists crane their necks to see the Big Trees in the more popular tourist areas such as Giant Forest, Garfield Grove remains cloaked in relative obscurity, awaiting discovery by the small number of devotees who are willing to make the 5-mile hike to the heart of the grove.

The trail begins in foothill woodland and climbs moderately through a diverse set of plant communities, including riparian zones and mixed coniferous forest, to reach

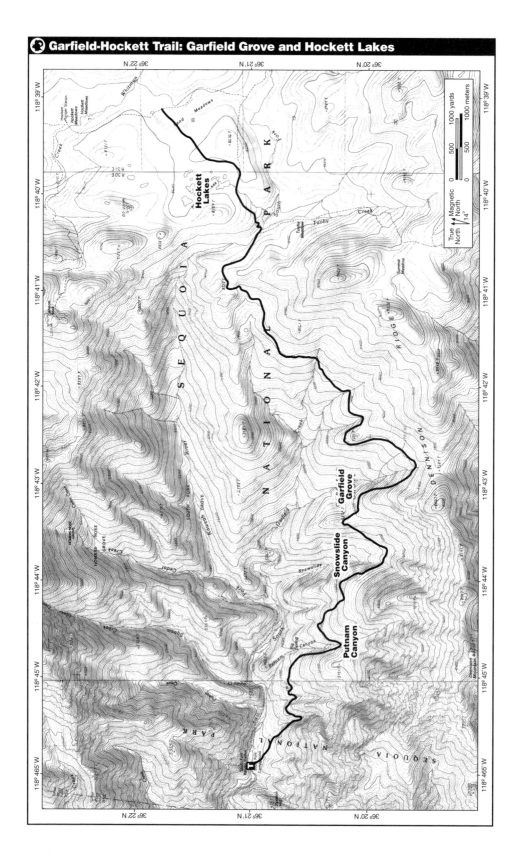

the Big Trees. Along with such diversity, the trip to the grove offers good views and refreshing streams. At the culmination of the 10-mile, 5000-foot climb backpackers reach first-rate camping and swimming at the serene Hockett Lakes.

While the low starting elevation provides an off-season opportunity for short dayhikes (see Trip 1), backpackers bound for the high country beyond will want to get an early start to avoid the typical summer heat. High daily temperatures sufficiently scare away many recreationists from using this trail, although it is the shortest route to Hockett Lakes. Perhaps the best bet for avoiding the stiff ascent during the heat of the day is to take advantage of a free night's stay at the trailhead in the no-fee South Fork Campground, in order to begin at the crack of dawn the next morning. In all seasons, hikers at these low altitudes should be on the lookout for poison oak, ticks, and rattlesnakes for the first 3 miles or so.

DIRECTIONS TO THE TRAILHEAD: Take State Highway 198 to the town of Three Rivers and turn east onto South Fork Road approximately 7 miles southwest from the Ash Mountain Entrance. Follow South Fork Road for about 9 miles to the end of the pavement and continue another 3 miles to the South Fork Campground. Proceed through the campground to a small parking area.

DESCRIPTION: Begin by following the description in Trip 1 to Snowslide Canyon. A short distance beyond Snowslide Canyon, you reenter mixed forest and continue the steady, moderate ascent through the heart of the Garfield Grove. After reaching the crest of a forested ridge, stately sequoias become more numerous, and the trail actually passes right by some of the larger trees in the grove. At the 5-mile point, you step across the first of five branches of Garfield Creek (7235´±) — the luxuriant flora and delightful, cascading streams in each of the five shady nooks provide inviting opportunities for rest stops.

The next 3 miles of trail take you to the far end of Garfield Grove on a mostly mild ascent through mixed forest and giant sequoias.

Leaving the Big Trees behind, a steeper climb takes you quickly to the crest of a red-fir-forested ridge, at 8322 feet. A brief descent from the ridge leads to the broad ford of the South Fork of the Kaweah River (8250´±), 9.25 miles from the trailhead, where you'll find several shady riverside campsites on the far bank.

From the South Fork crossing, you follow the river upstream to a signed junction with the little-used Tuohy Creek Trail, which fords the South Fork and continues south beyond park boundaries to a trailhead at Shake Camp Campground. From this junction, a winding, moderate climb leads you away from the river and up a hillside through light lodgepole-pine forest to the gentler slopes above. Just beyond the crossing of the outlet stream, a short lateral leaves the main trail and leads to the southernmost Hockett Lake (8590´±), 10.0 miles from South Fork Campground. The Garfield-Hockett Trail continues approximately 300 yards east to a junction with a connector trail across Sand Meadows and 1 mile farther to another junction with the Atwell-Hockett Trail (see Trip 5).

Hockett Lakes are a collection of shallow, grassy-banked lakelets surrounded by a light forest of lodgepole pines. A couple of primitive campsites near the southernmost lake testify to the lack of overnight visitors and the strong potential for solitude. The 5- to 8-foot-deep lakes make fine swimming holes.

Although not as extensive as in former days, a fine network of maintained trails provides a number of connections to additional trails on the Hockett Plateau. Along with the route described in Trip 5, seldom-used trails lead south and east to a variety of obscure destinations.

PERMITS: Wilderness permit required for overnight stays. (Quota: 15 per day)
CAMPFIRES: Yes

SOUTH FORK KAWEAH TRAILHEAD

TRIP **3**

Ladybug Camp and Cedar Creek

Ⓜ️Ⓢ ↗ DH/BP

DISTANCE: 1.75 miles one way to Ladybug Camp; 2.8 miles one way to Cedar Creek

ELEVATION: 3620/4300, +960´/-180´
3620/5050, +1800´/-325´

SEASON: All year to Ladybug Camp; March to December to Cedar Creek

USE: Light

MAPS: *Dennison Peak, Moses Mountain*

TRAIL LOG:

1.75 Ladybug Camp
5.0 Garfield Creek
2.75 Cedar Creek
10 Hockett Lakes

INTRODUCTION: The Ladybug Trail offers a fine opportunity for off-season hiking when the rest of the Sierra remains buried under the annual snowpack. During March and April, blooming wildflowers provide a fine complement to the green grasslands, both replenished by the winter rain that makes up the bulk of precipitation in the foothills. In spring, the deciduous trees and shrubs that compose the oak woodland zone leaf out and return signs of life to their bare branches. The South Fork Kaweah River is at full force, cascading and churning its way through the foothills to a much tamer fate in the Central Valley. Fall adds a dose of crisp air and a splash of autumn color to the leaves of the deciduous forest. Throw in the opportunity to experience the giant sequoias close up at Cedar Creek, and

you have the makings for a splendid off-season hike or backpack. Watch for ticks, rattlesnakes, and poison oak.

DIRECTIONS TO THE TRAILHEAD: Take State Highway 198 to the town of Three Rivers and turn east onto South Fork Road approximately 7 miles southwest from the Ash Mountain Entrance. Follow South Fork Road for about 9 miles to the end of the pavement and continue another 3 miles to the South Fork Campground. Proceed through the campground to a small parking area.

DESCRIPTION: From the trailhead parking area, head east upstream on a wide trail down to the wooden bridge across the South Fork Kaweah River. Across the bridge you begin a moderate ascent through oak woodlands and widely scattered boulders that leads you high above the river. Along the way, you step across the usually dry streambed of Pigeon Creek. Just before the stream, you may notice the remnants of an obscure old path that at one time led hikers steeply uphill to Homers Nose. This route has long been abandoned, one of many such trails in the southwest part of Sequoia National Park. Beyond the creek, you eventually emerge from the shaded cover of light forest to a fine view of 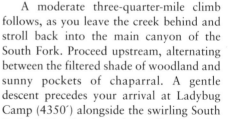 the South Fork below; ahead you can see Putnam Canyon and its cascading creek. A milder climb takes you back into oak woodlands and on to the log-and-boulder crossing of Squaw Creek, 0.9 mile from the trailhead.

A moderate three-quarter-mile climb follows, as you leave the creek behind and stroll back into the main canyon of the South Fork. Proceed upstream, alternating between the filtered shade of woodland and sunny pockets of chaparral. A gentle descent precedes your arrival at Ladybug Camp (4350´) alongside the swirling South Fork, 1.75 miles from the trailhead. Oaks, incense cedars, and a few ponderosa pines shade the pleasant campsites spread around the flat. Apparently, the area received its name from a wintering population of lady-bug beetles.

The main trail continues upstream a short distance to an unofficial junction. A use-trail proceeds straight ahead to an open area of rock slabs on a narrow bench. From this spot, directly above the river and across from the confluence of Garfield Creek, you have breathtaking views of the tumbling river, full of spring snowmelt, as it churns and plunges down the canyon.

From the unofficial junction with the use-trail, the main trail bends away from the river on a moderate climb across a grassy hillside dotted with oak and cedar. Through gaps in the trees, you have fine views of Homers Nose 4000 feet above, a granite dome dubiously named by a survey-or for its resemblance to the nose of his guide, John Homer. Careful inspection of the drainages across the canyon will reveal a smattering of giant sequoias, their charac-teristically rounded tops thrust skyward. These specimens from the Garfield Grove represent the lowest-elevation sequoias in the Sierra. The views eventually disappear in a thickening forest of oak and cedar, heralding your approach to Cedar Creek (5050′±). Along the banks, a number of

THE BRIDGE THAT ISN'T

You may notice some reinforcing steel protruding from the rock on either side of the river just above the confluence, remnants of an old bridge that used to span the South Fork. A trail once led from the bridge up the ridge to a connection with the Garfield-Hockett Trail, but was aban-doned after the bridge collapsed from heavy snows in 1969.

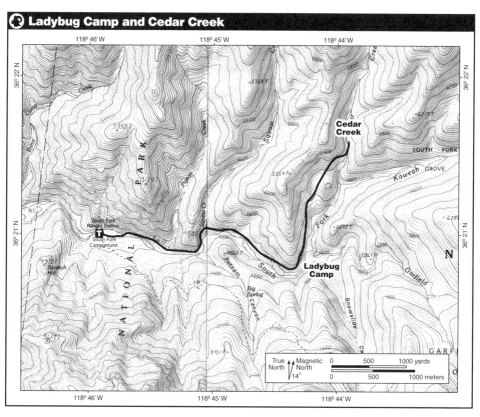

Ladybug Camp and Cedar Creek

giant sequoias tower over the surroundings and several younger sequoias are sprinkled throughout the drainage.

O At one time your options along the Ladybug Trail were relatively numerous, as a number of trails used to penetrate the backcountry beyond the currently maintained trail, which dead-ends at Cedar Creek. You can still follow the old trail beyond Cedar Creek without much difficulty. It leads up the hillside to an old Y-junction, where a metal sign with punched-out letters gives directions to Cahoon Meadow and South Fork. Since the 1970s, neither trail has been maintained, and both are overgrown with brush, blocked by deadfalls, and have washed-out sections.

The South Fork path descends to a grove of sequoias in the South Fork Kaweah River canyon and some old campsites at Whiskey Log Camp, about 2 miles from Cedar Creek, but the hiking is difficult and should be attempted only by parties experienced in bushwhacking cross-country travel.

R **PERMITS:** Wilderness permit required for overnight stay (Quota: 15 per day)
CAMPFIRES: Yes

Mineral King as seen from the Sawtooth Pass Trail

Introduction to Atwell Mill and Mineral King

One glimpse of the glacier-carved East Fork canyon, with its alpine-looking slopes and rim of striking peaks is enough to convince virtually anyone of Mineral King's picturesque riches. Ironically, however, these scenic virtues had less to do with the inclusion of the area into Sequoia National Park than did the lack of the region's material wealth.

Prompted by the well-publicized mining booms in other areas of California and Nevada, hopeful miners poured into the area (originally named Beulah) in the late 1800s in search of the next mother lode. Just enough ore was present to keep hopes alive, but never enough to make mining practical in such a remote location. The southern Sierra never yielded a significant strike of either gold or silver, and by the turn of the century the anticipated boom was a bust. The 1906 earthquake that destroyed San Francisco triggered massive avalanches that leveled structures in Mineral King and served as an exclamation point to the region's commercial woes.

The wood to rebuild the ruins had to come from somewhere. A nearby sawmill, now known as Atwell Mill, built by Collins and Redfield in 1879, provided the lumber for the buildings, as well as a million board feet of lumber to construct a flume used for hydroelectricity between Oak Grove and Hammond. Unfortunately, a number of massive sequoias were axed in the process, their stumps still visible today in the vicinity of Atwell Mill. The mill eventually suffered a death similar to the mining industry, as the cost of transporting lumber to viable markets in the San Joaquin Valley beyond Mineral King proved to be unprofitable.

Yet another commercial interest invaded Mineral King when the Mt. Whitney Power Company built a series of four rock-and-mortar dams at Crystal, Eagle, Franklin, and Monarch lakes between 1904

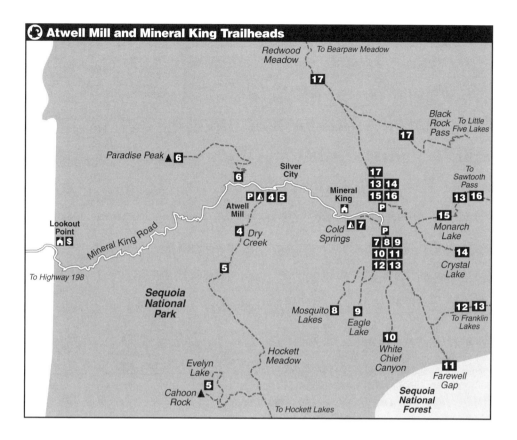

Atwell Mill and Mineral King Trailheads

and 1905. The dams were constructed to regulate the flow of water into the aforementioned flume in order to maximize the generation of electricity at the company's hydroelectric plant in Hammond. Unlike the mining and timber interests, the dams and the power plant are still in operation, currently owned by Southern California Edison.

Once mining and timber went by the wayside, the remaining inhabitants of Mineral King turned to the prospect of a resort community in order to earn an existence in their beloved mountains. The town was rebuilt after the 1906 earthquake, but failed to attain much fame as a resort, maintaining a rather sleepy existence until after World War II.

Mild winters and long-lasting snowpacks prompted the Tulare County Board of Supervisors to sponsor a snow survey in 1947, which resulted in a recommendation for development of Mineral King as a winter sports region. In 1949, the board solicited proposals from developers, but it wasn't until 1965 that Disney Enterprises of Burbank, California, was selected as the contractor. Disney planned to turn Mineral King into the foremost ski destination in the world, with a resort that would cater to over 10,000 skiers per day. With eager cooperation from the Forest Service, Disney proceeded with their plans.

Timing is everything: Plans for turning Mineral King into a mega-resort ran headlong into the budding environmental movement. Protracted legal battles and negative public opinion, along with the excessive costs of building an all-weather road and an increased awareness of Mineral King's avalanche potential combined to create forces that were too much for Disney to

Campgrounds							
Campground	Fee	Elevation	Season	Restrooms	Running Water	Bear Boxes	Phone
ATWELL MILL* (18 miles from Hwy 198)	$8	6650'	Memorial Day weekend to Oct. 31	Pit Toilets	Yes	Yes	Yes
COLD SPRINGS* (21.5 miles from Hwy 198)	$8	7500'	Memorial Day weekend to Oct. 31	Pit Toilets	Yes	Yes	Yes

*No trailers or RV's

overcome. In 1978, President Carter signed the bill finally incorporating the majestic region of Mineral King into Sequoia National Park. Today, the area is managed with the same sleepy atmosphere that prevailed through much of the 20th century.

ACCESS: (Open late May to November 1) Access to both Atwell Mill and Mineral King trailheads is via Mineral King Road, a steep, narrow, winding, and partially dirt road that proceeds up the canyon of the East Fork Kaweah River. Drivers must be alert for oncoming traffic, particularly during weekends. Plan on at least an hour and 15 minutes for the 25-mile, 6700-foot climb from Three Rivers to Mineral King. Be forewarned, gas is not available beyond Three Rivers.

Weather permitting, the road is open between November and late May for the first 16.5 miles to a locked gate, 2.5 miles before Atwell Mill Campground.

AMENITIES: The tourism-based community of Three Rivers, 37 miles east of Visalia, offers a wide range of services, including motels, restaurants, gas stations, and general stores.

The family-run Silver City Resort is generally open from late May into October, providing comfortable lodging in chalets and cabins, a limited selection of supplies (no ice or alcoholic beverages), dining, public showers, and ranger-led campfire talks on Thursday evenings. Call (559) 561-3223 (summer) or (805) 528-2730 (off-season) for more information, or visit their website at www.silvercityresort.com.

RANGER STATION: The Mineral King Ranger Station is located 22 miles from Hwy. 198 on Mineral King Road. The facility is generally staffed from late May to late September. Wilderness permits can be obtained in person during normal business hours (7 A.M. to 5:30 P.M., Thursday through Sunday; 7 A.M. to 3 P.M., Monday through Wednesday). Hours are reduced after Labor Day weekend, and eventually permits are self-issued later in the season. A limited selection of books and maps are for sale and bear canisters are available for rent. Call (559) 565-3768 for more information.

GOOD TO KNOW BEFORE YOU GO:

1. Backpackers leaving cars overnight at Mineral King trailheads should put all food and scented items in the storage shed directly opposite the ranger station, as bear boxes are not available at Tar Gap, Eagle-Mosquito, or Sawtooth-Monarch trailheads.

2. Marmots are plentiful at Mineral King, and some of these rodents have developed an unusual hankering for munching on car parts. For an inexplicable reason, Mineral King marmots are prone to nibbling on radiator hoses, fan belts, brake lines, and even radiators, sometimes rendering vehicles inoperable. Fortunately, this problem is usually limited to early season (May and June), and by July they turn to more nutritious fare. Check with the rangers at Mineral King on the current conditions. If your trip happens to coincide with car-munching season, you may want to take the precaution of encircling your vehicle with chicken wire from your local hardware store when you leave it at the trailhead.

3. If you plan on camping at either of the two campgrounds, check the board at the junction between Hwy. 198 and the Mineral King Road, and at the Lookout Point entrance to see if space is available. This could save you a very time-consuming trip if the campgrounds are full.

East Fork Kaweah Bridge

TRIP **4**

East Fork Grove

Ⓜ ↗ DH

DISTANCE: 2.5 miles one way

ELEVATION: 6600/6240, +525´/-820´

SEASON: Late May to November

USE: Light

MAP: *Silver City*

INTRODUCTION: Most hikers and backpackers who endure the rigors of driving the Mineral King Road are bound for the high country above the valley, thereby overlooking some of the lesser-known treasures nearby. Some of these neglected riches lie along the Atwell-Hockett Trail, which leads hikers to a classically picturesque river canyon and a nearly forgotten grove of giant sequoias. On a 2.5 mile hike, visitors will enjoy the turbulent East Fork Kaweah River cascading through a narrow cleft of granite, and a fine selection of the Big Trees sans crowds.

DIRECTIONS TO THE TRAILHEAD: From the east end of Three Rivers, leave State Highway 198 and turn onto Mineral King Road. Follow the narrow, twisting, road for 18 miles to the Atwell Mill Campground and then continue 0.2 mile farther to the turnoff into the signed trailhead parking area (with a bear box) at the east end of the campground.

DESCRIPTION: Walk down the campground road for about 250 yards from the parking area to the beginning of the signed Atwell-Hockett trail. Running water and pit toilets are available in the campground. You follow the path past redwood stumps to a small meadow filled with relics from the old Atwell Mill.

Through mixed forest of black oaks, white firs, sugar pines, ponderosa pines, incense cedars, and sequoias, you follow the trail as it veers away from the mill site. On a mild descent, the trail wraps around a hillside. Soon you drop to Deadwood Creek, a diminutive sliver of stream. The descent continues through the trees another half a mile to a stout steel-and-wood bridge spanning the granitic cleft of the East Fork Kaweah River (5955′±), 1.25 miles from the parking area. From the bridge, you take in a picture-postcard scene of the cascading stream as it plummets over slabs and boulders down a narrow, sequoia-lined gorge.

Beyond the bridge, you proceed through the East Fork Grove on a mild to moderate climb that leads away from the raucous sound of the creek. Deer Creek is a good turnaround point for your hike; the Atwell-Hockett Trail continues south to the unceremonious end of the East Fork Grove.

THE ATWELL MILL

In the 1870's, the Atwell Mill provided the town of Beulah (Mineral King) with lumber for buildings and mines. In the 1890s, the mill supplied a million board feet for a flume between Oak Grove and a hydroelectric facility in Hammond. The high cost of transporting lumber to the San Joaquin Valley doomed the mill by the turn of the century, but not before many stately giant sequoias surrounding the mill succumbed to the logger's axe. Ironically, most of the brittle sequoia lumber was found to be useful only for shakes and fence posts.

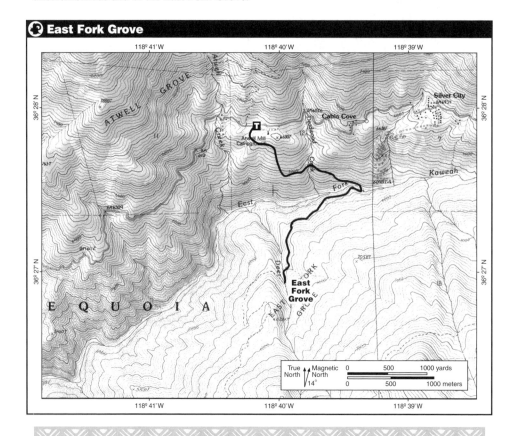

ATWELL MILL TRAILHEAD

TRIP **5**

Atwell-Hockett Trail: Hockett Plateau

Ⓜ ↗ BP

DISTANCE: 10 miles to Hockett Meadows

ELEVATION: 6600/8510, +3690'/-1785'

SEASON: June to late October

USE: Light

MAP: *Silver City*

TRAIL LOG:

1.25 E. Fork Kaweah River
2.5   Deer Creek
7.25 Clover Creek
8.5   Tar Gap Trail Jct.
8.75 Horse Creek
10.0 Hockett Meadow & Evelyn Lk/Cahoon Jct.

INTRODUCTION: Travelers along the Atwell-Hockett Trail pass cascading streams, giant sequoias and quiet forests on their way to Hockett Meadow, one of the largest and most scenic meadows in Sequoia National Park. Not many backpackers and horse packers visit the Hockett Plateau, and those who do generally enter from Mineral King on the Tar Gap Trail. Unfortunately, they miss the scenic canyon of the East Fork Kaweah River and the stately sequoias of the East Fork Grove on the Atwell-Hockett Trail.

After the first mile of descent to the East Fork, the remaining 9-mile trek is mostly a steady climb on a pleasant grade through mixed forest; breaks in the forest allow periodic views along the way.

Once at pastoral Hockett Meadow, backpackers will find pleasant camping, stunning scenery, and unmatched serenity.

A base camp on the Hockett Plateau is a fine outpost for additional hikes; you can visit attractive Evelyn Lake and tranquil Hockett Lakes, take in expansive views from Cahoon Rock, and explore more remote destinations along the southern fringe of the park. Another highlight of this trip is the wildlife; deer frequent the meadow around dusk and bears are occasionally seen along the trail.

DIRECTIONS TO THE TRAILHEAD: From the east end of Three Rivers, you leave State Highway 198 and turn onto Mineral King Road. Follow the road for 18 miles to the Atwell Mill Campground and then continue 0.2 mile farther to the turnoff taking you into the signed trailhead parking area (with a bear box) at the east end of the campground.

DESCRIPTION: The first segment of the trail takes you to Deer Creek, 2.5 miles from the trailhead. You walk down the campground road for about 250 yards from the parking area to the beginning of the signed Atwell-Hockett trail. Follow the path past redwood stumps to a small meadow filled with relics from the old Atwell Mill.

Through mixed forest, you follow the trail as it veers away from the mill site. On a mild descent, the trail wraps around a hillside and then drops to Deadwood Creek. The descent continues through the trees another half mile, to a stout steel-and-wood bridge spanning the granitic cleft of the East Fork Kaweah River (5955'±), 1.25 miles from the parking area.

Beyond the bridge, proceed through the East Fork Grove on a mild to moderate climb that leads away from the raucous sound of the creek. As you ascend, you pass a pair of creeklets on the way to Deer Creek.

Leaving Deer Creek, you continue along the Atwell-Hockett Trail on a steady climb through a mixed forest of sugar and ponderosa pines, white firs, incense cedars, black oaks, and giant sequoias. The trail switchbacks and then curves high above the Deer Creek drainage as you bid a final

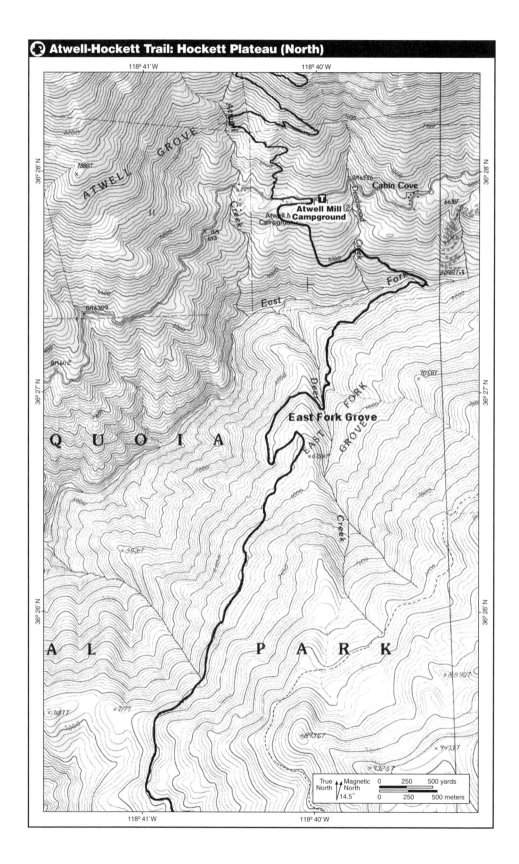

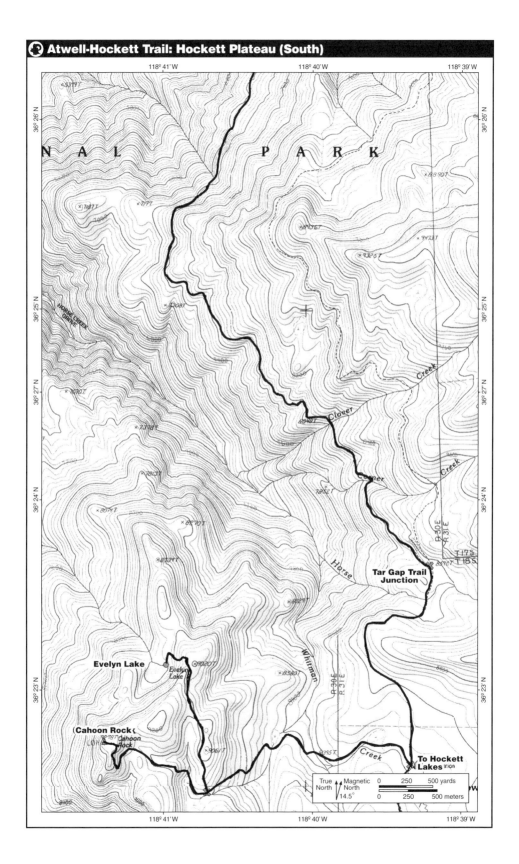

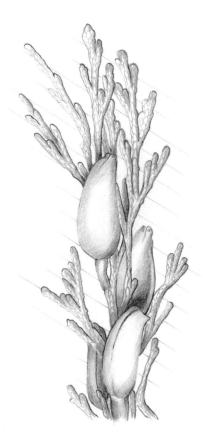

Incense cedar

farewell to the big sequoias of the East Fork Grove. Across a hillside above the East Fork Kaweah River, the ascent continues through mixed forest and an understory of chinquapin, mountain misery, thimbleberry, bracken fern, and hazel nut. Occasional breaks in the forest allow fine views down the East Fork canyon and out to the San Joaquin Valley (haze permitting), including cars snaking along Mineral King Road.

You round a ridge, and find yourself above the Horse Creek drainage, with periodic views of Cahoon Rock and the back side of Homers Nose. After crossing a number of tiny brooks, you eventually reach densely vegetated Clover Creek (8040′±), 7.25 miles from the parking area. Above

the near bank, a short use-trail leads to a solitary campsite.

From the creek, a steady, half-mile ascent takes you past a flower-filled, sloping meadow and on to the crossing of Corner Creek, where head-high wildflowers and plants carpet the drainage. You travel through fir forest and pockets of meadow for the next tree-quarters of a mile to the signed Y-junction with the Tar Gap Trail (8590′) to Mineral King, 8.5 miles from the start.

A few paces from the Tar Gap Trail intersection, you pass the indistinct junction with the abandoned Horse Creek Trail, which leads to Ansel Lake. The lake is quite scenic, but the route is extremely obscure and very hard to follow. An easier route to the lake is cross-country from White Chief basin (see Trip 10). Stay on the Atwell Mill Trail and descend gently to a series of spacious campsites alongside Horse Creek. Backpackers won't find a bear box, but an old-fashioned food-storage cable may thwart any marauding bears. A short distance beyond the camp, at 8.75 miles, you reach the ford of Horse Creek (8575′±).

From the creek, you cross a boggy area on a wood-plank bridge and begin a short climb around the nose of a red-fir-forested ridge. A gentle descent through lodgepole pine follows, leading you to the signed junction with the Evelyn Lake Trail near

HOCKETT RANGER STATION

The two-room, log cabin Hockett Ranger Station stands guard over the spacious meadow, assisted by a good-sized tack cabin and large corral. This gig must be a coveted assignment for park rangers, as the pastoral scenery and gentle surroundings are quite appealing. (Rangers are typically on duty here from June to early September.) Early evening almost guarantees a visit from the local deer herd to graze on the verdant meadow grass.

Thomas Winnett

Wild geranium

the northern fringe of a huge meadow. A short stroll from the junction brings you to the wide expanse of Hockett Meadow (8510′±), 10 miles from the Atwell Mill Campground.

The signed trail to Evelyn Lake/Cahoon Rock leads to campsites not far from Whitman Creek, with a toilet and a bear box. However, with a little effort, you can find better sites around the fringes of Hockett Meadow, with fine views of the meadow.

O **SIDE TRIP TO EVELYN LAKE:** Hockett Meadow provides a fine basecamp for exploring the hinterlands of the Hockett Plateau. First on the list of must-see features is Evelyn Lake—a 2.5-mile hike. From its junction with the Atwell-Hockett Trail, follow the Evelyn Lake Trail past lodgepole-shaded campsites to the crossing of Whitman Creek. Step across a meadow-rimmed smaller tributary of Whitman Creek 0.4 mile farther, and then make a moderate ascent to a signed Y-junction, 1.7

miles from the Atwell-Hockett Trail. Veer right at the junction and climb more steeply up a hillside of scattered trees and then along the crest of a ridge, which provides excellent views. At the end of the ridge you make a zigzagging descent through red firs to Evelyn Lake (8665′±).

You'll find campsites with a hitching post nearby along the northeast shore of the lake. There are more remote sites near the outlet, but most of the shoreline is covered with thick brush and a jumble of boulders that make travel around the lake a tad difficult. The picturesque cliffs of this rock-bound cirque make a fine backdrop to the lake's sparkling waters; the fishing is quite good and the swimming is very refreshing.
END OF SIDE TRIP

O **SIDE TRIP TO CAHOON ROCK:** To take in expansive views from the summit of Cahoon Rock, begin on the Evelyn Lake Trail from Hockett Meadow. At the Evelyn Lake/Cahoon Rock Y-junction, follow the left-hand trail alongside a diminutive stream through moderate forest cover. Eventually, you climb up the hillside to a sandy slope below the summit. Although the trail becomes ill-defined, the route is obvious—a short scramble over boulders to the top of Cahoon Rock (9278′), 1 mile from the junction.

The view from the summit is quite rewarding, especially if the normally hazy skies have just benefited from a cleansing shower or zephyr. The distant peaks of the Great Western Divide and the nearby summits of Quinn Peak, Soda Butte, and Vandeveer Mountain fill the eastern skyline. Dennison Ridge is visible in the south, and Homers Nose in the west, with the Central Valley beyond. **END OF SIDE TRIP**

O **SIDE TRIP TO HOCKETT LAKES:** To reach Hockett Lakes, continue on the Atwell-Hockett Trail past the ranger cabin and cross the wooden bridge over Whitman Creek. After a short climb up the hillside, you parallel Hockett Meadow on a long traverse through a lodgepole forest; the meadow remains hidden from view thanks to the trees. At a junction at the north end of Sand Meadow, 1.1 miles from the Evelyn Lake/Cahoon Rock junction, you turn right (southwest), leaving the Atwell-Hockett Trail.

Follow the path across the northern fringe of Sand Meadow to the resumption of lodgepole forest beyond. A mile from the junction, you encounter the Garfield–Hockett Trail, where you head west several hundred yards to the short lateral leading to the southernmost Hockett Lake (8950′±). The Hockett Lakes are a collection of shallow, grass-lined lakes and ponds fringed with lodgepole pines; the lakes offer quiet camping and pleasant swimming. **END OF SIDE TRIP**

O Although not as extensive as it once was, a fine network of trails extends from the Hockett Plateau to far-flung destinations scattered across the southern extremity of Sequoia National Park. A base camp at Hockett Meadow or Hockett Lakes allows forays on isolated trails to a variety

of seldom-seen areas. With arrangements for a shuttle from the South Fork trailhead, you could combine this trip with the Garfield-Hockett Trail, reversing the description from Hockett Lakes in Trip 2.

R **PERMITS:** Wilderness permit required for overnight stays. (Quota: 25 per day)

CAMPFIRES: Yes

ATWELL MILL TRAILHEAD

TRIP **6**

Paradise Peak

Ⓜ️ ↗ DH

DISTANCE: 4.8 miles one way

ELEVATION: 6600/9362, +2990'/-185'

SEASON: Mid-June to late October

USE: Light

MAP: *Silver City*

INTRODUCTION: You won't fight crowds on this trail, as only a few hardy souls undertake the steep ascent to Paradise Peak. But the climb up this south-facing slope to the site of the old lookout tower isn't as difficult as it seems, and the view from the top is superb. The giant sequoias in Atwell Grove are an added bonus, some of which are among the largest in existence.

DIRECTIONS TO THE TRAILHEAD: From the east end of Three Rivers, you leave State Highway 198 and turn onto Mineral King Road. Follow the road for 18 miles to the Atwell Mill Campground and then continue 0.2 mile farther to the turnoff taking you into the signed trailhead parking area (with a bear box) at the east end of the campground.

DESCRIPTION: From the parking area, head back down the Mineral King Road for a quarter of a mile to the signed PARADISE RIDGE TRAILHEAD. A single-track trail climbs moderately through a mixed forest of white firs, ponderosa and sugar pines, incense cedars, and young sequoias, with an understory of mountain misery and manzanita. Soon you begin a series of switchbacks that take you well up the hillside. Past an opening in the forest, medium-sized giant sequoias appear just before you step over a small fern-and-alder-lined seasonal rivulet. As you progress up the trail, you'll see larger sequoias, a few of which are some of the 20 or 30 largest in the Sierra.

The Great Western Divide, seen from Paradise Peak Trail

More zigzagging switchbacks take you steeply up the hillside and toward Atwell Creek—contrary to what is shown on the USGS quad, the trail approaches but does not cross the creek. If you need water, you'll have to thrash your way through brush to the creek, as it is the only reliable source of water along the entire route. Continue the switchbacking ascent away from the stream to a junction at the crest of Paradise Ridge, 3.75 miles from the parking lot.

In a light forest of red fir, where snowbush, chinquapin, and manzanita, grow in widely scattered patches, you turn west and follow the ridge toward Paradise Peak. The gentler grade of the trail is a welcome relief after the steep climb up the south-facing hillside to the ridgecrest. After passing to the north of Peak 8863, watchful eyes may be able to spot the crown of the highest growing sequoia (at the elevation of 8800′)

down the slope to the southeast. Proceed up the ridge and then wind your way toward the top over rocky terrain. The trail falters through here, so watch for ducks or simply head for the high point. From the summit of Paradise Peak (9362′), you have a fine view to the east, of the peaks of the Great Western Divide, and to the north, of the back side of Castle Rocks and the granite domes of Big and Little Baldy.

Any trip to Paradise Peak would be incomplete without experiencing the view from the site of the old lookout, directly southwest of the true summit. Work your way through brush and boulders to the base of the rock at the end of the ridge, climb the rock steps, and then scramble up a crack to the top. You may not have a splendid view of the Great Western Divide from here, thanks to the trees, but the vista to the west is most impressive, including a glimpse straight down the canyon of

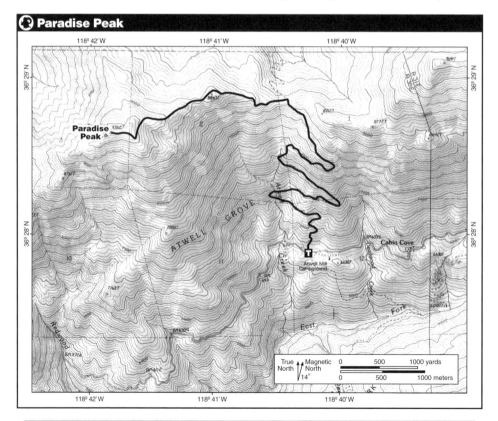

Paradise Creek to the Middle Fork Kaweah River. Also visible are Moro Rock, Alta Peak, and the Generals Highway. To the south is the Hockett Plateau. Although the lookout was dynamited back in the 1950s, a radio repeater nearby stands as an unwelcome reminder of contemporary human presence.

MINERAL KING TRAILHEAD

TRIP **7**

Cold Springs Trail

Ⓔ ↗ ↗ DH

DISTANCE: 1.2 miles one way

ELEVATION: 7480/7810, +350´/-20´

SEASON: Late May through October

USE: Moderate

MAPS: *Mineral King*
Mineral King, SNHA

INTRODUCTION: Most trails that emanate from Mineral King climb steeply out of the valley. The Cold Springs Trail is a rare exception, mildly ascending along the East Fork Kaweah River between the Cold Springs Campground and the Eagle-Mosquito trailhead parking area. Diehard backcountry enthusiasts won't find the short trail much of a challenge, but the pleasant path is well suited for a family hike or lazy afternoon stroll. Although the trail is easy and short, the alpine-like scenery of Mineral King is always rewarding. A detour on the short nature trail loop is an informative way to acquaint oneself with the ecology and history of the Mineral King area.

DIRECTIONS TO THE TRAILHEAD:
START: From the east end of Three Rivers, leave State Highway 198 and turn onto Mineral King Road. Follow the narrow, twisting road 22 miles to the turnoff to Cold Springs Campground, which is 2.5 miles past Silver City. Cross the bridge over the East Fork Kaweah River and turn left at the first intersection. Travel 0.1 mile to the small parking area near the signed trailhead, by campsite 6.
END: To reach the Eagle-Mosquito trailhead parking area, follow the directions above; when you reach the campground, continue up Mineral King Road, 1.2 miles

past the ranger station to the parking area at the end of the road.

DESCRIPTION: Head upstream along the south bank of the East Fork Kaweah River. The gently graded trail crosses a grassland dotted with aspens, cottonwoods, and a plethora of wildflowers. About 0.1 mile from the trailhead, the Cold Springs Nature Trail branches to the right and then quickly loops back to the main trail. The nature trail has interpretive signposts with information on the flora, geology, and mining activity of the Mineral King area.

The main trail continues upstream, past delightful pools and tumbling cascades that are well suited for fishing or wading. Farther on, switchbacks take you away from the river and into a stand of red fir. Beyond the trees, you emerge onto drier, sagebrush-covered slopes. You cross several streams on wood walkways and then

descend some rock steps. The final stretch of trail passes a number of old cabins from the settlement of Mineral King to reach the Eagle-Mosquito parking area. If you didn't make shuttle arrangements, retrace your steps to the Cold Springs Campground.

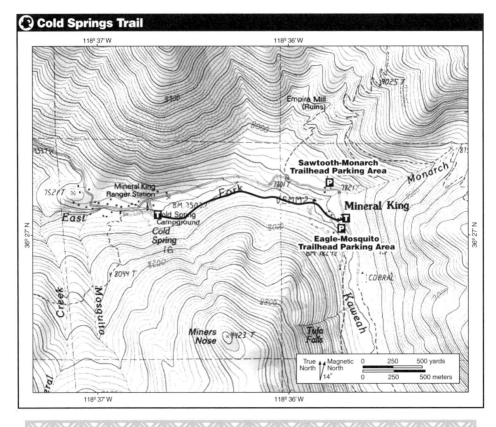

TRIP **8**

Mosquito Lakes

Ⓜ ↗ DH/BP

DISTANCE: 3.5 miles one way to
Mosquito Lake No. 1;

ELEVATION: 7815/9585, +2135'/-375'

SEASON: Early July to mid-October

USE: Moderate

MAPS: *Mineral King*
Mineral King, SNHA

TRAIL LOG:

1.0 White Chief Canyon Trail Jct.
1.75 Eagle Lake Trail Jct.
3.25 Mosquito Lake No. 1

INTRODUCTION: The six fascinating Mosquito Lakes range from densely forested to barren and rockbound. The lakes used to be extremely popular destinations, until several changes made them less accessible: the steep but short 1.5-mile trail from Cold Springs Campground was abandoned; camping was prohibited at Mosquito Lake No.1; and the trail above the first lake was allowed to regress into a cross-country route. Nowadays, a smattering of day hikers make the trek up the newer trail to the first lake, but only a few travel to the higher lakes, and a high percentage of backpackers seem intimidated by the off-trail climb to the permissible camping at the upper lakes. The result is that visitors to the Mosquito Lakes, whether by day or for the night, can enjoy the surroundings without crowds.

The scenery is sublime at each of the lakes, swimming is refreshing, and brook trout fishing is reportedly good. The best campsites are at Lake No. 3. Traces of the old trail to the upper lakes still exist, marked by ducks, which makes the mostly cross-country route easy to follow. Getting lost would be difficult, as you would have

Mosquito Lake No. 3 from the Mosquito Lakes Trail

to make a very steep climb to get out of the canyon. One word of caution: these lakes received their name for a reason—be prepared for hordes of the nasty pests in early summer.

DIRECTIONS TO THE TRAILHEAD: From the east end of Three Rivers, leave State Highway 198 and turn onto Mineral King Road. Follow the narrow, twisting road 23.5 miles to the end of the road at the Mosquito-Eagle trailhead parking area.

DESCRIPTION: South of the parking area a dirt road begins past the trailhead signboard and the Honeymoon Cabin. Follow the road on a mild climb up the East Fork Kaweah River canyon through open sagebrush vegetation, dotted with red firs, mountain maples, and an occasional juniper. After a quarter of a mile, you cross Spring Creek on a removable wooden

bridge made of 2″ x 6″ planks. Within earshot but out of sight is Tufa Falls, which is visible from the Farewell Gap Trail across the valley. The creek originates higher up the hillside and travels through a subterranean band of marble before its sudden emergence a few hundred feet above the trail.

Just beyond Spring Creek, you pass an unsigned lateral that descends to the river; continue on your trail, taking in views across the valley of cascading Crystal Creek. Step across willow-lined Eagle Creek and shortly arrive at the signed White Chief Canyon Trail junction (8255′±), 1 mile from the parking area.

Turn right at the junction and wrap around the hillside to a set of steep switchbacks that climb through alternating pockets of meadow and stands of red fir and lodgepole pine. The grade eases as you approach Eagle Sink Hole, where part of

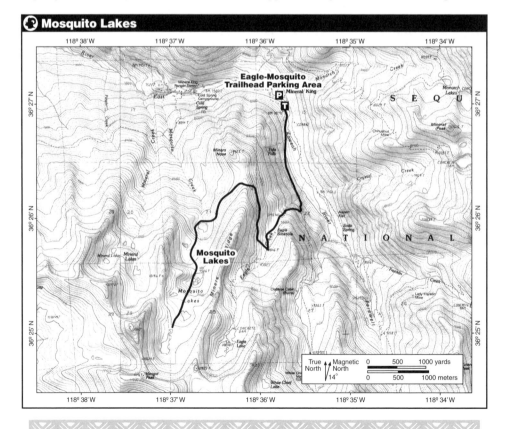

Eagle Creek mysteriously disappears. You start to climb again and soon pass the Eagle Lake Trail junction (9016´), 1.75 miles from the trailhead.

Ascend through red firs to the forested crest of Miner's Ridge, where you begin a 0.75-mile descent, aided by switchbacks, to Mosquito Lake No. 1 (9030´±), 3.25 miles from the trailhead.

Oval-shaped Mosquito Lake No. 1 is backed by a talus slope and surrounded by lodgepole pine. Camping has been banned for many years to allow overused sites to recover. The absence of tents and of overnight visitors adds to the tranquility of the surroundings. Fishing for brook trout is reported to be quite good.

UNMAINTAINED TRAIL

Old signs near the outlet stream mark a junction with the unmaintained trail that descends Mosquito Creek to a connection with the Tar Gap Trail, a half mile from the trailhead at Cold Springs Campground. This old trail was a shorter but much steeper route from Mineral King to the lakes.

A now unmaintained trail used to climb up the canyon to the other Mosquito Lakes, but over time it has deteriorated. Parts of the old path are still evident as far as Lake No. 3, and the route is fairly easy to follow. From the outlet of Mosquito Lake No. 1, follow a distinct path around the west shore and then head south up a steep hillside above the lake. Blazes on lodgepole pines and an assortment of ducks help guide you. On the east side of tiny Mosquito Lake No. 2 (campsites), you make another steep but short climb to Mosquito Lake No. 3 (9586´). Two small islands dot this scenic lake, and an amphitheater of towering white rock cliffs rims it. Slabs on the south shore entice sunbathers and swimmers. Anglers may ply the

waters in search of good-sized resident brook trout. A sparse forest of lodgepole pine shades idyllic campsites around the lakeshore.

Above the third lake, signs of the old trail disappear and the route becomes mostly cross-country. Ducks will help guide you up the next hillside to the right of a rocky slope. Pass well to the east of diminutive Mosquito Lake No. 4 and continue to Mosquito Lake No. 5 (9885´±), an irregular-shaped lake surrounded by a grassy shoreline and scattered lodgepoles, and tucked against the cliffs of Miners Ridge.

The route to the austere, treeless Mosquito Lake No. 6 (10,005´±), the last lake in the chain, continues a quarter of a mile up the canyon.

⊙ Off-trail enthusiasts can make a short but challenging loop back to the trailhead. An extremely steep ascent leads over rock-strewn Miners Ridge to Eagle Lake. See Trip 9 for the trail description from to Eagle Lake back to Mineral Spring.

Mineral Lakes can be accessed over a saddle that lies directly west of Mosquito Lake No. 4.

R **PERMITS:** Wilderness permits required for overnight stays. (Quota: 25 per day)
  CAMPFIRES: No
  CAMPING: No camping at Mosquito Lake No. 1.

TRIP 9

Eagle Lake

Ⓜ ↗ DH/BP

DISTANCE: 3.25 miles one way

ELEVATION: 7815/10,045, +2285´/-55´

SEASON: Early July to mid-October

USE: Moderately heavy

MAPS: *Mineral King*
Mineral King, SNHA

TRAIL LOG:

1.75 Mosquito Lakes Jct.
3.25 Eagle Lake

INTRODUCTION: Crystalline Eagle Lake, reposing majestically in a deep cirque, draws flocks of anglers, photographers, day hikers, and backpackers in the summer. The lake's popularity is well deserved, and the journey is only 3.25 miles, although the stiff climb requires that visitors be in reasonable shape.

In the early 1900s, the Mt. Whitney Power and Electric Company dammed Eagle Lake to regulate water flow for power production at their generating plant in Hammond. Similar dams were constructed at Crystal, Franklin, and Monarch lakes. Eagle Lake is regulated today by Southern California Edison Company; be forewarned that the water level drops dramatically toward the end of the season, somewhat diminishing the beauty of the lake.

DIRECTIONS TO THE TRAILHEAD: From the east end of Three Rivers, leave State Highway 198 and turn onto Mineral King Road. Follow the narrow road 23.5 miles to the end, at the Mosquito-Eagle trailhead parking area.

DESCRIPTION: South of the parking area a dirt road begins past the trailhead signboard and the Honeymoon Cabin. Follow the road on a mild climb up the East Fork

Crossing a talus slide on the Eagle Lake Trail

Kaweah River canyon through open vegetation, dotted with red firs, mountain maples, and an occasional juniper. After a quarter mile, you cross Spring Creek on a removable wooden bridge made of planks.

Just beyond Spring Creek, you pass an unsigned lateral that descends to the river; 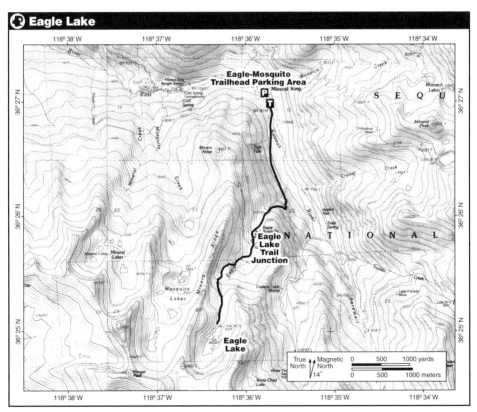 continue on your trail, taking in views across the valley of cascading Crystal Creek. Step across willow-lined Eagle Creek and shortly arrive at the signed White Chief Canyon Trail junction (8255′±), 1 mile from the parking area.

Turn right at the junction and wrap around the hillside to a set of steep switchbacks that climb through alternating pockets of meadow and stands of red fir and lodgepole pine. The grade eases as you approach Eagle Sink Hole, where part of Eagle Creek mysteriously disappears. You start to climb again and soon reach the Eagle Lake Trail junction (9016′), 1.75 miles from the trailhead.

From the junction, you climb mildly alongside Eagle Creek to the far end of the meadow. A steeper, switchbacking ascent up a red-fir and lodgepole-pine forested hillside leads to an expansive talus slope. You begin a long ascending traverse across the talus toward the lip of the Eagle Lake basin. Along the way the open topography grants excellent views of Mineral Peak, Sawtooth Peak, and the silver thread of cascading Crystal Creek.

The grade eases beyond the talus slope, and you pass through pockets of grasses and shrubs, scattered boulders, and rock slabs amid a light forest of lodgepole pine. A short climb leads by the concrete dam and along the west shore of Eagle Lake (10,010′), 3.25 miles from the trailhead.

The stunning scenery of the steep-walled cirque is complemented by the soaring summit of Eagle Crest (11,110′±), immediately to the south. Opposite, a row of multi-colored peaks rims the deep cleft of Mineral King. Just beyond the dam, a lateral trail leads uphill to the screened pit toilet, placed here in an attempt to minimize the pollution at this popular lake. Camping is not allowed between the trail and the lake, and the best sites are located about midway down the west shoreline. Anglers will enjoy fishing for the small-to-medium-sized brook trout.

O Cross-country enthusiasts can climb Miners Ridge to reach the Mosquito Lakes basin. The route is short, but quite steep and particularly rocky on the Mosquito Lakes side. The least difficult crossing is directly up the slope from the dam. See Trip 8 for the trail description to Mosquito Lakes.

R **PERMITS:** Wilderness permit required for overnight stays. (Quota: 20 per day)

CAMPFIRES: No

CAMPING: No camping between the lakeshore and the trail.

MINERAL KING TRAILHEAD

TRIP **10**

White Chief Canyon

S ✓ DH / BP / X

DISTANCE: 3.75 miles to upper meadow

ELEVATION: 7815/10,030, +2360′/-150′

SEASON: Early July to mid-October

USE: Light to moderate

MAPS: *Mineral King*
Mineral King, SNHA

TRAIL LOG:

1.0 Eagle Lake Trail Jct.
2.0 White Chief Meadow
3.75 Upper meadow

INTRODUCTION: All trails from the Mineral King area are blessed with nearly indescribable scenery. The White Chief Canyon Trail is no exception, with wonderful vistas, rockbound canyons, delightful meadows, and off-trail routes to exquisite lakes. To top it off, this trip offers a feature not found on other trails — caves. Some of these are naturally occurring stone caverns, and others were mines, but all of them are potentially dangerous. If caving or spelunking is on your agenda, you should consult the rangers at the Mineral King ranger station before embarking on your adventure. In addition, some of the mines are located on private inholdings, which require permission from the owner to enter.

DIRECTIONS TO THE TRAILHEAD: From the east end of Three Rivers, leave State Highway 198 and turn onto Mineral King Road. Follow the narrow road 23.5 miles to the end, at the Mosquito-Eagle trailhead parking area.

DESCRIPTION: South of the parking area a dirt road begins past the trailhead signboard and the Honeymoon Cabin. Follow

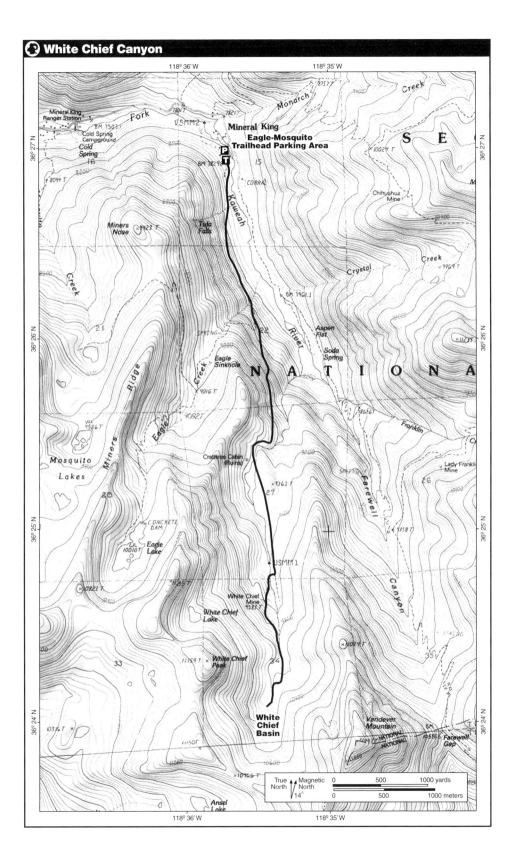

White Chief Meadow, on the White Chief Canyon Trail

the road up the East Fork Kaweah River canyon through open vegetation, dotted with red firs, mountain maples, and an occasional juniper. After a quarter mile, you cross Spring Creek on a removable wooden bridge made of planks.

Just beyond Spring Creek, you pass an unsigned lateral that descends to the river; continue on your trail, taking in views across the valley of cascading Crystal Creek. Step across willow-lined Eagle Creek and shortly arrive at the signed White Chief Canyon Trail junction (8255´±), 1 mile from the parking area.

From the junction, head south on the White Chief Canyon Trail. If you thought the mile-long climb to the junction was tough, just wait; the next stretch of trail is as steep as any section of maintained trail in the park. The excellent view of the canyon and the peaks above may provide a temporary distraction from the grueling climb.

Eventually, the grade moderates as you emerge from the canyon of White Chief

Creek. As you continue up the trail, through sagebrush-covered slopes dotted with junipers and beside outcroppings of dark metamorphic rock instead of the typical granite, you may feel you are somewhere other than the Sierra. The grade eases even more as you approach White Chief Meadow (9170´±), 2 miles from the trailhead.

The remains of Crabtree Cabin are on a low rise just west of the lower end of White Chief Meadow. Supposedly built by John Crabtree, the cabin was used as a bunkhouse for miners working the White Chief Mine. The trail quickly crosses the creek and proceeds along the fringe of the flat. Numerous avalanches over the years have littered the meadow with snags and swept clean the slopes above. The path soon climbs a rib to a bench overlooking the meadow, where campsites nestle beneath red firs, and lodgepole and foxtail pines. A resident deer herd is often seen in this vicinity.

Quickly leaving the trees behind, you cross open, view-filled slopes carpeted with wildflowers in season, including gentian, paintbrush, yarrow, and bluebell. The creek plays a game of cat and mouse in the canyon below, frequently disappearing and then reappearing. Such seemingly erratic behavior is typical of streams in areas of porous marble and limestone. At 2.75 miles, the trail crosses White Chief Creek (9420′±).

Once across, you ascend the far hillside and pass through tailings directly below the White Chief Mine, which was blasted out of a huge vein of white marble. The mine is private property and should not be explored without obtaining permission from the owners.

Past the mine, you ascend rocky slopes across the west wall of the canyon. The trail may be difficult to follow, but ducks help keep you on track. Continue up the canyon, passing numerous mine shafts, sinkholes, and caves, to another crossing of the creek. Now on the east side of the drainage, you climb across a grassy slope before returning to the creek. The trail follows the creek to a meadow-rimmed tarn at the head of the canyon. In the upper basin there are ruins from old mining cabins and natural marble caverns.

🔲 From the upper meadow, you can continue on a 0.75-mile, easy cross-country route to White Chief Lake (10,425′±), where you'll find a few windswept campsites. The route heads northwest across a talus-filled slope beneath White Chief Peak to reach the lake. From the lake, there is a straightforward route up White Chief Peak (11,159′) from the saddle between the peak and Eagle Lake (11,085′±). A challenging off-trail loop takes you on a descent from the same saddle west to the broad pass (10,650′±) south of Eagle Lake. From there, drop to the lake and follow the Eagle Lake Trail back to Mineral King (see Trip 9).

You can reach isolated, beautiful Ansel Lake (10,540′±) either from the vicinity of White Chief Lake, or by a 0.75-mile off-trail route from the upper meadow of White Chief Canyon over the crest (10,966′) and down to the lake. Although many people logically conclude that the lake was named for famed photographer Ansel Adams, the name refers to Ansel Franklin Hall, a Sequoia Park ranger from 1916 to 1917.

🔲 **PERMITS:** Wilderness permit required for overnight stays. (Quota: 25 per day)
CAMPFIRES: No

WHITE CHIEF MINE

The story of White Chief Mine's origin is a colorful bit of history. John Crabtree and two companions claimed that a giant Indian spirit led them on an all-night vision quest to a natural marble cave that contained veins of pure gold. As ridiculous as the tale may now seem, when they related their experience in the San Joaquin Valley, it sparked the first wave of gold-rush fever in Mineral King. Despite all the hoopla and millions of investment dollars, the mines never produced a single bar of gold or silver.

MINERAL KING TRAILHEAD

TRIP ▌▌

Farewell Gap

🔵 ↗ DH

DISTANCE: 5.5 miles one way

ELEVATION: 7815/10,680, +3320′/-455′

SEASON: Mid-July to mid-October

USE: Light

MAP: *Mineral King*
Mineral King, SNHA

TRAIL LOG:

3.25   Franklin Lakes Jct.
5.5   Farewell Gap

INTRODUCTION: The Farewell Gap Trail was a popular route into the Kern River backcountry, until construction of the trail over Franklin Pass. Nowadays, only the stretch of trail to the Franklin Lakes junction remains well traveled. However, well-conditioned day hikers in search of supreme views will find this 5.5-mile route a very rewarding climb. Mineral King's splendid scenery is even more stunning from the lofty aerie of Farewell Gap, as is the vivid panorama of the upper basin of the Little Kern River.

DIRECTIONS TO THE TRAILHEAD: From the east end of Three Rivers, leave State Highway 198 and turn onto Mineral King Road. Follow the narrow road 23.5 miles to the end, at the Mosquito-Eagle trailhead parking area, where you should leave your car, unless space is available in the small parking area near the East Fork Kaweah River bridge.

DESCRIPTION: If you parked in the Eagle-Mosquito parking area, backtrack down the Mineral King Road to the East Fork Kaweah River bridge. Across the bridge, an unsigned single-track trail climbs to the pack station access road. Follow the road up the canyon to the pack station, where you'll find the first sign indicating that you're on the Franklin Lakes/Farewell Gap Trail. Continue up the gently graded old road, past the corrals, through the open East Fork Kaweah River valley. Sagebrush, gooseberry, and currant grow in the valley; grasses and willows line the river bottom; and the colorful slopes above hold a very sparse mixed forest.

At 1.1 mile from the Eagle-Mosquito parking area, you ford Crystal Creek and, just beyond, you veer onto single-track trail at an unsigned junction; the old roadbed to the right follows the river through Aspen Flat to Soda Spring. A mild-to-moderate 0.75-mile climb beyond the junction brings you to Franklin Creek and the beginning of a steeper switchbacking climb, interrupted by an ascending traverse near the midpoint. Enjoyable views of the multi-colored hues of the peaks and valleys of the Mineral King area help to distract you from the grind. Above the switchbacks, at 3.25 miles, you reach a junction with the Franklin Lakes Trail (9358′).

Continue south up the Farewell Gap Trail, high above the dwindling East Fork. You soon reach a set of over 20 switchbacks that take you high up the canyon. The final leg of the climb is a quarter-mile traverse that culminates at V-shaped Farewell Gap, 5.5 miles from the parking lot.

The view from Farewell Gap is certainly awe-inspiring. Through the notch of Farewell Canyon, the entire Mineral King area spreads out before you, rimmed by majestic, vibrantly colorful peaks. To the south, the equally colorful headwaters of

> **MINERAL KING VALLEY**
>
> Because of its sparse tree cover, the Mineral King valley gives the impression of an alpine environment; however, periodic avalanches that clear the slopes of trees are responsible for the alpine ambience.

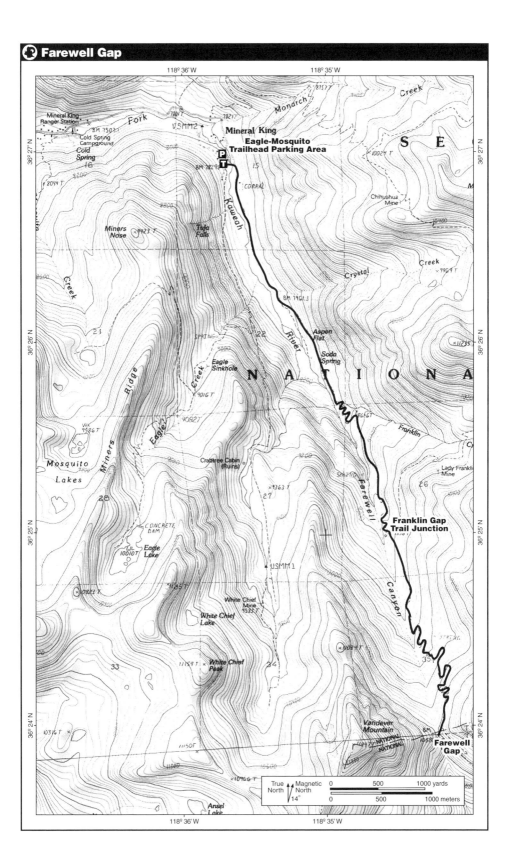

the Kern River create a picture-postcard scene. If the often-present winds fail to drive you from the gap, the hours will drift away as you stop and enjoy the dramatic surroundings.

O The trail is infrequently used beyond Farewell Gap, especially since camping at nearby Bullfrog Lakes has been banned. Adventurous souls in search of solitude will find plenty of routes in the surrounding Golden Trout Wilderness and Kern River backcountry.

Vandeveer Mountain is a straightforward climb from Farewell Gap.

MINERAL KING TRAILHEAD

TRIP **12**

Franklin Lakes

M ↗ DH/BP

DISTANCE: 5.5 miles

ELEVATION: 7815/10,335, +2910´/-465´

SEASON: Early July to mid-October

USE: Heavy

MAPS: *Mineral King*
Mineral King, SNHA

TRAIL LOG:

3.25   Farewell Gap Trail Jct.
5.5   Lower Franklin Lake

INTRODUCTION: Scores of backpackers and day hikers travel the Franklin Pass Trail to reach beautiful Franklin Lakes, cradled in a dramatic cirque basin beneath the Great Western Divide. This route's popularity will deflate most weekend backpacker's expectations for solitude.

Like most trails in the Mineral King area, this one makes a steady climb away from the valley. Rainbow-colored metamorphic rock in Farewell and Franklin canyons provides optical delights during the ascent and at the lakes.

DIRECTIONS TO THE TRAILHEAD: From the east end of Three Rivers, leave State Highway 198 and turn onto Mineral King Road. Follow the narrow road 23.5 miles to the end, at the Mosquito-Eagle trailhead parking area, where you should leave your car, unless space is available in the small parking area near the East Fork Kaweah River bridge.

DESCRIPTION: If you parked in the Eagle-Mosquito parking area, backtrack down the Mineral King Road to the East Fork Kaweah River bridge. Across the bridge, an unsigned single-track trail climbs to the pack station access road. Follow the road up the canyon to the pack station, where you'll find the first sign indicating that you're on the Franklin Lakes/Farewell Gap Trail. Continue up the road, past the corrals, through the open East Fork Kaweah River valley.

At 1.1 mile from the Eagle-Mosquito parking area, you ford Crystal Creek and, just beyond, you veer onto single-track trail at an unsigned junction; the old roadbed to the right follows the river through Aspen Flat to Soda Spring. A mild-to-moderate 0.75-mile climb beyond the junction brings you to Franklin Creek and the beginning of a steeper switchbacking climb, interrupted by an ascending traverse near the midpoint. Above the switchbacks, at 3.25 miles, you reach a junction with the Franklin Lakes Trail (9358′).

At the junction, turn to the left and follow the Franklin Lakes Trail on a long ascending traverse across the slope below Tulare Peak. Views down to Mineral King and up to red-and-orange-hued Franklin Canyon abound. With sharp eyes you may be able to detect the tailings and shaft of the Lady Franklin Mine, on the slope above a pair of switchbacks. At 4.4 miles, you reach a crossing of willow-lined Franklin Creek (9860′±).

Continue on switchbacks above the creek, toward the lower Franklin Lake. The rock-and-mortar dam soon springs into view, with the dramatic backdrop of the Great Western Divide, including aptly named Rainbow Mountain. A use-trail heads downhill to some exposed campsites alongside the creek just below the dam. You continue climbing to high above lake level and reach the first of a pair of paths that leads to campsites on the hillside above the lake.

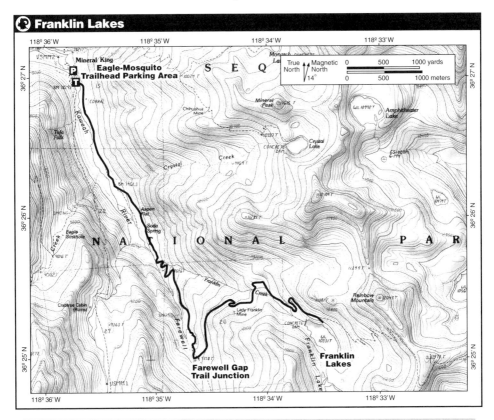

Lower Franklin Lake (10,331′), 5.5 miles from the Eagle-Mosquito parking lot, nestles in a picturesque basin below the multi-colored peaks of the Great Western Divide. However, campsites that meet the 100-foot regulation are in short supply, leaving only semi-level sites on a steep hill-side above the north shore. The popularity of the area combined with the marginal campsites insures that the lake is more like a trailer park than like the backcountry. Don't expect solitude!

Both camp areas on the north side are shaded by a smattering of foxtail pines and have bear boxes. A pit toilet is located down the southernmost use-trail. Brook trout inhabit both Franklin Lakes, but the crowd at the lower lake may prevent anglers from landing any trophy-sized fish.

Backpackers who haven't expended all their energy in reaching the first campsites may escape some of the crowds by continuing another half a mile to the bench between the upper and lower lake. Campsites on the bench are treeless and exposed, but see far fewer visitors. A short romp over boulders from here will take you to Upper Franklin Lake (10,578′) directly below the steep cirque wall between Florence and Tulare peaks.

O For a description of the continuation of the Franklin Pass Trail beyond Franklin Lakes, see Trip 13.

Mountaineers can ascend class 2 routes to either Rainbow Mountain (12,043′) or Florence Peak (12,432′) from Franklin Pass (11,760′±).

R **PERMITS:** Wilderness permit required for overnight stays. (Quota: 30 per day)
  CAMPFIRES: No

MINERAL KING TRAILHEAD

TRIP **13**

Franklin Pass and Sawtooth Pass Loop

Ⓢ ↻ BPx/X

DISTANCE: 27.5 miles loop

ELEVATION: 7815/11,760/8605/11,710/ 7815, +9250′/-9250′

SEASON: Mid-July to mid-October

USE: Light

MAPS: *Mineral King, Chagoopa Falls*

TRAIL LOG:

5.5	Lower Franklin Lake
7.4	Franklin Pass
10.5	Forester Lake
11.75	Little Claire Lake
16.4	Sawtooth Pass Trail Jct.
18.0	Big Five Lakes Trail Jct.
21.5	Columbine Lake
22.3	Sawtooth Pass
24.0	Lower Monarch Lake
24.75	Crystal Lake Trail Jct.
26.9	Timber Gap Trail Jct.

INTRODUCTION: A bare minimum of three days will provide an opportunity to experience one of Mineral King's classic loop trips. Alpine and subalpine lakes, deep forests, picturesque meadows, tumbling streams, and stunning views atop two passes on the Great Western Divide combine to provide plenty of scenic delights. The red and orange hues of metamorphic rock surrounding Mineral King will complement and contrast with the characteristic Sierra granite. Crossing both Franklin and Sawtooth passes insures that backpackers will get a workout, especially Sawtooth, which follows an unmaintained "route" on a difficult climb from Columbine Lake and

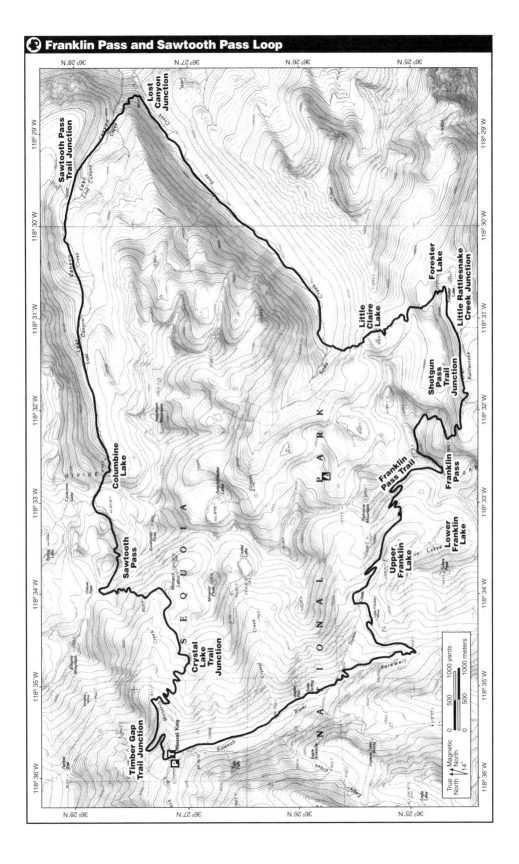

Franklin Pass and Sawtooth Pass Loop

a tedious descent to Monarch Lakes. Managing this demanding stretch requires more than rudimentary skills, making this a trip for experienced backpackers.

Travelers with extra time will want to take advantage of the short side trip to the Big Five Lakes. The siren call of grand scenery and relative seclusion at the lakes may lure hikers off the loop for an extended stay. Anglers will enjoy the temptations offered by good-sized brook trout. Connections to other trails and potential climbs of some of the surrounding high peaks provide extra diversions.

DIRECTIONS TO THE TRAILHEAD: From the east end of Three Rivers, leave State Highway 198 and turn onto Mineral King Road. Follow the narrow road 23.5 miles to the end, at the Mosquito-Eagle trailhead parking area, unless space is available in the small parking lot near the East Fork Kaweah River bridge.

DESCRIPTION: If you parked in the Eagle-Mosquito parking area, backtrack down the Mineral King Road to the East Fork Kaweah River bridge. Across the bridge, an unsigned single-track trail climbs to the pack station access road. Follow the road up the canyon to the pack station, where you'll find the first sign indicating that you're on the Franklin Lakes/Farewell Gap Trail. Continue up the road, past the corrals, through the open East Fork Kaweah River valley.

At 1.1 mile from the Eagle-Mosquito parking area, you ford Crystal Creek and, just beyond, you veer onto single-track trail at an unsigned junction; the old roadbed to the right follows the river through Aspen Flat to Soda Spring. A mild-to-moderate 0.75-mile climb beyond the junction brings you to Franklin Creek and the beginning of a steeper switchbacking climb, interrupted by an ascending traverse near the midpoint. Above the switchbacks, at 3.25 miles, you reach a junction with the Franklin Lakes Trail (9358′).

At the junction, turn to the left and follow the Franklin Lakes Trail on a long ascending traverse across the slope below Tulare Peak. At 4.4 miles, you reach a crossing of willow-lined Franklin Creek (9860′±).

Continue on switchbacks above the creek, toward the lower Franklin Lake. The rock-and-mortar dam soon springs into view, with the dramatic backdrop of the Great Western Divide. A use-trail heads downhill to some exposed campsites alongside the creek just below the dam. You continue climbing to high above lake level and reach the first of a pair of paths that leads to campsites on the hillside above the lake.

From the lake, ascend the Franklin Pass Trail southeast to the well-graded switchbacks that have replaced the old zigzagging trail. At the top of the switchbacks, a long ascending traverse takes you near the crest of the ridge. A few short switchbacks lead to the final approach to the pass, which turns out to be north of the low point. At 7.4 miles, you stand atop Franklin Pass (11,760′±) at the spine of the Great Western Divide. Alpine scenery spreads across the horizon, including Mt. Whitney 18 miles northeast above the deep cleft of Kern Canyon, and the Kaweah Peaks less than 10 miles north.

From the pass, you wind your way down barren, sandy slopes. Eventually, very widely scattered, stunted pines begin to appear prior to some switchbacks that lead down to a small meadow in the Rattlesnake Creek drainage. On the way, you pass a signed junction with the faint Shotgun Pass Trail to your right. Skirting the meadow, you continue downstream another 0.5 mile to a junction between the Rattlesnake Creek and Soda Creek trails (10,190′±), 10.0 miles from the parking area. Take the left-hand Soda Creek Trail and proceed through light lodgepole-pine forest on a mild ascent to Forester Lake (10,354′) at 10.5 miles. The lake is rimmed by grass and pine, with plenty of campsites spread around the shore. Fair-sized brook trout will tempt the angler.

A moderate climb, interrupted briefly by a small meadow, takes you to the top of a rise; after a moderate descent you reach Little Claire Lake (10,420′), 11.75 miles from the parking area. Along the south shore, a large sandy slope dotted with fox-tail pines makes a fine camping area, with an excellent view across the lake of 12,210-foot Needham Mountain. Average campsites can be found on the north shore near the outlet, close to the lip of the steep canyon of Soda Creek. Anglers can ply the waters for good-sized brook trout.

From Little Claire Lake, the trail drops 900 vertical feet in a mile of switchbacks to the crossing of Soda Creek. For the next 3.25 miles you make a mild, featureless descent alongside Soda Creek through predominantly lodgepole-pine forest, with cleared pockets where avalanches have swept the sides of the canyon. Nearing the Lost Canyon junction, you enter more of a mixed forest composed of red firs, and western white, Jeffrey, and lodgepole pines. At 16.4 miles, you reach the signed Sawtooth Pass Trail junction (8604′).

Heading northeast from the junction, you climb steeply up an exposed slope that can be scorching on a sunny afternoon. Fortunately, the Park Service has scheduled this stretch of trail to be rerouted in the near future. In another act of supreme mercy, the trail eventually enters cool forest and leads you to the crossing of Lost Canyon Creek, a pleasant oasis following the blistering ascent. Beyond the creek, the trail resumes a steep zigzagging climb through light forest cover until you reach a meadow with a campsite nearby. A more moderate climb continues up Lost Canyon past the meadow to the Big Five Lakes Trail junction (9580′), 18 miles from the parking area. Campsites (with a bear box) are a short distance up the Sawtooth Pass Trail near the crossing of Lost Canyon Creek.

SIDE TRIP TO BIG FIVE LAKES: From the junction, switchbacks lead you up a hillside covered with chinquapin and lodgepole pine. You reach a bench where a tepid tarn offers the possibility of a fine swim and secluded camping above the heather-lined shore. Beyond the pond, you resume a moderate climb amid boulders and slabs to the apex of a ridge overlooking the deep cleft holding the Big Five Lakes. A rocky, steep descent brings you to the first of the lakes (9830′), 2 miles from the junction. Good campsites are located near the outlet and along the north shore. Follow the trail around the north side of the lake to an informal junction; take the right fork up a short, steep, zigzag to a T-junction (10,450′) with the trail to Little Five Lakes.

From the junction, descend southwest to the north shore of the second lake (10,260′), smallest in the chain, where you'll find more excellent campsites. A short descent leads to the third and largest lake (10,192′) and then along the north shore through boggy meadows. An easy climb takes you to the fourth lake (10,214′) where you'll find more good campsites near the outlet. The trail becomes faint past the fourth lake, but the route is clear to the uppermost lake.

The Big Five Lakes have much to offer, not the least of which is that all five of the lakes are strikingly beautiful. In addition, solitude is a reasonable expectation as the hordes are kept at bay due to the relatively long distances from trailheads and the steep passes that must be conquered to get over the Great Western Divide. Anglers will appreciate the opportunity to fish for good-sized brookies. **END OF SIDE TRIP**

From the Big Five Lakes junction, continue upstream past campsites to the crossing of Lost Canyon Creek. One-third mile farther you hop back over to the north side of the creek and proceed up the mostly forested canyon. Eventually, you break out into the open to fine views across the boulder-strewn meadow of upper Lost Canyon to Needham Mountain, Sawtooth Peak, and the crest of the Great Western Divide. Scattered campsites beckon travelers to linger in the upper basin.

The steep wall at the end of the canyon signals the end to the mild climb, as the terrain forces you to climb more moderately

Upper Lost Canyon on the Sawtooth Pass Trail

towards the lake and the pass above. You follow switchbacks up the slope to the lip of the basin, where Columbine Lake (10,970′) immediately springs into view, 21.5 miles from the parking lot. Columbine Lake is a classic alpine lake, reposing in a deep rockbound bowl of granite slabs and boulders. The deep blue waters reflect the rust-colored, metamorphosed rock of the surrounding jagged peaks. Cramped pockets of decomposed granite offer passable campsites near the trail, but the best sites will be found above the southwest shore.

The Park Service-maintained trail ends at Columbine Lake and does not resume again until Monarch Lakes, well down the other side of Sawtooth Pass. Consequently, finding the best route to the pass can be something of a challenge, as a number of different paths offer variations on a theme. Fortunately, no matter which route you happen to follow from Columbine Lake, they eventually all converge on the sandy slope below the pass. A final set of switchbacks brings you to Sawtooth Pass

(11,725′±), 22.3 miles from the Eagle-Mosquito parking lot.

Views from the windswept pass are stunning. The nearby summits of Empire Mountain and Sawtooth Peak dominate the foreground, while Mt. Whitney, Mt. Langley, and Cirque Peak punctuate the eastern horizon. Perhaps most impressive is the view straight down the Monarch Creek drainage to Mineral King.

From the pass, you make a seemingly interminable, obnoxious descent across a steep, constantly shifting slope of loose dirt, sand, and scree, where myriad paths crisscross the slope in seemingly haphazard fashion. Eventually, just short of forever, you reach more stable ground below, where you can pour out buckets of accumulated mountain debris from your boots. In a vain attempt to put a positive spin on the situation, you may hear survivors utter this familiar retort, "At least we didn't have to climb up that way."

After such a descent, the more stable, single-track path to the Monarch Lakes creates an illusion of being one of the best trails ever built, despite being an unmaintained trail. You pass a bear box and fair campsites fashioned out of the rocky terrain just before reaching the west shore of Lower Monarch Lake (10,395´), at 24 miles. A path leads along the north shore and to the larger upper lake, where campsites are virtually nonexistent. The environs of the lower lake are a flutter of activity, with backpackers crowding into the limited campsites and day hikers from Mineral King languishing along the shoreline.

Leaving Monarch Lakes behind, you cross the outlet and begin a mildly descending traverse below rust-colored cliffs and across a rocky slope devoid of plant life. The trail crests a sub-ridge, where you leave the harsh surroundings and continue the mild descent through scattered pines and wildflowers, including lupine and paintbrush. After a pair of switchbacks, you encounter the Crystal Lake Trail junction (10,024´), at 24.75 miles.

Long-legged switchbacks continue the lengthy descent toward Mineral King. Prior to the crossing of Crystal Creek at 25.9 miles (8757´), you encounter lush vegetation carpeting the hillside. Beyond the creek, you descend along the edge of the canyon, where a burst of water falls right out of the opposite wall. Through open slopes of sagebrush, manzanita, chinquapin, and gooseberry, you continue down the canyon and then across the final slope above Mineral King. At a switchback, you reach the junction with the Timber Gap Trail (8320´±), at 26.9 miles, and continue 0.6 mile to the Sawtooth-Monarch trailhead near the Mineral King road. Complete your journey by walking up the road to your vehicle.

[O] Many options are available for trip extensions, including forays deep into the heart of Sequoia National Park along the Rattlesnake, Big Arroyo, and Kern River trails.

A pair of difficult cross-country routes leaves the Big Five Lakes basin. The first climbs over Cyclamen Pass (11,145´) at the Great Western Divide and on to Cyclamen and Columbine Lakes. The second climbs over Bilko Pass (11,480´) and around the east side of the Great Western Divide to Columbine Lake.

Mountaineers may attempt a number of class 2 routes: Florence Peak or Rainbow Mountain from Franklin Pass, Sawtooth Peak from Sawtooth Pass, Empire Mountain via Glacier Pass, or Mineral Peak from the Monarch Lakes.

[R] **PERMITS:** Wilderness permit required for overnight stays. (Quota: 30 per day)

CAMPFIRES: Yes at Forester Lake, Soda Creek to Lost Canyon. No at Little Claire Lake.

MINERAL KING TRAILHEAD

TRIP **14**

Crystal Lake

(MS) ↗ **DH / BP**

DISTANCE: 3.75 miles one way

ELEVATION: 7820/10,995, +3675'/-500'

SEASON: Mid-July to mid-October

USE: Light

MAPS: *Mineral King*
Mineral King, SNHA

INTRODUCTION: The Sawtooth Pass Trail is often crowded with hikers and backpackers, but few continue past the junction with the Crystal Lake Trail. Apparently, an extra half-mile and 600 vertical feet are enough to dissuade travelers from climbing to Crystal Lake; most opt for the slightly easier route to Monarch Lakes instead. Beyond the junction, the tailings and shaft from the Chihuahua Mine are reminders of the high expectations that miners had for the Mineral King area—expectations that were never realized. The lake itself is quite picturesque, backdropped by steep, multicolored peaks. Whether you're out for the day or for an overnight, the rewards of Crystal Lake are sure to please.

DIRECTIONS TO THE TRAILHEAD: From the east end of Three Rivers, leave State Highway 198 and turn onto Mineral King Road. Follow the narrow, twisting road 23 miles to the Sawtooth-Monarch trailhead parking area, 0.8 mile past the ranger station.

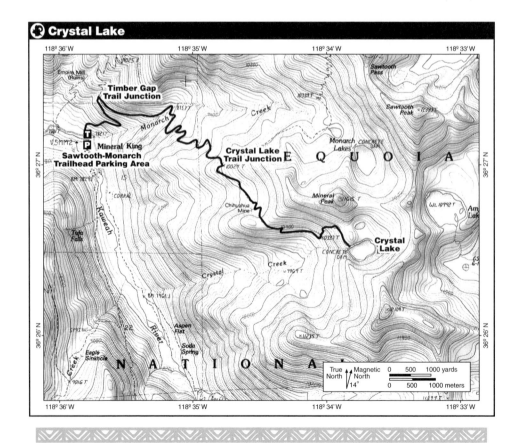

Crystal Lake

DESCRIPTION: Climb steeply away from the trailhead up a hillside carpeted with sagebrush, manzanita, chinquapin, and gooseberry to the junction with the Timber Gap Trail (8320′±) at 0.6 mile. Turn right at the junction and continue on the Sawtooth Pass Trail, as the ascent assumes a more reasonable grade following long-legged switchbacks up the slope. About 1.2 miles from the parking lot, you encounter Groundhog Meadow, slightly misnamed for the ubiquitous yellow-bellied marmot, a relative of the eastern woodchuck that inhabits the meadows and rocky slopes of the subalpine Sierra. Near the meadow, you hop across Crystal Creek and begin a series of switchbacks that lead you in and out of red fir forest to the Y-junction with the Crystal Lake Trail (10,024′), 2.4 miles from the trailhead. A small sign marks the somewhat indistinct junction.

Just after the junction, veer left onto the lightly used Crystal Lake Trail and climb across the barren, avalanche-ridden slopes of Chihuahua Bowl. On a flat near the far end, remains of the Chihuahua Mine are visible. Beyond the bowl, you climb over the crest of a ridge to excellent views amid scattered foxtail pines. A short descent from the crest leads to an ascending traverse across Crystal Creek canyon, followed by a steep, switchbacking climb up to the narrow outlet of Crystal Lake.

CRYSTAL LAKE DAM

As at Franklin, Monarch, and Eagle lakes, the Mt. Whitney Power Company built a concrete dam at Crystal Lake around 1905 for power production downstream at their plant near Hammond. Southern California Edison Company currently operates the dam.

A lack of trees around the shoreline sends most backpackers to campsites on a terrace just below the lake, where gnarled foxtail pines offer a modicum of protection from the elements. Brook trout will test the patience of anglers.

O A faint path leaves the Crystal Lake Trail to descend alongside Crystal Creek. From there, a straightforward trip to the dwarfish Cobalt Lakes begins.

Although the maintained trail dead-ends at Crystal Lake, a short scramble over bluffs to the northeast leads to Little Crystal Lake (11,030′±), tucked into the slope below Crystal Peak. A direct off-trail route to the Monarch Lakes heads north from the upper lake, climbing 400 vertical feet to a saddle (11,180′±) overlooking the upper Monarch Lake, where a steep but straightforward descent leads down a chute to the lakeshore.

A short, class 3 cross-country route connects Crystal Lake to Amphitheater Lake (10,992′) over Crystal Pass (11,405′±).

R **PERMITS:** Wilderness permit required for overnight stays. (Quota: 20 per day)
CAMPFIRES: No

MINERAL KING TRAILHEAD

TRIP 15

Monarch Lakes

Ⓜ ↗ DH

DISTANCE: 3.25 miles to Lower
Monarch Lake

ELEVATION: 7820/10,395, +2740′/-200′

SEASON: Mid-July to mid-October

USE: Heavy

MAPS: *Mineral King,*
Mineral King, SNHA

INTRODUCTION: The reward for this hike's stiff climb is a pair of subalpine lakes cradled in a picturesque cirque beneath multi-

colored peaks of metamorphic rock. Not only is the destination stunningly beautiful, but the vistas of the Mineral King area during the ascent are equally impressive. Despite the climb—2500 feet in 3-plus miles—this trip up the Sawtooth Pass Trail is quite popular with hikers and backpackers alike. Since the overused campsites become quite cramped during peak season, my advice is to view this trip as a day hike only. If you insist on an overnight visit, don't expect peace and quiet. Experienced off-trail enthusiasts can enjoy more serene camping and the added bonus of a loop trip by staying at nearby Crystal Lakes and following the cross-country route over a saddle to Monarch Lakes (see Options below).

DIRECTIONS TO THE TRAILHEAD: Follow directions in Trip 14 to the Sawtooth-Monarch trailhead.

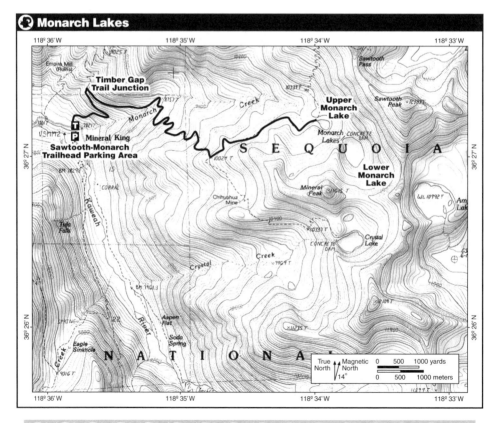

Hikers at Lower Monarch Lake

DESCRIPTION: Follow the description in Trip 14 to the Crystal Lake Trail junction, 2.4 miles from the trailhead.

From the junction, continue the climb up the Sawtooth Pass Trail. After a pair of switchbacks, you cross a sub-ridge at the edge of Chihuahua Bowl and begin a mildly ascending traverse across a barren rock slope well above Monarch Creek. Eventually, the trail curves toward more hospitable surroundings to meet the meadow-lined creek just below the outlet of the lake, quickly reaching Lower Monarch Lake at 3.25 miles. Sandwiched between multi-hued Sawtooth and Mineral peaks, the Monarch Lakes nestle into a scenic cirque basin. Scratched out of the rocky slopes to the west of the lakes are overused campsites with bear box.

Upper Monarch Lake is another Mineral King lake that was dammed in the early 1900's by the Mt. Whitney Power Company to regulate flow in the East Fork for power generation at a plant near Hammond. Southern California Edison Company currently operates the dams.

To reach the upper lake, find the use-trail near the inlet in a patch of willows and follow the path up the steep hillside to the larger of the two lakes (10,635′±).

⟦O⟧ For a description of the Sawtooth Pass Trail beyond the lakes, see Trip 13.

A steep but relatively straightforward off-trail route connects the Monarch Lakes with Crystal Lakes. From the upper lake, head south and ascend a steep chute to the saddle (11,170′±) above. Descend toward the smallest lake below and then find the use-trail leading to the shore of the lower Crystal Lake.

⟦R⟧ **PERMITS:** Wilderness permit required for overnight stays. (Quota: 20 per day)
CAMPFIRES: No

MINERAL KING TRAILHEAD

TRIP 16

Little Five and Big Five Lakes Loop

Ⓜ Ⓠ BPx

DISTANCE: 26.5 miles loop trip

ELEVATION: 7820/9511/7124/11,670/ 9580/7820, +9930/-9930

SEASON: Mid-July to mid-October

USE: Moderate

MAPS: *Mineral King, Mineral King, SNHA*

TRAIL LOG:

2.25   Timber Gap
5.0   Black Rock Pass Jct.
7.5   Pinto Lake
10.7   Black Rock Pass
11.5   Little Five Lakes
12.5   Big Five Lakes Trail Jct.
14.1   Big Five Lakes
17.1   Sawtooth Pass Trail Jct.
20.5   Columbine Lake
21.25 Sawtooth Pass
23.0   Monarch Lakes

INTRODUCTION: This loop exposes backpackers to the best that Mineral King has to offer. Both the Little Five and Big Five lakes basins contain picturesque lakes with excellent camping and good fishing. Flower-carpeted meadows, tumbling steams, and quiet forests in the shadow of the Great Western Divide provide plenty of scenic delights along the way. Add alpine Columbine Lake, with the far-reaching views from nearby Sawtooth Pass, and you have nearly every component of a classic Sierra trip. Mountaineers and cross-country types will have much from which to choose as well.

Such stunning attributes are not without a price, as three passes of increasing difficulty require steep climbs. Timber Gap is a relatively straightforward climb, gaining 1700 feet in 2.25 miles, while Black Rock Pass requires a 3000-foot climb in 3 miles. The difficulty of Sawtooth Pass is not as much its distance and elevation as the condition of the "trail," which isn't really a trail at all, but an unmaintained route. Backpackers must pick one of many paths and scramble up a steep mountainside on the east side of the pass, and then endure a nasty descent across loose dirt, sand, scree, and rock on the opposite side. Anyone considering this trip should be in good physical condition.

DIRECTIONS TO THE TRAILHEAD: From the east end of Three Rivers, leave State Highway 198 and turn onto Mineral King Road. Follow the narrow road 23 miles to the Sawtooth-Monarch trailhead parking area, 0.8 mile past the ranger station..

DESCRIPTION: Climb steeply from the trailhead up a hillside carpeted with sagebrush, manzanita, chinquapin, and gooseberry to the junction with the Sawtooth Pass Trail (8320′±) at 0.6 mile. Turn left and continue a less severe climb across open slopes up the Timber Gap Trail, which soon switchbacks through a swath of red firs that provide pockets of welcome shade. Near 9200 feet, you leave the trees and make a long ascending traverse toward Timber Gap. Before you reenter red-fir forest below the gap, take in the grand view toward Mineral King one last time. You reach the forested saddle of Timber Gap (9511′) at 2.25 miles from the trailhead.

Descend from the gap through red-fir forest on switchbacks to a crossing of Timber Gap Creek, where a long swath of flower-bedecked meadow bordering the stream supplants the mixed forest. Continue on the trail down the verdant canyon, quickly recrossing the creek and a number of lush, spring-fed side streams. Eventually, you leave the Timber Creek drainage, make a short climb over the northeast lip of the canyon, and follow a switchbacking descent toward Cliff Creek.

Little Five and Big Five Lakes Loop

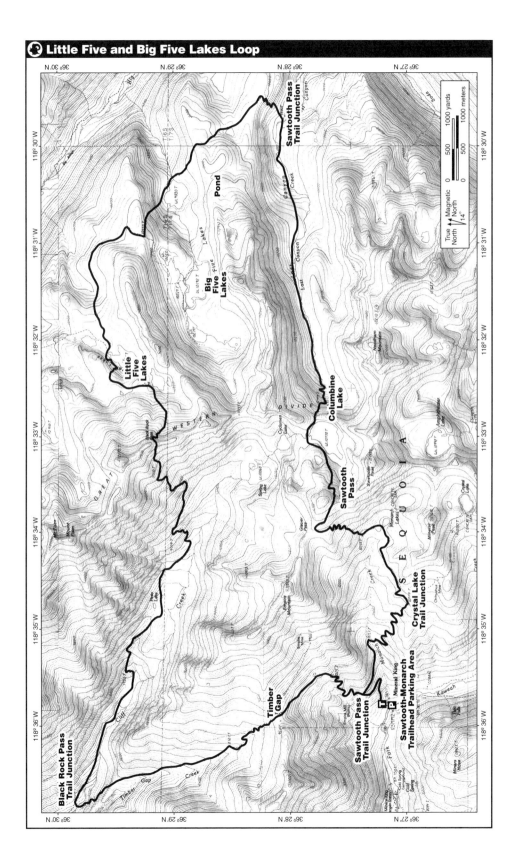

Upper Cliff Creek Basin on the Black Rock Pass Trail

At 5.0 miles you boulder-hop Cliff Creek (7124´) and reach campsites with a bear box under red firs near the signed junction with the Black Rock Pass Trail.

From the junction, ascend southeast up the Black Rock Pass Trail through wildflowers, shrubs, and scattered firs across a number of small rivulets lined with lush foliage. Farther up the canyon, you emerge from the forest to an extensive area of boulders where the creek seems to take a temporarily subterranean course. Up ahead, you get a glimpse of a ribbon-like fall spilling down a rock wall on the south side of the canyon.

Switchbacks lead you along the left-hand branch of the creek up the wall of the lower canyon to a crossing of the stream and on to the meadows surrounding Pinto Lake. At 7.5 miles, you encounter an unmarked junction with a use-trail branching to campsites on your right (bear box). Nearby, Pinto Lake (8685´±) hides in a pocket of thick willows, offering surprisingly pleasant swimming.

Past a series of meadows, you begin to climb again through open terrain of shrubs, including sagebrush, chinquapin, and willow. Early summer hosts quite a flower display, with forget-me-nots, paintbrush, lupine, phlox, wallflower, yampa, larkspur, senecio, and Bigelow sneezeweed. Soon you encounter the first of many switchbacks that will take you to the pass, over 2000 feet above. The interminable slog is made more tolerable by the incredible scenery along the way. As you climb, first Spring Lake comes into view backdropped majestically by the sheer face of Peak 11,480, followed by Cyclamen Lake and then Columbine Lake. Finally, you can catch your breath at Black Rock Pass (11,670´±), 10.7 miles from the trailhead. From the pass, Little Five and Big Five basins spill into the cleft of Big Arroyo, which is backdropped dramatically by the Kaweah Peaks. Mt. Whitney and surrounding summits cap the horizon to the east.

A zigzagging descent from the pass leads to the first of the Little Five Lakes (10,740´±), at 11.5 miles. Fine campsites at the north shore of the lake will tempt back-packers, just as brook trout will tantalize any anglers in your group. You reenter lodgepole and foxtail pine forest on the descent to the second highest lake (10,476´), where more delightful campsites are found above the north shoreline. Just after crossing the outlet, you reach the Big Five Lakes Trail junction (10,475´±) at 12.5 miles. By continuing north on the Black Rock Pass Trail for another mile to the out-let, you can access the remaining Little Five Lakes, where a faint use-trail heads west to the lakes. Solitude is almost guaranteed at the northern group of the Little Five Lakes.

From the Big Five Lakes junction, take the left-hand trail and head east over rolling terrain through lodgepole-pine for-est. Eventually, you bend south as the trail contours around the ridge separating the Little Five Lakes from the Big Five Lakes. At 14.1 miles, you come to a junction (10,450´) with the trail that accesses four of the Big Five Lakes.

To visit Big Five Lakes Nos. 2 through 5, descend southwest from the junction to the north shore of the second lake (10,260´), smallest in the chain, where you'll find excellent campsites. A short descent leads to the third and largest lake (10,192´) and then along the north shore through boggy meadows. An easy climb takes you to the fourth lake (10,214´), where you'll find more good campsites near the outlet. The trail becomes faint past the fourth lake, but the route is clear to the uppermost lake. Good-sized brook trout in all the Big Five Lakes should provide anglers with plenty of challenges.

From the Big Five Lakes junction, the Big Five Lakes Trail zigzags down a pine-covered hillside to an informal T-junction near the north shore of Lake No. 1 (9830´), where you'll find good campsites scattered around the lake. Bear left (southeast) from the junction and continue around the north shore to the outlet crossing. As you bid farewell to the Big Five Lakes basin, a mod-erately steep climb takes you away from the lake and up a rock-strewn hillside to the

crest of the ridge above. After a short descent, the trail levels at a bench holding a tepid, heather-fringed pond that provides excellent swimming and secluded camping. Newly constructed switchbacks past the pond take you down the hillside to a junc-tion with the Sawtooth Pass Trail (9580´) in Lost Canyon, 17.1 miles from the trailhead. A short distance up the trail are campsites with bear box near the crossing of Lost Canyon Creek.

From the Big Five Lakes/Sawtooth Pass junction, follow the description in Trip 13 the 9.5 miles to the trailhead at the Sawtooth-Monarch parking area.

⊡ Easy options abound for exploration of Big and Little Five Lakes basins, especially from a base camp at one of the lakes.

Cross-country enthusiasts can chose among routes to a variety of destinations. From Timber Gap, a .75-mile traverse southeast along the Historic Wagon Road leads to the ruins from the Empire Camp (9966´) and the site of the Empire Mine (10,400´±).

You can access strikingly beautiful Spring Lake (10,040´) from either the Black Rock Pass or the Sawtooth Pass Trails. The easiest route leaves the Black Rock Pass Trail near 10,000 feet to contour 0.9 mile to the lake basin. A more difficult track leaves the unmaintained section of the Sawtooth Pass "Trail" near 11,200 feet to traverse easily 0.1 mile to Glacier Pass (11,080´±). The next section is the crux of the route, where you must descend a short but steep cliff (class 3) to easier slopes that

EMPIRE CAMP

The Empire Camp bunkhouse was destroyed in 1880 by an avalanche while 20 miners slept inside. Four men were seriously injured, but fortu-nately no one was killed. The mine itself was not so lucky, as work ceased for good after the following summer.

lead to the north shore of the lake. Be prepared for snow on the north side of the pass until late in the season following average winters.

Two difficult cross-country routes leave the Big Five Lakes basin. The first climbs over Cyclamen Pass (11,145′) at the Great Western Divide and continues to Cyclamen and Columbine Lakes. The second climbs over Bilko Pass (11,480′) and around the east side of the Great Western Divide to Columbine Lake.

Mountaineers have a variety of peaks to bag as well. Mt. Eisen (12,160′±) is class 1–2 from the Black Rock Pass Trail or the pass itself. A class 3 couloir on the north side of Needham Mountain (12,210′) leads to easier climbing along the east ridge. Sawtooth Peak (12,343′) is class 2 from Sawtooth Pass. The southeast ridge of Empire Peak (11,550′) is class 2 via Glacier Pass. Mineral Peak is class 2 from the Monarch Lakes.

R **PERMITS:** Wilderness permit required for overnight stays. (Quota: 25 per day)

CAMPFIRES: Permitted along lower Timber Gap Creek, along Cliff Creek below Pinto Lake, in Big Five Lakes basin, and in Lost Canyon.

MINERAL KING TRAILHEAD

TRIP **17**

Redwood and Bearpaw Meadows

Ⓜ ╱ BP

DISTANCE: 8.5 miles to Redwood Meadow; 12.9 miles to Bearpaw Meadow/High Sierra Trail

ELEVATION: 7820/9511/6035, +2170′/-3925′ 7820/9511/7750, +4360′/-4340′

SEASON: July to late October

USE: Light

MAPS: *Mineral King, Triple Divide Peak, Lodgepole*

TRAIL LOG:

5.0	Black Rock Pass Trail Jct.
8.3	Redwood Meadow and Atwell-Redwood Trail Jct.
8.5	Bearpaw Trail Jct.
10.6	Middle Fork Kaweah River
11.6	Little Bearpaw Meadow
12.5	Bearpaw Meadow Campground
12.9	High Sierra Trail junction

INTRODUCTION: Solitude is a nearly constant companion along this mostly forested route, at least until Bearpaw Meadow, which is a frequent stop for travelers along the High Sierra Trail (HST). Although the Timber Gap Trail is one of the easiest routes from Mineral King, a stiff 1700-foot climb in the first 2.25 miles is necessary to reach the easier terrain beyond, where picturesque meadows, churning streams, and giant sequoias lure those in search of serenity. Beyond Redwood Meadow, backpackers will find some steep sections of trail following the ford of the Middle Fork Kaweah

River, which may be a difficult crossing in early season. Bearpaw Meadow provides highly civilized camping and a variety of options for further wanderings along the HST.

DIRECTIONS TO THE TRAILHEAD: From the east end of Three Rivers, leave State Highway 198 and turn onto Mineral King Road. Follow the narrow, twisting road 23 miles to the Sawtooth-Monarch trailhead parking area, 0.8 mile past the ranger station.

DESCRIPTION: Climb steeply from the trailhead up a hillside to the junction with the Sawtooth Pass Trail (8320´±) at 0.6 mile. Turn left and continue a less severe climb across open slopes up the Timber Gap Trail, which soon switchbacks through a swath of red firs that provide pockets of welcome shade. Near 9200 feet, you leave the trees and make a long ascending traverse toward Timber Gap. You reach the forested saddle of Timber Gap (9511´) at 2.25 miles from the trailhead.

Descend from the gap through red-fir forest on switchbacks to a crossing of Timber Gap Creek, where a long swath of meadow bordering the stream supplants the mixed forest. Continue on the trail down the verdant canyon, quickly recrossing the creek and a number of lush, spring-fed side streams. Eventually, you leave the Timber Creek drainage, make a short climb over the northeast lip of the canyon, and follow a switchbacking descent toward Cliff Creek. At 5.0 miles you boulder-hop Cliff Creek (7124´) and reach campsites with a bear box under red firs near the signed junction with the Black Rock Pass Trail.

From the junction, continue down the canyon of Cliff Creek on a moderate descent through a dense forest of pines, firs, cedars, and oaks. The trail initially hugs the banks of the creek, but after crossing a mud-lined side stream, it favors the forested slopes away from the creek. You make a brief return to Cliff Creek at the next side-stream crossing, but quickly veer away again on a mildly descending stretch of trail. Soon, a more moderate descent resumes and leads you to the low point of your journey, where the trail crosses another small tributary at the 7-mile mark.

You climb steeply away from the tributary until you undertake a mildly ascending traverse that wraps around the forested hillside. Sugar and Jeffrey pines join the mixed forest, and where the trail bends into a side canyon, you begin to see the first giant sequoia specimens of the Redwood Meadow Grove.

You suddenly leave the forest and the Big Trees behind as the trail exits the side canyon and reaches a rocky promontory dotted with manzanita and oak. From the promontory you have an impressive view of Moro Rock, Alta Peak, and Tharps Rock above the Middle Fork Kaweah River. Beyond the viewpoint, the trail descends moderately through a light mixed forest with an understory of manzanita and mountain misery. Soon, you find yourself back in thick forest cover sprinkled with more giant sequoias. At 8.3 miles from the trailhead, you reach Redwood Meadow (6035´±) and the signed junction with the Atwell-Redwood Trail. A variety of signs give mileages to assorted destinations, including the camping area, which is 0.2 mile farther up the trail.

A short stroll along the tree-rimmed meadow leads to some primitive campsites.

REDWOOD MEADOW

A large log cabin occasionally houses the seasonal rangers, who spend part of their summers in the serenity of Redwood Meadow. Numerous scratch marks on the exterior walls are a testament to the resident bear population. Nearby, a tack shack, hitching post, and corral contribute to the pastoral atmosphere. The namesake meadow is a thin pocket of verdant vegetation surrounded by a thick forest of mixed conifers dotted with giant sequoias.

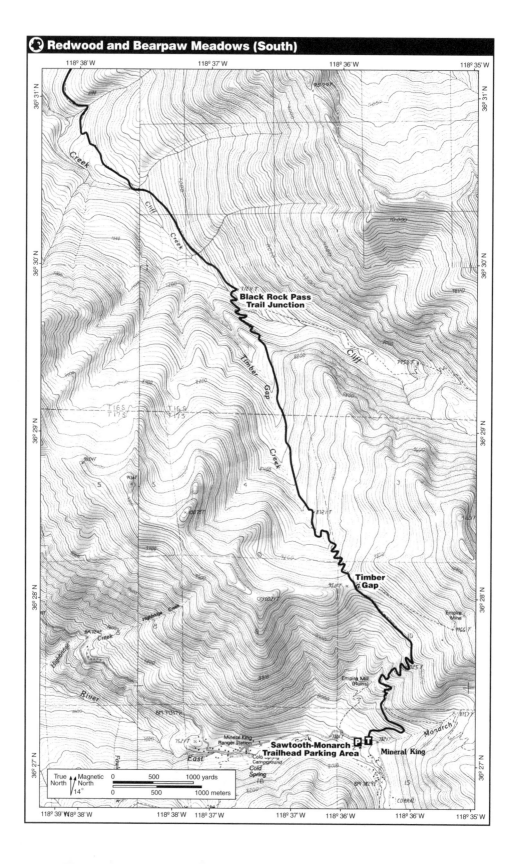

118° 38' W 118° 37' W 118° 36' W 118° 35' W

36° 31' N

9500 T

Creek

Cliff Creek

10,000

36° 30' N

7184 T

Black Rock Pass Trail Junction

Cliff

7853 T

Timber Gap

T16S / T17S   T16S / T17S

9641 T

9347 T

1007 T

8121 T

Creek

Timber Gap

9511 T   Empire Mine

7966 T

10025 T

Highbridge Creek

Empire Mill (Ruins)

8151 T

Creek

BM 7249

Highbridge River

925 T

Monarch

BM 7033 T

7521 T   Mineral King Ranger Station   7321 T

Sawtooth-Monarch Trailhead Parking Area

Mineral King

East   Cold Spring Campground

Cold Spring

36° 27' N

True North   Magnetic North
14°

0   500   1000 yards
0   500   1000 meters

BM 7829 T

CORRAL

118° 39' W 118° 38' W 118° 38' W 118° 37' W 118° 36' W 118° 36' W 118° 35' W

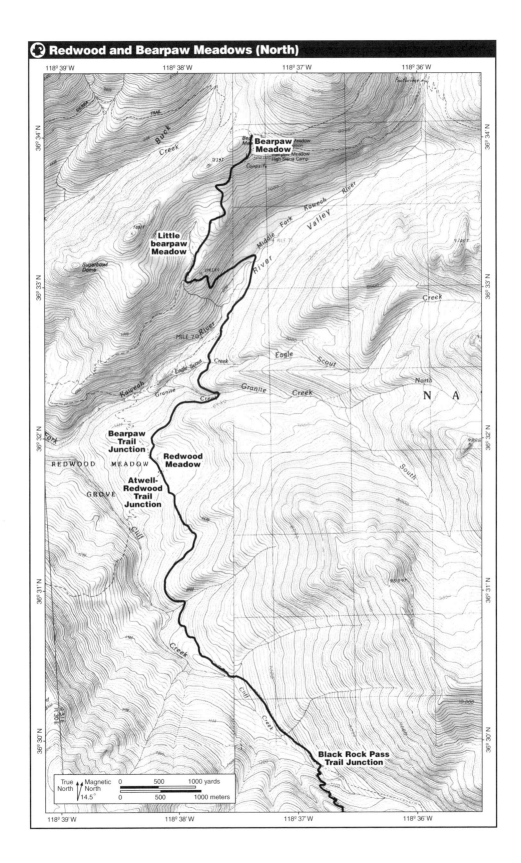

Domes, seen from Timber Gap Trail

A water faucet provides drinking water, but only during the height of summer when rangers are on duty. Aside from the faucet, water is hard to come by at Redwood Meadow, especially late in the season. An outhouse is a stone's throw away. Just beyond the campsites, the trail crosses a low wooden bridge over a boggy drainage and comes to a junction with the Bearpaw Trail and a connector to the Middle Fork Trail, 8.5 miles from the trailhead.

Take the right-hand path, the Bearpaw Trail, and climb through a mixed forest to the crest of a low ridge. Beyond the ridge, you traverse a lightly forested hillside of black oaks, incense cedars, red firs, and pockets of manzanita with periodic views of Moro Rock, Alta Peak and some interesting granite domes. One mile from the ranger station, you reach the rocky chasm of turbulent Granite Creek. You negotiate the chasm easily with the aid of a stoutly built, wooden plank-and-rail bridge.

Beyond Granite Creek, you follow the trail on an easy traverse around the nose of an oak-shaded ridge to the crossing of cascading Eagle Scout Creek (possibly a difficult ford in early season). Pass a small campsite above the far bank and contour over to a junction with the Middle Fork Trail. A gentle half a mile ascent leads to the broad ford of the Middle Fork Kaweah River (6205´±), 10.6 miles from the trailhead. Check with the Park Service regarding conditions of the river before embarking on your trip, as the ford is potentially dangerous in early season when the river is high and swift. On the far side of the river are pleasant campsites shaded by alders and sugar pines.

The Bearpaw Trail turns west beyond the river and makes a stiff, winding climb up the dry, south-facing wall of the canyon through black oaks, red firs, and incense cedars. Near the top of the climb, you reach a junction with a lateral trail that connects with the Middle Fork Trail. Turn right (north) and make the easier climb to Little Bearpaw Meadow (6840´±), 11.6 miles from the trailhead. As you skirt the fern-carpeted meadow, you'll find secluded campsites next to the gently flowing stream.

The trail once again assumes attack mode beyond the serene glade, as you make a moderate-to-moderately steep climb through incense cedars and red firs. Your mile-long ascent leads you to the shady backpackers' campground near Bearpaw Meadow (7640´±), where amenities include numbered sites with bear boxes, pit toilets, and faucets with running water. About the only missing items from the typical auto-accessible Park Service campground are picnic tables and fire pits.

From a signed junction at the edge of the campground, you may take the left-hand fork directly up a steep climb to the HST, or the right-hand branch that leads through the campground to the Bearpaw Meadow ranger station and the High Sierra Camp. Heading along the left-hand trail, you encounter a junction between the High Sierra Trail (7750´±) and the Over the Hill Trail, a short distance before the ranger station and 12.9 miles from the Sawtooth-Monarch trailhead.

O From Redwood Meadow, you can vary your return route by following the Atwell-Redwood Trail back to the Atwell Mill trailhead. However, this route necessitates a 5-mile shuttle back to the Sawtooth-Monarch trailhead.

Numerous trip extensions can be made from the junction with the High Sierra Trail to a variety of destinations (see Trips 31–32). One of the most straightforward and intriguing possibilities follows the HST past Hamilton Lakes and Nine Lakes Basin to a junction with the Black Rock Pass Trail in Big Arroyo. From there, you could visit Little and Big Five lakes before connecting with the Sawtooth Pass Trail for a return to the Sawtooth-Monarch trailhead (see Trip 13). A slightly shorter variation follows the Black Rock Pass and Timber Gap trails back to the trailhead (see Trip 16).

R **PERMITS:** Wilderness permit required for overnight stays. (Quota: 25 per day)

CAMPFIRES: Yes, except no fires at Timber Gap.

CAMPING: Restricted to designated sites at Bearpaw Meadow.

Introduction to Foothills

Most of the Sierra Nevada is inaccessible during the winter, at least to those who don't wish to don cross-country skis or snowshoes. Fortunately, Sequoia National Park has a low-elevation area with a handful of all-year trails. Hikers in the foothills may enjoy their pursuit no matter what the season of the year, even when the bulk of the Sierra is buried under the annual snowpack. However, summers are generally unbearably hot on most of these trails, and many recreationists spend more time in the water than on the trail during the blistering summer days of 90°F–100°F. While fall and winter provide wonderful times to enjoy the foothills, spring is perhaps the ideal season, when winter rains have turned the grassy hills a verdant green, wildflowers add a complementary display of brilliant color, and the trees and shrubs of the oak woodland have sprouted new growth.

The pleasant climate of the foothills was first enjoyed by Native Americans, who established their villages near the streams and rivers, evidenced by the numerous pictographs and bedrock mortars scattered throughout the area. Game was more

plentiful in this zone, as were nuts, seeds, and berries. Today, much of the limited tourist traffic in the foothills is tied to sites highlighting the presence of Native Americans in the park.

Generally, vegetation in the foothills is outside of the conifer belt, composed mainly of grasslands, chaparral, and oak woodland. Those unfamiliar with the landscape may consider it rather scrubby, but more perceptive eyes will see a diverse flora, especially along riparian areas. While the characteristic granite of the Sierra appears sporadically in this zone, most of the rock is metamorphic, lending a decidedly different feel than what is normally associated with the Sierra Nevada.

In addition, much of the foothills terrain is not only brush-filled, but also steep and virtually inaccessible without the aid of a trail. While lines of motorists speed through the foothills on their way to the famous sequoias above, hikers who stop and take the time will see much more than brushy, dry, rocky, inhospitable terrain. The foothills region of Sequoia National Park is filled with dramatic rivers, tumbling streams, splendid vistas, and exquisite terrain.

Modern-day visitors who plan on enjoying the many pools of the rivers and streams should exercise caution, as conditions can be quite dangerous, especially in spring and early summer. The low elevations may present additional concerns, including rattlesnakes, ticks, and poison oak.

ACCESS: Principal access for foothills trails is via State Highway 198, which becomes the Generals Highway within the park.

AMENITIES: The resort-driven community of Three Rivers offers the basic necessities for tourists visiting the national parks and

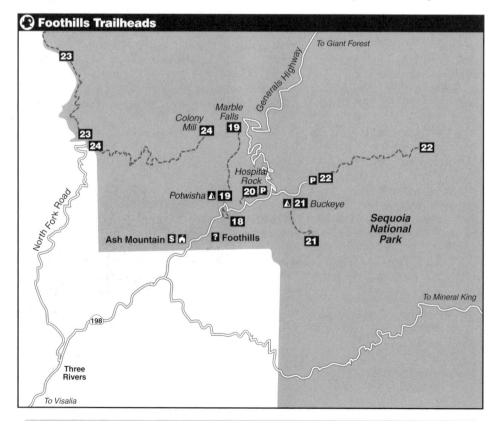

Campgrounds

Campground	Fee	Elevation	Season	Restrooms	Running Water	Bear Boxes	Phone
POTWISHA	$14	2100'	Open all year	Flush Toilets	Yes	Yes	Yes
BUCKEYE	$14	2800'	Mid-May to mid-October	Flush Toilets	Yes	Yes	No

Lake Kaweah, including motels, cafes, and restaurants, general stores, gas stations, and automobile repair shops. Visalia is a larger city, 20 miles west, with a much wider range of services.

RANGER STATION: The Ash Mountain Visitor Center, which is 0.7 mile from the Ash Mountain Entrance, is the year-round headquarters for Sequoia National Park. Wilderness permits may be obtained during normal office hours. The visitor center also offers various books, maps, and gifts.

GOOD TO KNOW BEFORE YOU GO: Although the Ash Mountain Entrance remains open all year, the Generals Highway between Hospital Rock and Giant Forest may require chains during winter conditions. In addition, the Generals Highway between Sequoia and Kings Canyon may be closed at various times during the winter.

California black oak

POTWISHA TRAILHEAD

TRIP 18

Potwisha Pictographs Loop

E ↻ DH

DISTANCE: 0.5 mile

ELEVATION: 2095/2070/2160, +205′/-205′

SEASON: All Year

USE: Light

MAP: *Giant Forest*

INTRODUCTION: An easy half a mile jaunt, suitable for just about anyone, the Potwisha Pictographs Loop is not much of a hike by most hikers' standards. However, an extensive display of bedrock mortars, in which the native Monache ground nuts and seeds, and a set of pictographs add an interesting historical glimpse into the lifestyles of the first peoples to inhabit this scenic area. During the warmer half of the year, sandy beaches and granite slabs provide swimmers and sunbathers with a lovely setting along the banks of the picturesque Middle Fork Kaweah River, which glides over slabs, tumbles in cataracts, and swirls through delightful pools. A wooden suspension bridge over the river will be of special interest to the young and the young at heart. While the trail is easy enough for groups with small children, caution should be exercised at all times, as the river can be treacherous for both young and old, particularly in spring and early summer.

DIRECTIONS TO THE TRAILHEAD: Follow the Generals Highway 3.8 miles from the Ash Mountain Entrance to the turnoff into Potwisha Campground. Take the road opposite the campground that heads toward the dump station. Instead of continuing down the dump-station loop, where you'll find the Middle Fork trailhead, follow the gravel surface to the end of a broad clearing above the river and park near a trio of garbage cans.

Suspension Bridge, Potwisha Pictographs Trail

MONACHE ARTISTS

The Monache used bedrock mortars to grind acorns from the native oaks into meal, a staple of their diet. Since only women were involved in this task, anthropologists assume female members of the tribe drew the nearby pictographs; the meanings of the rock drawings remain a mystery.

DESCRIPTION: Find the unmarked path near the garbage cans and head down toward the Middle Fork Kaweah River. You quickly encounter a series of granite slabs, site of numerous Indian bedrock mortars. An overhanging rock to the south has several Indian pictographs on the underside surface.

From the mortars and pictographs, proceed through granite boulders above the river to a wooden suspension bridge. On the far side, a series of granite slabs provide excellent views of the pools and cataracts along the Middle Fork, and fine spots for sunbathing after a refreshing dip. If you swim, exercise caution, as the Middle Fork can be hazardous when the turbulent waters are running swift and high. The path quickly dead-ends above the bridge near a flume.

Recross the bridge and veer to the right on a trail heading toward a large-diameter steel pipe. A faint path follows the pipe on a short, steep climb up the hillside to an informal junction with the Middle Fork Trail. Turn left at the junction and follow the trail high above the Middle Fork through typical oak woodland back to the dump station. From the dump station, walk the gravel surface back to your car.

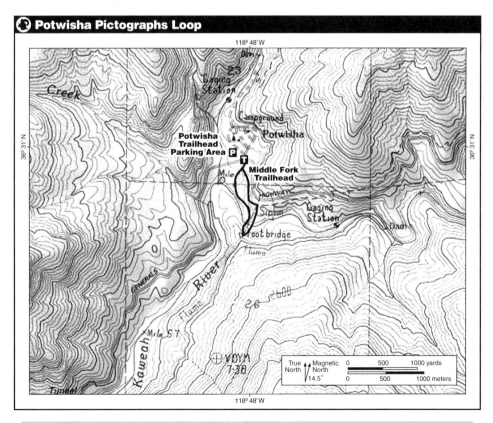

Potwisha Pictographs Loop

TRIP **19**

Marble Falls

Ⓜ ↗ DH

DISTANCE: 3.3 miles one way

ELEVATION: 2160/3760, +1750'/-295'

SEASON: All year (best March to May)

USE: Light

MAP: *Giant Forest*

INTRODUCTION: The trail to Marble Falls provides year-round opportunities to enjoy the outdoors, and is especially delightful in spring, when the rest of the Sierra remains buried beneath a blanket of snow. While most of the park's backcountry is accessible only to cross-country skiers and snow-shoers, the foothills region offers restless hikers a chance to shake off the winter doldrums and experience the beauty of the mountains sans snow. This trip has an abundance of beautiful sights, including the raging torrent of the Marble Fork Kaweah River, coursing and cascading through aptly named Deep Canyon, and a series of dramatic waterfalls surrounded by glistening marble slabs and boulders. Patches of verdant grass and an assortment of wildflowers are added bonuses of springtime visits.

Foothills hiking poses a trio of concerns that are uncommon in the high country, namely, ticks, poison oak, and rattlesnakes.

DIRECTIONS TO THE TRAILHEAD: Follow the Generals Highway 3.8 miles from the Ash Mountain Entrance to the turnoff into Potwisha Campground. Turn into the campground and follow the loop road to the dirt access road at the northwest end. Turn on the short access road and quickly find the trailhead parking area.

DESCRIPTION: Walk up the access road from the parking area to a wood plank bridge over a concrete-lined flume. Continue up the dirt road, paralleling the flume, until you reach a stream-flow gauging device and a fenced control gate. The signed trail officially begins opposite this gate, 0.2 mile from the parking area.

Leave the road behind and head uphill on moderate switchbacks that take you across a hillside dotted with typical foothill woodland trees and carpeted with vibrant wildflowers. Poison oak is prevalent along this initial section of trail. Beyond the switchbacks, you leave the trees behind and proceed through chaparral, climbing high above the Marble Fork around ridges and seams on the east side of Deep Canyon. Views down to the turbulent Marble Fork greet you as you ascend chaparral-covered hillsides, although the views are interrupted briefly by forays into small woodland groves at crossings of the numerous tiny

Cascading Marble Falls, on the Marble Falls Trail

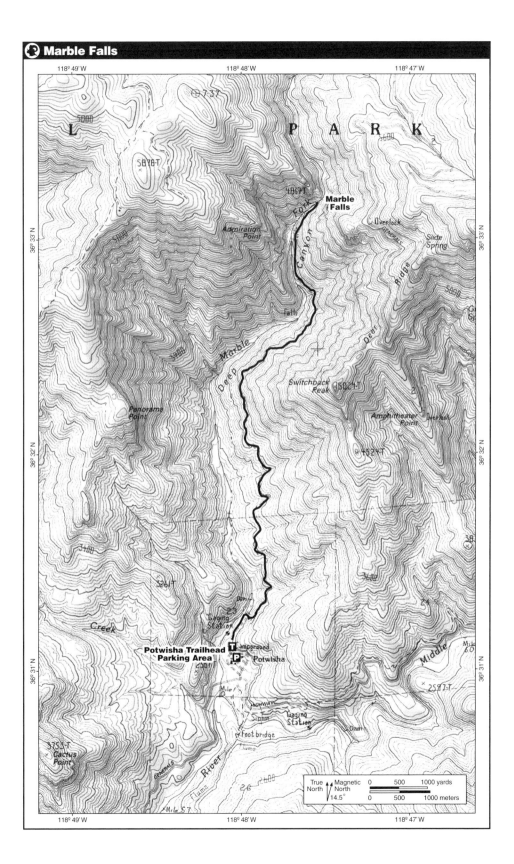

streams and seasonal drainages en route. The Marble Fork provides dramatic scenery in spring, as the swollen stream cascades over rock steps and swirls through churning pools, producing a raucous thunder that reverberates up the steep walls of Deep Canyon to the trail above. You continue the steady climb up the east side of the canyon to the crossing of the last stream that drains down the southwest slopes of Switchback Peak. Amid woodland, you wrap back around into the main canyon and climb across the hillside to meet the river at the abrupt ending of the trail, where a jumble of boulders and slabs impedes further progress.

Although the name "Marble Falls" specifically applies to the uppermost falls in Deep Canyon, a series of picturesque falls extend from the end of the trail over a narrow, quarter-mile section of the upper canyon. Across the gap, Admiration Point stands guard over the thunderous clamor the stream creates as it spills over glistening marble precipices into wildly churning pools. The most accessible vantage point is just down the trail, where short paths lead to impressive views from thin grassy benches of the lower falls. By scrambling over boulders, slabs, and steep portions of the canyon wall, you can make limited progress up the canyon to further views, but the terrain can be quite treacherous and moving across it should be attempted only by those skilled in such travel. The terrain becomes even more difficult farther up the canyon.

TRIP **20**

Middle Fork Kaweah River: Hospital Rock to Potwisha

Ⓜ ⟋ DH

DISTANCE: 2.4 miles one way

ELEVATION: 2695/2100, +345′/-935′

SEASON: All Year (Best September to June)

USE: Light

MAP: *Giant Forest*

INTRODUCTION: Although unbearably hot in summer, the Middle Fork Trail offers pleasant hiking the remainder of the year, when the high country is typically buried by snow. This short trail offers fine views of the Middle Fork Kaweah River canyon, as well as periodic glimpses of Moro Rock and Castle Rocks. A nice cross-section of foothill vegetation rewards hikers as they pass through oak woodland, chaparral, and grasses. Late winter and early spring bring green hillsides and splashes of color from a pleasant array of wildflowers.

DIRECTIONS TO THE TRAILHEAD:

START: Take the Generals Highway to the Hospital Rock parking lot, 6.1 miles from the Ash Mountain Entrance.

END: Follow the Generals Highway 3.8 miles from the Ash Mountain Entrance to the turnoff into Potwisha Campground. Take the road opposite the campground that heads toward the dump station. Instead of taking the dump-station loop, where you'll find the Middle Fork trailhead, follow the gravel surface to the end of a broad clearing above the river and park near a trio of garbage cans.

DESCRIPTION: The signed trail begins on the far, uphill side of the picnic area, near a small concrete and wood structure.

Moro Rock as seen from Hospital Rock

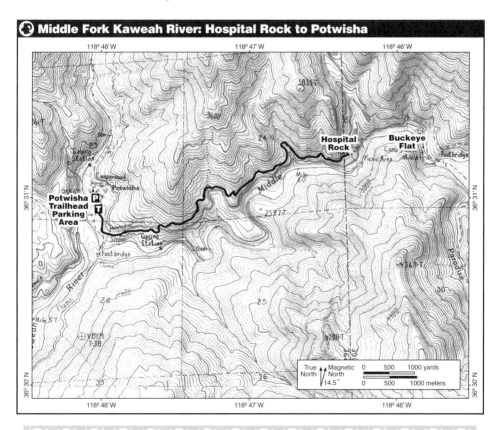

Middle Fork Kaweah River: Hospital Rock to Potwisha

Through shady oak woodland, proceed away from the picnic area, quickly breaking into the open, where a nearly continuous downstream view of the Middle Fork Kaweah River canyon begins. You follow an undulating traverse across the north side of the canyon through mostly open terrain, interrupted occasionally by brief dips into the narrow folds of side streams and seasonal drainages. As you continue down the canyon, don't neglect the periodic views behind of Moro Rock and Castle Rocks. Near the 1.75-mile mark, switchbacks lead down to the crossing of the Generals Highway.

The path resumes on the downhill side of the road and continues westbound after a switchback. The oak woodland mostly obscures views of the river and the canyon on the lower side of the highway. Easy hiking leads to the Potwisha dump station access road and the conclusion of the trail.

HOSPITAL ROCK TRAILHEAD

TRIP **21**

Paradise Creek Trail

E ╱ DH

DISTANCE: 2.3 miles one way

ELEVATION: 2685/3385, +975′/-280′

SEASON: All year

USE: Light

MAP: *Giant Forest*

INTRODUCTION: The Paradise Creek Trail is a little-known gem that provides a relatively temperate hike in the summer and a low-elevation alternative during months when the high country is snowbound. One of the few all-year trails in the park, a dense forest cover with lush understory keeps hikers from suffering the intense heat common to other foothills trails during the summer. Late winter and early spring provide extra greenery and a nice assortment of wildflowers, although hikers should keep a wary eye open for ticks during those months.

After the bridged crossing of the tumbling Middle Fork Kaweah River, the path ascends the narrow side canyon of Paradise Creek on a mild-to-moderate climb. The Park Service built the Paradise Creek Trail in the 1920s, extending it all the way to Mineral King. After the Mineral King Road was improved, the trail suffered from a lack of use, and the upper portion was abandoned in the 1960s. Nowadays, only about 2.5 miles are maintained.

DIRECTIONS TO THE TRAILHEAD: Take the Generals Highway to the Hospital Rock parking lot, 6.1 miles from the Ash Mountain Entrance.

DESCRIPTION: Unless you are camped at Buckeye Creek, you must walk the 0.6-mile access road, as day-use parking is not allowed within the campground. Follow the paved access road eastbound from Hospital Rock for half a mile to the Y-junction with the dirt road heading to the Middle Fork trailhead. Take the paved road downhill into the campground and find the signed trailhead on the east side, opposite campsite No. 28. Through dense oak woodland, you follow a single-track trail, initially on a mild ascent, until a short descent leads to the bridged crossing of the Middle Fork, 0.9 mile from the parking lot.

Once across the stout, wood plank-and-rail-bridge, you soon reach an informal junction with short paths that follow the river upstream and downstream. If you have a few extra minutes, detour on the upstream trail to a picturesque fall with a huge pool at the base, surrounded by colorful rock formations. The path on the right leads to a small waterfall and swimming pool on Paradise Creek. Your trail is the middle one, the Paradise Creek Trail, which

climbs mildly on a pair of switchbacks through dense oak woodland with a lush understory. High above the river, you have good views of the cataracts and cascades of the Middle Fork below. Quickly, you encounter another informal junction, where the main trail veers left and is marked by a sign reading, TRAIL MAINTAINED FOR 3 MILES ONLY.

At 1.9 miles from Hospital Rock, the trail makes the first crossing of Paradise Creek, which may be a wet ford in early season. After 0.1 mile on the west bank, the trail recrosses the creek and continues upstream. Beyond the second crossing, the unmaintained trail is steeper and becomes faint and brushy, but determined hikers may be able to continue to a pretty 15-foot fall on the unnamed tributary east of the main fork of the creek. Along the way, the vegetation opens up, allowing good views of Paradise Canyon and Ridge.

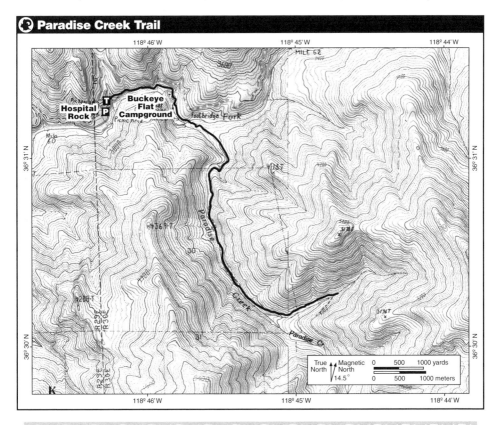

Paradise Creek Trail

HOSPITAL ROCK TRAILHEAD

TRIP **22**

Middle Fork Kaweah River: Hospital Rock to Panther Creek

Ⓜ ↗ DH / BP

DISTANCE: 2.75 miles to Panther Creek (+1.8 miles when road is closed)

ELEVATION: 3220/3875, +1325'/-670'

SEASON: All year

USE: Light

MAP: *Giant Forest*

INTRODUCTION: Many hikers and backpackers consider spring the best time to take the trail up the Middle Fork Kaweah River. The low elevation provides snow-free travel throughout the course of an average year, but the mild temperatures, splendid array of wildflowers, and swollen river combine to make this journey a fine vernal experience. No matter what the season, stunning views of Moro Rock, Castle Rocks, and the Great Western Divide provide excellent scenery. Good campsites offer an opportunity for off-season backpacks as well, with the possibility of extending the trip farther up the Middle Fork (see Options below).

The route up the south-facing wall of the canyon is exposed most of the way, which makes this a hot trip when the typical southern Sierra sunshine bathes the area. Therefore, an early start is advisable when the forecast is for fair skies. Travel in the foothills also includes potential encounters with such hazards as ticks, rattlesnakes, and poison oak.

When the nearby Buckeye Campground is open, hikers and backpackers can drive 1.8 miles up the access road to the official trailhead (note that the sign gives this dis-

tance as 1.3 miles). However, if the gate is closed at the highway, you must park at the Hospital Rock parking lot and walk that distance to the trailhead.

DIRECTIONS TO THE TRAILHEAD: Take the Generals Highway to the Hospital Rock parking lot, 6.1 miles from the Ash Mountain Entrance. If the road into Buckeye Campground is open, drive an additional 0.5-mile to a Y-junction and follow the dirt road to the left, signed MIDDLE FORK 1.3, to the trailhead.

DESCRIPTION:

FROM HOSPITAL ROCK: Cross the Generals Highway and walk the paved access road toward Buckeye Campground for half a mile to a Y-junction. Follow the upper road to the left and proceed on a steady climb up the dirt road across grassy hillsides dotted with oaks and lined with wildflowers. You have excellent views of the cascading and careening Middle Fork below, as well as the Great Western Divide up the canyon. At 1.8

Great Western Divide from the trail

miles from Hospital Rock, you reach the official trailhead for the Middle Fork Trail.

FROM MIDDLE FORK TRAILHEAD: On single-track trail, you quickly descend to a crossing of Moro Creek, which you may have to ford in early season rather than boulder hop. You enjoy an attractive scene, as the refreshing creek dances over a series of slanted rock slabs, backdropped nicely by the narrow, V-shaped canyon framing the granodiorite dome of Moro Rock, 3500 feet above. A tangle of alder and laurel lines the banks.

You climb moderately on a sandy track, proceeding up-canyon across the open, chaparral-covered slopes. Soon, you wrap around into the drainage of an unnamed creek and easily cross the lively but diminutive stream. Beyond the creek, you follow the serpentine course of the Middle Fork on a steady climb, weaving around the folds and creases of the canyon. Patches of poi-

son oak may appear along the fringe of the trail. For the most part, the mighty river is distant enough from the trail to remain hidden by the intervening terrain, but the raucous torrent is constantly within earshot. Across the canyon, the spires and pinnacles of Castle Rocks lend a craggy feel to the scrubby surroundings. Before Panther Creek, three switchbacks take you to a vantage point and vistas of the Great Western Divide, Moro Rock, Castle Rocks, and the turbulent Middle Fork below. Continue the moderate climb, until a short, moderately steep descent brings you to Panther Creek (3840′±).

Conveniently placed rocks provide a relatively easy boulder hop across the shallow but quickly moving creek, although the crossing may be a bit intimidating in light of the precipitous fall immediately downstream. The creek hurtles through a narrow chute of slick rock to plummet a hundred

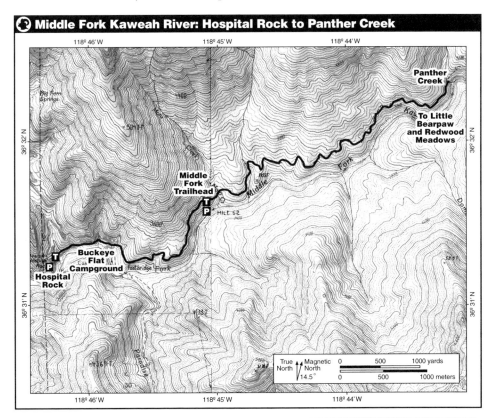

Middle Fork Kaweah River: Hospital Rock to Panther Creek

feet down the steep canyon wall toward a rapid union with the turbulent Middle Fork. Take extra precautions at the crossing, and while swimming in the inviting pools above the fall. Some nice campsites reside on a bench above the far side of the creek, next to slabs near the lip of the canyon, and provide scenic views of the Middle Fork below and the Great Western Divide to the east.

O The trail continues past Panther Creek up the canyon of the Middle Fork to junctions with trails leading to Little Bearpaw and Redwood meadows, providing a rare opportunity for an extended off-season backpack. Beyond the creek you pass through a transition forest of oaks and cedars to a junction with the unmaintained Castle Creek Trail, 2.5 miles from Panther Creek. Campsites are available a short way down the old trail at Mehrten Creek and 0.4 mile farther along the Middle Fork. The Middle Fork Trail continues an undulating course, past campsites at Mehrten Creek and toward more camping near the bridged crossing of Buck Creek, 2.75 miles from the junction. A 1.8-mile climb leads to a junction with a lateral trail to Little Bearpaw Meadow. The next mile involves more climbing, followed by a sustained descent that leads to a crossing of the Middle Fork Kaweah River and a junction with the trail to Redwood Meadow (see Trip 17).

R PERMITS: Wilderness permit required for overnight stays. (Quota: 25 per day)
CAMPFIRES: Yes

NORTH FORK TRAILHEAD

TRIP **23**

North Fork Trail

M ✗ DH

DISTANCE: 4.2 miles one way

ELEVATION: 1800/2355, +1415′/-555′

SEASON: September to June

USE: Light

MAP: *Shadequarter Mountain*

INTRODUCTION: Following the route of an old fire road built by the Civilian Conservation Corps (CCC) in the 1930s, the seldom-used North Fork Trail offers solitude and splendid views of the namesake canyon. Although the fire road once extended nearly 14 miles to Hidden Springs, nowadays only the first 6 miles of the trail are in good enough condition for pleasant hiking. While a scorcher in the summer, the North Fork Trail provides splendid off-season opportunities in the foothills for hikers itching to stretch out their legs.

DIRECTIONS TO THE TRAILHEAD: From the town of Three Rivers, leave State Highway 198 and drive north on North Fork Drive, immediately crossing the Middle Fork Kaweah River. Continue past the community of Kaweah, where the road narrows and begins a winding climb up the canyon. Six miles from the highway, you enter the Bureau of Land Management's North Fork Recreation Area and continue another 1.5 miles to the end of the pavement. Now on a dirt road, you encounter a Y-junction after about 10 miles. The uphill fork on the right is the Colony Mill Road. Veer left at the junction and proceed downhill for another 0.7 mile, crossing the boundary of Sequoia National Park. There is plenty of parking at a broad, flat area at the end of the road.

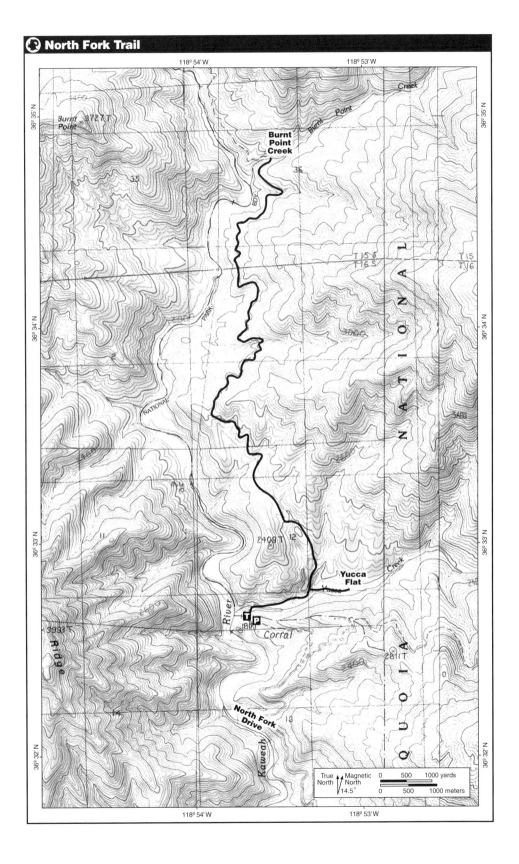

Kaweah Post Office

canyon of the North Fork. Now roughly paralleling the river, you traverse the folds and creases on the east side of the canyon, periodically veering into small, forested side canyons on the way. You'll have plentiful views of the North Fork, including Burnt Point, as you proceed upstream.

At 3.8 miles, you reach an unnamed creek, half a mile before the crossing of Burnt Creek, where sloping granite slabs offer a pleasant spot for a rest. A gently graded trail leads away from the smaller creek to Burnt Creek, which is heavily shaded and flows through a culvert below the old road. Hikers can continue up the mild path through similar terrain for another couple of miles, enjoying views of the river along the way. The trail eventually becomes brushy and less distinct as it climbs more steeply toward Pine Ridge and Hidden Spring.

DESCRIPTION: From the flat, cross the wood-beam and single-rail bridge over Yucca Creek and follow the old roadbed above the north bank across a grassy slope dotted with oaks. About 0.3 mile from the trailhead, you reach an unmarked junction with a short trail on the right that leads to Yucca Flat, which was occupied by a succession of inhabitants, including Native Americans, members of the Kaweah Colony, and ranchers, before its eventual purchase by the Park Service.

Steeper climbing beyond the junction leads away from the creek and up a series of hillsides. In the midst of the climb, a short use-trail leads to a pair of small concrete bunkers, once used by the CCC to store explosives. Continuing the ascent, you pass through an old steel gate as the trail climbs over grassy hills carpeted with wildflowers in spring. As the trail eases, you pass through another old gate and eventually work your way above the main

TRIP **24**

Colony Mill Road: North Fork to Colony Mill Ranger Station

Ⓜ ↗ DH / BP

DISTANCE: 8 miles one way

ELEVATION: 2360/5445, +5170′/-1085′

SEASON: March to November

USE: Light

MAPS: *Shadequarter Mountain, Giant Forest*

INTRODUCTION: Modern-day hikers can enjoy the history of Colony Mill Road while experiencing the views and foliage of the foothill zone. Chaparral, woodland, and riparian flora provide plenty of diversity over the first 6.5 miles before the trail enters the starkly contrasting belt of the mixed coniferous forest that lies just below the Colony Mill Ranger Station. The low-elevation trailhead provides off-season opportunities for fine ramblings when the backcountry above is covered with snow. During the height of summer, expect hot daytime temperatures. Early spring hikers typically will see a bountiful display of wildflowers. On the way to the trailhead, plan on a short stop at the historic Kaweah Post Office.

DIRECTIONS TO THE TRAILHEAD: From the town of Three Rivers, leave State Highway 198 and drive north on North Fork Drive, immediately crossing the Middle Fork Kaweah River. Six miles from the highway, enter the Bureau of Land Management's North Fork Recreation Area and continue another 1.5 miles to the end of the pavement. After about 10 miles on the dirt road, you encounter a Y-junction The uphill fork on the right is the Colony Mill Road.

Bear right at the junction and continue climbing on a narrow dirt road for another 0.4 mile to a closed gate at the park boundary. Park your vehicle either near the gate or at the Y, as conditions allow.

DESCRIPTION: Walk through the pedestrian bypass at the locked gate and follow the old roadbed of the Colony Mill Road on a steady climb through typical foothill vegetation. Except for the narrow footpath, the road is now covered with grasses, small plants, and spring wildflowers. The well-graded road follows the folds and creases of Yucca Creek canyon far above the stream. Sporadic views through gaps in the deciduous woodland lining the road allow views down to Yucca Flat and up toward forested Colony Peak.

At 0.6 mile, you encounter the first of the many streams and seasonal creeklets that feed Yucca Creek. In keeping with the excellent quality of the construction of the Colony Mill Road, all these streams pass safely below the roadbed through well-placed culverts. Another 0.6 mile brings you into the densely forested canyon of a spring-fed creek, where a small concrete room with a metal door is built into the hillside on the uphill side of the road. A larger rock structure missing a roof, which was used to store explosives, appears a short distance away.

Away from the creek, the vegetation diminishes considerably, allowing good views of the canyon for a short while. Soon, you return to a thickly vegetated area and follow the road on a winding, easterly course. Near the 2-mile mark, you swing south to enter the canyon of Maple Creek, where a dense tangle of maples and alders shades the road. After crossing the stream at 2.5 miles, follow the road out of the canyon and around the nose of a hill, marked as *4234* on the *Giant Forest* topo. Well below the crest of Ash Peaks Ridge, the road curves around to cross an unnamed tributary of Cedar Creek at 4.7 miles.

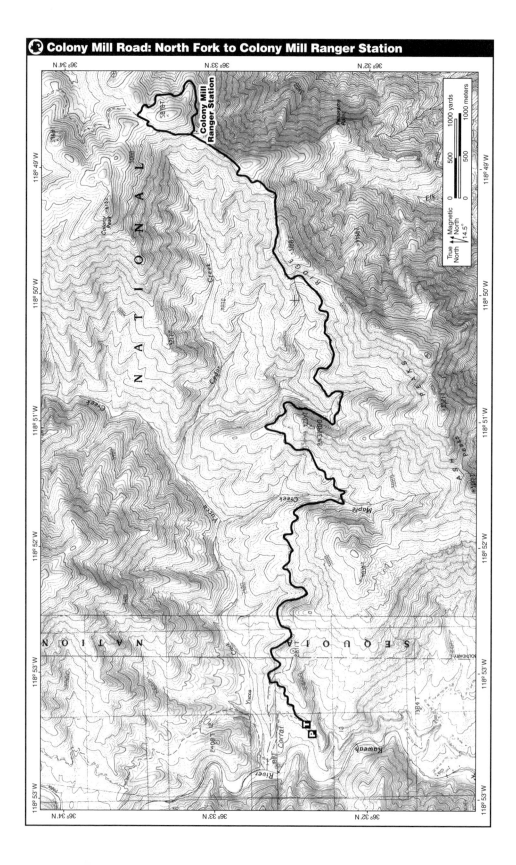

Still heading roughly east, you follow the path on an ascending traverse across the northwest face of Ash Peaks Ridge, above the canyon of Cedar Creek. Eventually, the road draws near the creek and a few of the namesake conifers make an appearance, the first evergreens along the trail so far. You wrap around a hill and quickly pass a second branch of Cedar Creek, where another small concrete room is built into the hillside. Beyond the last stream, the road makes a steady climb toward a saddle at the crest of Ash Peaks Ridge, where you have an excellent view down the canyon of Elk Creek.

After an easy stroll along the ridgecrest, you quickly resume climbing and ascend a moderately forested hillside, composed of ponderosa pines and incense cedars — a stark contrast to the foothills woodland you've been traveling through for the past 6.5 miles. Beyond the hill, you stride easily across the crest of Ash Peaks Ridge once again, this time admiring views down the

COLONY MILL ROAD

Perhaps no other route through Sequoia National Park is replete with more history than the journey along the Colony Mill Road. In 1885, a group of San Francisco-based radicals formed the Kaweah Colony in an attempt to create a utopian society based on socialist principles. They established a group of community land claims in the giant sequoia groves and constructed a wagon road from the area above Three Rivers to the Giant Forest plateau. Their plan was to transport timber from the groves to a mill, where they would ship the lumber to market for sale. The profits from the lumber would be used to finance their utopian dream.

From a base near the present community of Kaweah, the colonists began work on their road, using nothing more than hand tools. Despite their lack of modern machinery, they performed an admirable job of construction, evidenced by the excellent grade of the road and the fine quality of workmanship in the many hand-stacked retaining walls. After four years, they completed the road through chaparral and foothill woodland to a small flat just inside the mixed coniferous forest zone, near 5400 feet. The colonists erected a steam-powered, portable sawmill at the flat, which operated for a brief period, milling a rather modest quantity of lumber.

A number of factors combined to ultimately dash the dream of the Kaweah Colony, including growing concerns over forest destruction from ranchers and preservationists, the government disputing their land claims, and internal disputes among the colonists themselves. Due primarily to legal battles, the mill was a short-lived proposition; the colonists abandoned it and quickly tried to regroup by leasing Atwell's Mill near Mineral King. Additional disputes with the government over the new mill eventually deflated the last of the colonists' resolve, and by 1892, Kaweah Colony was formally disbanded.

Although the Kaweah Colony had a short run, their road lived on for many years. Upon creation of the park, the U.S. cavalry extended the road from the former mill site into the Giant Forest in 1903. For the next 23 years, the Colony Mill Road would be the only access for visitors to the giant sequoia grove. The narrow road permitted only one-way traffic, and vehicles had to travel by convoy from the Kaweah Post Office, past the entrance station at Colony Mill, and then into Giant Forest before the convoy of departing traffic could leave. With completion of the Generals Highway in 1926, use of the old road began diminishing. Since 1969, only the section of road between Giant Forest and Crystal Cave is periodically open to vehicular traffic, with the remaining 10 miles of old road seeing a very limited amount of foot traffic.

precipitous canyon of the Marble Fork Kaweah. More climbing leads to a junction, where a little-used old road veers to the left (north), ascending the west side of point 5878. You bear to the right and continue up the road past some overturned outhouses to the dilapidated Colony Mill Ranger Station, near the site of the old mill.

Few visitors reach the old ranger station anymore, which has been left to crumble and decay in relative obscurity. The view from the old porch down the Marble Fork to Potwisha Campground and the Middle Fork Kaweah River, and to the multiple ridges of the foothills region, is fairly impressive, although probably not as grand as when the vegetation surrounding the structure was less mature. Although it was a lonely outpost, the rangers who served here had excellent accommodations to go along with the views, including indoor plumbing and hot running water. Nowadays, the few backpackers who plan on an overnight stay will find a fire pit and perhaps a stack of wood in front of the ranger station, but no water nearby.

O To continue along the old road to the upper trailhead at the Crystal Cave Road, see Trip 26.

R **PERMITS:** Wilderness permit required for overnight stays. (Quota: none)

Introduction to Giant Forest

Upon seeing the splendor of this giant sequoia forest, famed naturalist John Muir dubbed the area "Giant Forest." His appellation certainly rings true, since four of the five largest sequoias in the world reside in the Giant Forest Grove (General Sherman, Washington, President, and Lincoln), as well as hundreds of other deserving specimens. Muir's adulation wasn't for the Big Trees alone, as he also declared Crescent Meadow to be the "gem of the Sierra." Nowhere else in the Sierra Nevada are so many verdant, flower-filled meadows found within a single sequoia grove. A greater sight than the full profile of a towering sequoia across a beautiful meadow is hard to imagine, and the Giant Forest offers many such scenes.

Another attribute of the Giant Forest plateau is the gentle terrain, which is unlike the topography in the rest of the park. An extensive network of trails graciously covers this plateau, offering hikers a plethora of opportunities for exploring the area on diverse routes and loops. Aside from the popular General Sherman, Congress, and Crescent Meadow trails, the Big Trees and picturesque meadows can be enjoyed with a certain amount of solitude. On many of the trails that crisscross the plateau, hikers may humbly stand beneath the towering monarchs, amid serene surroundings. In addition to the meadows and the Big Trees, the Giant Forest has far-reaching vistas and plenty of wildlife.

The giant sequoias and lush meadows of Giant Forest captured the fascination of white men from the moment they saw them, which led to both good and bad results. Ultimately the Big Trees received a portion of the protection they deserved, but not before overcoming serious threats from logging and grazing. Once the lumbermen, sheepherders and cattlemen were driven from the newly created park, a subtler foe of the sequoias emerged: development. To support visitors' increasing interest in the Big Trees, a variety of campgrounds, lodges, and other commercial buildings were erected in Giant Forest over the years, not to mention a number of administrative facilities. People poured into the area in increasing numbers, and their presence had a severe impact on the health of the environment. Giant Forest became the focal point of Sequoia's tourism, as the proliferation of man-made structures testified.

Although many people recognized the destructive influence of excessive tourism on Giant Forest and were concerned about degradation of the area, what to do about it was altogether another matter. As early as 1929, Park Superintendent John White considered ridding Giant Forest of all human-made improvements as a way of restoring the health of Giant Forest, but visionaries like him were a small minority.

Concessionaires opposed such a radical idea, and visitors desired access to the facilities they deemed necessary for their full enjoyment of the Big Trees and meadows. By the 1950s, the concessionaire managed more than 400 structures at Giant Forest. The Park Service had over a dozen of its own, plus four campgrounds, a picnic area, and an assortment of support facilities such as sewage plants, water cisterns, and an amphitheater. Traffic jams had become a constant summertime ritual. The battle over development in Giant Forest would rage on for a good part of the 20th century.

Starting in 1962, the Park Service began steps to minimize their own influence on Giant Forest by closing the Firwood Campground. A new visitor center was completed at Lodgepole in 1966, with a gas station and post office following four years later. The remaining three campgrounds, Paradise, Sunset Rock, and Sugar Pine, were

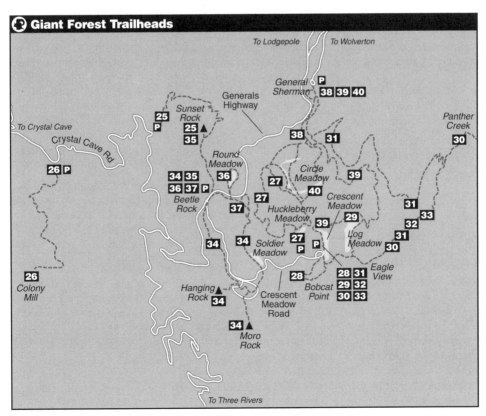

closed in 1971, along with the Hazelwood Picnic Area. Maintenance facilities were moved to Red Fir. Eventually, the Park Service's presence in the area was reduced to restrooms, an information station, and one cabin. However, the commercial presence was as strong as ever, with no end in sight.

Prompted by research on the detrimental effects of development on the sequoias, a growing environmental awareness by the public, and economics, the Park Service set in motion a plan that would ultimately attempt to restore health to Giant Forest. Over the course of several decades, all viable commercial facilities were eventually relocated to Lodgepole and Wuksachi, and the remaining dilapidated structures and needless asphalt were removed. As of summer 2002, the doors of the Giant Forest Museum and Beetle Rock Environmental Education Center were open to the public, improved parking facilities were available for motorists, and rehabilitated trails were reopened. In addition, less obvious parts of the Giant Forest restoration include soil restoration, regrading, revegetation, and fire management. Hopefully, generations of admirers to come will be able to enjoy a revitalized Giant Forest.

ACCESS: *(Open all year from Ash Mountain; subject to weather closures from Big Stump)* The Generals Highway provides access to the roads and trails of Giant Forest. The museum at the heart of Giant Forest is 16.75 miles from the Ash Mountain Entrance, much of that distance up a winding and steep section of the Generals Highway between Hospital Rock and Giant Forest (recommended maximum vehicle length is 22 ft.). From the opposite direction, the museum is 29 miles south of the Wye (a major Y in the road).

The Moro Rock-Crescent Meadow Road leaves the Generals Highway at the museum, heading southeast to a variety of trailheads (Trips 27–33). The Crystal Cave Road departs the Generals Highway 2 miles south of the museum to trailheads for Trips 25 and 26.

SHUTTLE BUS: The long-term commitment of Sequoia National Park is to provide a shuttle-bus system between various points in Giant Forest to facilities at Lodgepole and Wuksachi. After the completion of the Giant Forest restoration, the details of the shuttle-bus program were in a state of flux. Check with the Park Service for current conditions.

AMENITIES: Since the completed restoration, few amenities are available at Giant Forest. Aside from the museum, which houses an SNHA bookstore, you will have to travel 4.5 miles north to Lodgepole for stores, laundry, showers, food service, and post office. The nearest gasoline is over 20 miles away in Three Rivers.

The Beetle Rock Environmental Education Center, operated by a division of SNHA, is located across the Generals Highway from the museum down a short access road (see Appendix VII for more information on the SNHA).

CAMPGROUNDS: In the past, most of the lodging and camping in Sequoia National Park took place in Giant Forest, but the recent restoration has moved facilities out of Giant Forest. The nearest campground is now located at Lodgepole (4.5 miles north) and lodging is at Wuksachi (6 miles north).

RANGER STATION: Although the Giant Forest Museum is the new centerpiece of the Giant Forest area, the closest ranger station at which you can obtain a wilderness permit is at Lodgepole.

GOOD TO KNOW BEFORE YOU GO: The extensive network of trails crisscrossing the Giant Forest plateau are exclusively for day hiking. The only backpacking route follows the High Sierra Trail, with the first legal campsites at Panther Creek, well beyond the Big Trees.

CRYSTAL CAVE ROAD TRAILHEAD

TRIP **25**

Marble Fork Bridge to Sunset Rock

Ⓜ ↗ DH

DISTANCE: 2.4 miles

ELEVATION: 5160/6412, +1350´/-100´

SEASON: June to November

USE: Light

MAP: *Giant Forest*

INTRODUCTION: While scores of tourists of varying descriptions lumber up the Sunset Rock Trail from Giant Forest Museum, very few hardy souls make the stiff climb from the other side. The hike from the Marble Fork Bridge to the top of Sunset Rock is definitely the road less traveled, requiring three times the distance and over 10 times the elevation gain to achieve the same goal. In fact, the Park Service has abandoned the trail and removed the trailhead signs. Nevertheless, for hikers who are in good condition and can find their own way, the serenity more than compensates for the extra effort. The view of the western part of Sequoia National Park is quite pleasant, and sunsets can still be dramatic under the right conditions. An abundance of dogwood along the trail graces the shady forest with attractive white flowers in spring and brilliant red leaves in autumn.

DIRECTIONS TO THE TRAILHEAD: Two miles south of the Giant Forest Museum, leave the Generals Highway at a sharp curve and head north on the Crystal Cave Road. After a 1.5-mile descent, you reach the Marble Fork Bridge. Parking is extremely limited along the narrow shoulder of the road. You'll find better spots across the bridge and down a short dirt road, on a flat above the river. Be aware that the Crystal Cave Road is closed at the Generals

Dogwoods in autumn, Sunset Rock Trail

Highway after the first significant snowfall of the season.

DESCRIPTION: The trail to Sunset Rock begins on the east side of the bridge (no trailhead sign). You climb moderately away from the bridge through a mixed forest of black oaks, cedars, and white firs, quickly reaching the first of many switchbacks that zigzag up the west-facing hillside. The steady ascent takes you high above the river, where sugar pines and scores of dogwoods eventually join the shady forest and patches of mountain misery threaten to overgrow the seldom-used trail. The unrelenting climb curves around the slopes below Sunset Rock to a saddle directly south of the summit, whence a short stroll leads over to the top of the dome.

An expansive view greets you from the top, including the deep chasm of the Marble Fork Kaweah River canyon. Forested Colony Peak and Ash Peaks Ridge compose the southwestern skyline. To the north is another granite dome, Little Baldy. Undoubtedly, Sunset Rock received its name for a reason, and the sunsets can be awe-inspiring when the atmospheric conditions cooperate.

Pick a day after cleansing rains or strong winds have diminished the nearly perpetual San Joaquin Valley haze, and you may still be able to appreciate a stunning sunset from atop Sunset Rock.

⊙ Arrangements for pick-up would allow hikers to avoid backtracking to the Marble Fork Bridge by descending the more popular Sunset Rock Trail to the Giant Forest Museum (see Trip 35).

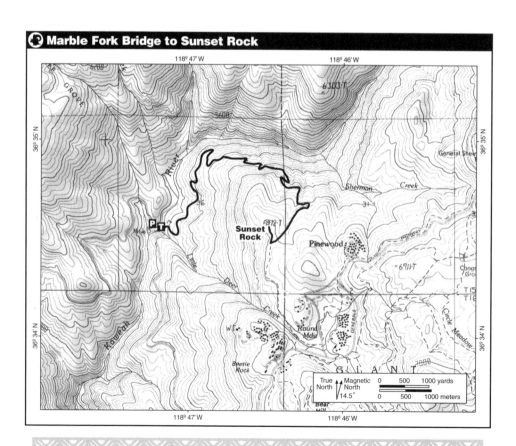

CRYSTAL CAVE ROAD TRAILHEAD

TRIP **26**

Colony Mill Road: Crystal Cave Road to Colony Mill Ranger Station

Ⓜ / DH

DISTANCE: 2 miles one way (+2.5 miles if road closed)

ELEVATION: 5300/5610, +865'/-245'

SEASON: May to November

USE: Light

MAP: *Giant Forest*

COLONY MILL

The Kaweah colonists' goal was to construct a road from Three Rivers to a mill site near marketable timber. They eventually erected a steam-driven mill named Ajax, which ultimately produced very little lumber. After the dream of the colonists was dashed, the U.S. Cavalry extended the road in 1903 from the defunct mill to the Giant Forest, and the road remained the main access for visitors until the Generals Highway was completed in 1926. The Park Service built a ranger station on the old mill site to take advantage of the far ranging view, but it too eventually was abandoned.

INTRODUCTION: History buffs and solitude seekers will reap big rewards on this short hike to the site of the Colony Mill Ranger Station. From 1886 to 1890, as part of their dream for a utopian society, the Kaweah colonists hand-built the Colony Mill Road through the rugged western hills of what would one day be known as Sequoia National Park.

Modern-day hikers can walk a portion of this old road, still in remarkably good condition, from the Crystal Cave Road to an abandoned ranger station and the site of the old mill.

The old Colony Mill Ranger Station

The Crystal Cave Road is subject to daily and seasonal closures. In summer, a gate immediately past the Marble Fork Bridge opens in the morning and closes in the late afternoon to allow passage for motorists to and from tours of the Crystal Cave. Hikers must plan their trip to coincide with the opening and closing of the gate (hours are posted on a sign near the gate). After the last tour in late October, the gate is closed for the season and hikers will have to walk an additional 2.5 miles of the Crystal Cave Road from the Marble Fork Bridge to the beginning of the Colony Mill Road. After the first major snowfall, the Crystal Cave Road is closed at the Generals Highway.

DIRECTIONS TO THE TRAILHEAD: Two miles south of the Giant Forest Museum, leave the Generals Highway at a sharp curve and head north on the Crystal Cave Road. Reach the Marble Fork Bridge at 1.5 miles. If the gate is closed, park your vehicle in the parking area down a dirt road on the far side of the bridge. If the gate is open, continue another 2.5 miles to the start of the Colony Mill Road. The road is not marked, but if you keep a close watch you should be able to spot it on the left side, where the usually steep-sided shoulder of the Crystal Cave Road briefly widens. Parking is very limited, but seems adequate for the infrequent cars that stop here.

DESCRIPTION:

FROM MARBLE FORK BRIDGE: Hike the easy grade of the paved road from the parking area under the shade of a mixed forest, following the course of the road as it weaves around hillsides and dips into small side canyons, where lushly lined streams trickle down the slope. After 2.5 miles of gentle

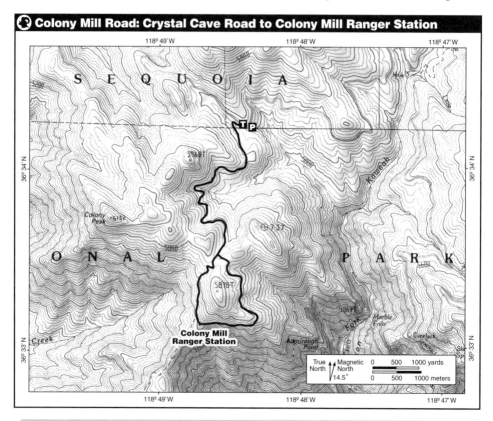

Giant sequoia and wildflowers

road, you reach the Colony Mill Road, angling away to your left.

FROM COLONY MILL ROAD TRAILHEAD: You begin hiking along the old road through thick vegetation of thimbleberry and maple, under a mixed forest, including dogwood. Fortunately, the dense foliage quickly recedes to the edge of the roadbed, as you climb mildly to moderately along the well-graded road. After a pleasant 1.5-mile stroll, you encounter a fork with a brush-filled old road that heads up the hillside to your right.

Remain on the main road to the left and continue to climb to the crest of a saddle. Beyond the saddle, you make a gently descending traverse that curves across the hillside. Along this traverse, the trees part just enough in places to allow nice views down the steep canyon of the Marble Fork Kaweah River. You follow the road as it bends west and quickly arrive at a small flat and the abandoned Colony Mill Ranger

Station, 2 miles from the Crystal Cave Road.

The run-down old structure appears to have provided fine accommodations in its day, with a shower, separate bedroom, enclosed porch, and an outhouse nearby, not to mention the incredible bird's-eye view. Before the ranger station was built, a steam-driven lumber mill operated by the Kaweah colonists in the late 1800s stood approximately 100 yards to the northwest. Today, the site offers the infrequent visitor the same excellent view that the colonists and the rangers enjoyed, along with a brief glimpse into the past.

⊡ Retracing your steps back to the Crystal Cave Road is by far the easiest route of return to the trailhead. However, if you don't mind a significant amount of brush-beating, you can follow the trail that the *Giant Forest* quad shows looping around the west side of Peak *5878-T* back to a fork with Colony Mill Road. Leave the main road at a sharp curve about 0.1 mile north of the old ranger station and follow an abandoned, shrub-and-brush-filled road heading north on a steep half-mile climb to the crest of a ridge. From there, a short descent leads back to the main road again.

From the ranger station, Colony Mill Road continues on an 8-mile descent along the north side of Ash Peaks Ridge to the lower trailhead at the end of North Fork Drive (see Trip 23).

CRESCENT MEADOW TRAILHEAD

TRIP **27**

Huckleberry Meadow Loop

Ⓔ ↻ DH

DISTANCE: 3.75 miles

ELEVATION: 6700/6970/6700, +840´/-840´

SEASON: June to November

USE: Moderate

MAPS: *Giant Forest, Lodgepole Giant Forest, SNHA*

INTRODUCTION: This pleasant loop sees little traffic, sandwiched as it is between two of the more popular trails in Giant Forest, the Crescent Meadow Trail on the south and the Congress Trail to the north. Along the way, you get to sample three delightful meadows (Huckleberry, Circle, and Crescent) and plenty of Giant Forest's famous sequoias, including the world's second largest—the Washington Tree. A log cabin built in the 1880s, and rock mortars at the site of an old Indian village, provide a bit of historical interest. Options abound for extending your travel through Giant Forest, as you will encounter nine trail junctions along this loop.

DIRECTIONS TO THE TRAILHEAD: From the Generals Highway near the Giant Forest Museum, turn onto the narrow Crescent Meadow Road and drive 1.2 miles to the junction with the road to Moro Rock. Continue on the Crescent Meadow Road another mile to the small parking area for the Huckleberry Trail, 0.3 mile before Crescent Meadow.

DESCRIPTION: In mixed forest of giant sequoias, white firs, and sugar pines, you follow the Huckleberry Meadow Trail on a mild climb to the Dead Giant, one of the few examples of a sequoia that actually succumbed to fire. The thick bark of the sequoia usually provides adequate protection against all but the most intense forest

Tharp's Log, Crescent Meadow Loop Trail

fires. A short distance beyond, you pass diminutive Huckleberry Meadow, carpeted with verdant grasses and decorated by splashes of color from an assortment of wildflowers. At the far edge of the meadow, beneath the shade of towering trees, is the Squatters Cabin.

Near the cabin, you reach a junction, one-third mile from the road.

Bear left at the junction and make a winding ascent to the crest of a ridge, where Jeffrey pines and manzanita thrive under these drier conditions. On a moderate descent, you return to damper surroundings beneath a mixed forest of sequoias, sugar pines, white firs, and dogwoods, with an understory of azaleas, wildflowers, and ferns. At 1.25 miles, you meet the Alta Trail at a well-signed junction.

Turn north and follow the Alta Trail on a mild, half-mile ascent through mixed forest to the next intersection, with an abandoned 0.3-mile spur trail that used to connect to the Rimrock Trail. A short distance past this junction a sign points the way to bedrock mortars, where Native Americans once ground acorns and seeds. Nearby, the trail crosses Little Deer Creek, a reliable source of water until late summer. Soon, you come to another fork in the trail, 2.0 miles from the parking lot.

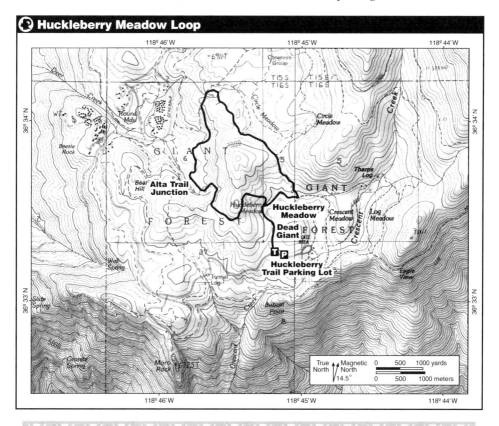

Huckleberry Meadow Loop

Leave the Alta Trail, following signed directions for the Washington Tree. A mild ascent alongside patches of azalea brings you to a second crossing of Little Deer Creek, bordered by a narrow swath of dense foliage. Beyond the stream, you may notice a profusion of young sequoias, the beneficial results of a prescribed burn in the late 1970s. A signed, short lateral trail leads to the base of the Washington Tree, with a volume of 47,850 cubic feet, second only in size to General Sherman. Washington stands 255 feet tall and has a circumference of 101 feet.

After your short detour to the Washington Tree, make a moderate ascent over a low rise and then quickly drop down to a fork in the trail near the edge of Circle Meadow, 2.5 miles from the trailhead. Although this description follows the path to the right, a short walk up the left-hand trail takes you to the Bear's Bathtub.

BEAR'S BATHTUB

Bear's Bathtub consists of two sequoias which have grown together. Early in the season, a fire-scarred hollow is filled with dank water. An implausible legend tells the tale of an old-timer who saw a bear wallowing in this water.

Head southeast along the fringe of Circle Meadow and then make a short climb to the crest of a hill and the next junction, a quarter mile from the previous one. Continue southeast on a 0.3-mile descent to a Y-junction, at 3.1 miles, where you can see the northern tip of Crescent Meadow through the trees to the south. Turn right (west) on a nearly level path that quickly reaches and then follows the northern edge of Huckleberry Meadow back to your first trail junction, near Squatters Cabin. From there, retrace your steps one-third of a mile back to the trailhead.

CRESCENT MEADOW TRAILHEAD

TRIP **28**

Bobcat Point Loop

E ↺ DH

DISTANCE: 1.25 miles

ELEVATION: 6720/6530/6720, +255/-255

SEASON: May to November

USE: Light

MAPS: *Lodgepole, Giant Forest, Giant Forest, SNHA*

INTRODUCTION: Crescent Meadow is a hub of activity on a typical summer day, with bevies of tourists picnicking, sightseeing, and strolling along the surrounding paths. Despite the minimal distance, this trip, combining the Bobcat Point and Sugar Pine trails, will take you away from the

A majestic giant

crowds. You won't see flower-filled meadows or towering sequoias, but you will have awesome views of the Middle Fork Kaweah River, Moro Rock, and Castle Rocks from Kaweah Vista and Bobcat Point. For those interested in Native American life, the trail passes a couple of locations where once they ground acorns and seeds in bedrock mortars. A journey to the top of Moro Rock is an easy extension to this trip.

DIRECTIONS TO THE TRAILHEAD: From the Generals Highway near the Giant Forest Museum, turn onto the narrow Crescent Meadow Road and drive 1.2 miles to the junction with the road to Moro Rock. Continue on the Crescent Meadow Road another 1.3 miles to the end of the road at the Crescent Meadow parking lot.

DESCRIPTION: Start your adventure on the High Sierra Trail, which begins at the east end of the Crescent Meadow parking lot near the restroom building. After a pair of wooden bridges over Crescent Creek, you quickly come to a junction with the Crescent Meadow Trail to your left. Remain on the High Sierra Trail for approximately another 25 yards to a second junction, signed to your right BOBCAT POINT 0.4, MORO ROCK 1.5. Turn right (south) and climb up a lightly forested hillside. Follow the trail as it bends west, drops into a saddle, and then climbs along a ridge high above the Middle Fork Kaweah River. Emerging from the light forest at the rock outcrop known as Kaweah Vista, you have a splendid view of the deep canyon 3000 feet below and the Great Western Divide to the east. A short distance farther, you come to Bobcat Point, 0.6 mile from the trailhead. Directly southwest, a mere three-

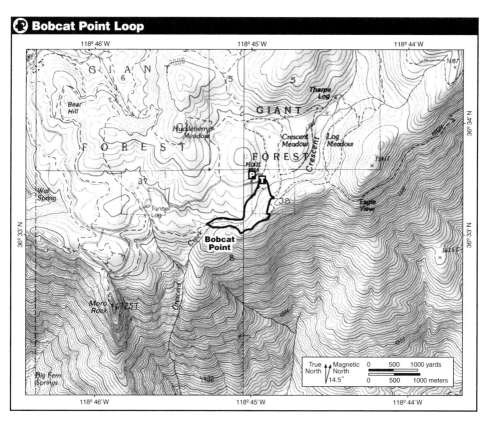

Bobcat Point Loop

quarters of a mile away, stands the impressive granite dome of Moro Rock. Across the yawning chasm of the Middle Fork are the crags and spires of Castle Rocks.

Turning away from Bobcat Point, you head back into the trees to a crossing of Crescent Creek, which flows over a broad, sloping slab of granite. Nearby are a number of bedrock mortars. Beyond the creek, you quickly reach a junction with the Sugar Pine Trail, on which an easy, 0.9-mile traverse provides a nice detour to the base of Moro Rock. To head back toward Crescent Meadow, you bear right at the junction and make a steady climb through light forest, swiftly approaching a signed spur for the Indian mortars. A mild ascent follows through a mixed forest that includes a number of stately sugar pines.

You reach the end of the loop at the Crescent Meadow Road, near the west end of the parking lot.

SUGAR PINE
(Pinus lambertiana)

Although Giant Forest received its name from the largest living tree on the planet, the giant sequoia, the forest is home to the largest species of pine as well. The huge cones on the forest floor, some as long as 20 inches, have dropped from the stately sugar pine, which can reach heights well over 200 feet. The sugar pine grows in the montane zone, and some of the massive trees have lived as long as 600 years.

CRESCENT MEADOW TRAILHEAD

TRIP **29**

Crescent and Log Meadows Loop

E ⟳ DH

DISTANCE: 2.2 miles

ELEVATION: 6720/6900/6720, +435′/-435′

SEASON: June to November

USE: Heavy

MAPS: *Lodgepole Giant Forest, SNHA*

INTRODUCTION: Although the Crescent Meadow Trail is one of the busiest paths in the Giant Forest, two flower-filled meadows and numerous majestic sequoias make this loop worth the crowds. Mid-summer is the best time to view the verdant sedges and grasses of Crescent and Log meadows, complemented by a palette of colors from the copious varieties of wildflowers. But the majesty of the sequoia can be appreciated in all seasons. Add a visit to Tharps Log — the oldest structure in the park — and you have the quintessential Giant Forest experience.

DIRECTIONS TO THE TRAILHEAD: From the Generals Highway near the Giant Forest Museum, turn onto the narrow Crescent Meadow Road and drive 1.2 miles to the junction with the road to Moro Rock. Continue on the Crescent Meadow Road another 1.3 miles to the end of the road at the Crescent Meadow parking lot.

DESCRIPTION: The High Sierra Trail begins at the east end of the parking area near the restroom building. Follow the paved trail across a pair of wooden bridges over Crescent Creek and past junctions with the Crescent Meadow and Bobcat Point trails. Beyond the second junction, the trail turns to dirt as you make a mild ascent across the north side of a low hill. You pass a few scattered sequoias and arrive at a fork in a forested saddle near the Burial Tree, a half mile from the parking lot.

Descend northwest from the junction, quickly dropping to a junction near the edge of Log Meadow, a grass-and-flower-filled glade ringed by giant sequoias and lesser conifers. Head north from the junction, walking along the eastern fringe of the meadow through ferns and azaleas underneath a mixed forest cover. Near the north end of the dell, 1.0 mile from the trailhead, you reach a signed T-junction with the Trail of the Sequoias.

THARPS LOG

Obtaining an accurate sense of the true size of a mature sequoia is often quite difficult while the tree is still standing. When one of the old giants topples from old age and extends across the forest floor, a better feel for the immensity of the Big Trees is possible. Tharps Log is such a tree, large enough for the fire-hollowed inside to have been used as a summer cabin in the late 1800's. Modern-day visitors may view the restored cabin, complete with rock fireplace, bed, plank table, and rough-hewn benches and chairs. Signs provide some history and a warning to respect the historical nature of the structure by remaining outside. Benches positioned around the clearing invite guests to linger.

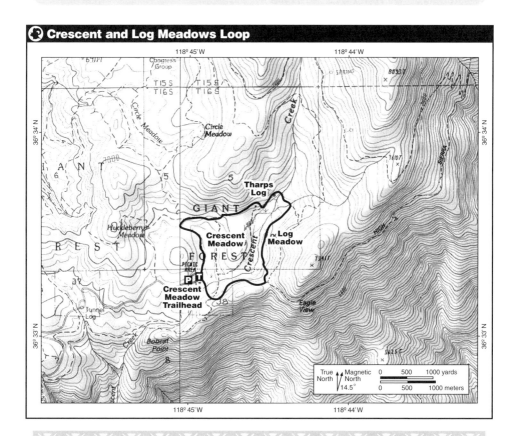

Crescent and Log Meadows Loop

Proceed straight ahead from the junction, step over a sliver of a stream to a forested flat and quickly come to a second crossing of a stream on a wood-plank bridge, where a number of stately sequoias dot the drainage. Heading west around the northern fringe of Log Meadow, you soon encounter Tharps Log, nestled in a small clearing, and a trail junction at 1.3 miles.

At the junction near Tharps Log, turn north toward the Chimney Tree and climb away from Log Meadow, quickly ascending stairs hewn out of a fallen sequoia. At the top of the climb, you surmount the low ridge separating Log and Crescent meadows and make a mild descent to a pair of trail junctions. At the first fork, a short lateral leads to the base of the Chimney Tree, where visitors can stand inside the fire-hollowed snag of a dead sequoia. The giant apparently met its doom at the hands of a careless camper in 1919. About 25 feet farther you reach a second junction and bear right to skirt the north side of Crescent Meadow. A quick detour down the left-hand branch leads to the Cleveland Tree, one of the larger sequoias in Giant Forest.

A stroll through the forest brings you to a Y-junction, 1.75 miles from the trailhead. Turn left (south) and follow the west side of picturesque Crescent Meadow a half mile back to the parking lot.

WHO WAS THARP?

Located near the fringe of Log Meadow, Tharps Log recalls a simpler time. Michigan native Hale D. Tharp settled near Three Rivers in 1856, where he quickly befriended the native Yokuts, who told their new friend tales of giant trees. Two years later, Tharp was led by way of the Middle Fork and Moro Rock to Log Meadow, and was later credited with being the first white man to see Giant Forest. A rancher and cattleman, Tharp eventually homesteaded Log Meadow, driving his cattle into the mountains to graze on the lush meadows, and using the log as a summer cabin from 1861 to 1890. The restored Tharps Log remains the oldest man-made edifice in the park.

CRESCENT MEADOW TRAILHEAD

TRIP **30**

High Sierra Trail: Crescent Meadow to Panther Creek

E ✗ DH

DISTANCE: 2.7 miles one way

ELEVATION: 6720/7045/6650, +850′/-800′

SEASON: Late April to November

USE: Moderate

MAPS: *Giant Forest, Lodgepole, Giant Forest, SNHA*

INTRODUCTION: The High Sierra Trail is one of the better known trails in the park, taking backpackers on a 70-mile journey from the Big Trees (giant sequoias) to the big mountain (Mt. Whitney). Day hikers can enjoy the initial portion from Crescent Meadow to Panther Creek, with grand views of the Great Western Divide, Middle Fork Kaweah River, and surrounding landmarks along the way. Thanks to the National Park Service, which built the trail between 1927 and 1932, the grade is quite pleasant, and the southern exposure makes this a fine spring or fall experience. Summer hikers will want to get an early start to beat the heat.

DIRECTIONS TO THE TRAILHEAD: From the Generals Highway near the Giant Forest Museum, turn onto the narrow Crescent Meadow Road and drive 1.2 miles to the junction with the road to Moro Rock. Continue on the Crescent Meadow Road another 1.3 miles to the end of the road at the Crescent Meadow parking lot.

DESCRIPTION: The High Sierra Trail begins at the east end of the parking area near the restroom building. Follow the paved trail

Panther Creek

across a pair of wooden bridges over Crescent Creek and past junctions with the Crescent Meadow and Bobcat Point trails. Beyond the second junction, the trail turns to dirt as you make a mild ascent across the north side of a low hill. You pass a few scattered sequoias and arrive at a fork in a

---

THE BUCKEYE FIRE

In October of 1988, a chaparral-covered slope near the Leaning Tree was the site of the Buckeye Fire, ignited by a cigarette discarded at the bottom of the canyon. After a cost of 2.5 million dollars and the efforts of 1200 firefighters, the weeklong blaze was extinguished, but not before it consumed over 3000 acres. A policy of controlled burning in Giant Forest was credited with slowing the advance of the fire into the Big Trees.

forested saddle near the Burial Tree, a half mile from the parking lot.

Continue east as the trail swings across an open hillside high above the Middle Fork Kaweah River.

Nearly level hiking brings you to aptly named Eagle View at 0.75 mile. From this aerie 3300 feet above the Middle Fork, you have a grand view of the canyon, Moro Rock, Castle Rocks, and the glacier-sculpted peaks of the Great Western Divide.

You then traverse the south-facing hillside, where open areas with great views alternate with stretches of light, mixed forest, including black oaks, white firs, Jeffrey pines, and incense cedars. A series of four switchbacks interrupts the gentle trail, be-

yond which you continue toward the high point of the journey, near the 2-mile mark. From the high point, you make a general descent through light forest, past a short rock wall to the signed junction with the Wolverton Cutoff at 2.5 miles. From the junction, you should be able to hear the roar from the first branch of Panther Creek, 0.2 mile away. A short walk brings you to the banks of refreshing Panther Creek, where a ribbon of water spills over moss-covered rocks and down a steep channel tangled with logs and lush vegetation. Hikers with plenty of vigor can continue farther up the High Sierra Trail, past the multiple branches of Panther Creek and on to the first campsites, at Mehrten Creek, 5.5 miles from the trailhead (see Trip 32).

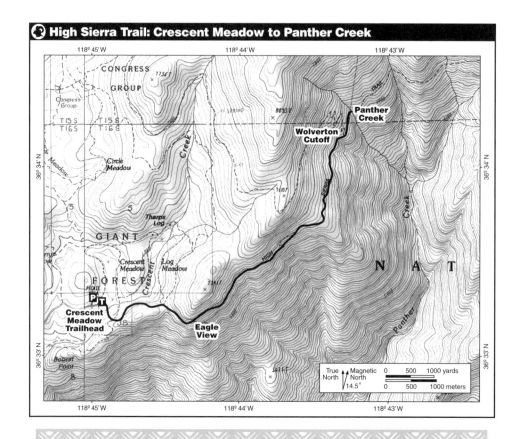

High Sierra Trail: Crescent Meadow to Panther Creek

CRESCENT MEADOW TRAILHEAD

TRIP **31**

Giant Forest East Loop

Ⓜ ↻ DH

DISTANCE: 8.5 miles

ELEVATION: 6720/7600/6720, +2370′/-2370′

SEASON: May to November

USE: Light to moderate

MAPS: *Lodgepole, Giant Forest, Giant Forest, SNHA*

INTRODUCTION: This trip utilizes the extensive network of trails that crisscrosses the Giant Forest plateau, offering hikers the best that Giant Forest has to offer. You'll see plenty of the giant sequoias for which the area is known, as well as a pair of picturesque meadows. In addition, the initial segment along the High Sierra Trail offers grand views of the Great Western Divide, Moro Rock, and Castle Rocks from an overlook above the Middle Fork Kaweah River canyon. While most of the loop follows a gently graded trail, a one-mile climb up the little-used Wolverton Cutoff is steep and scorching in the afternoon heat. The path takes travelers on a serene journey through a seldom-seen section of Giant Forest, with numerous magnificent examples of the Big Trees. Water is somewhat scarce along this route, especially later in the season, so you may want to stash an extra bottle in your pack.

DIRECTIONS TO THE TRAILHEAD: From the Generals Highway near the Giant Forest Museum, turn onto the narrow Crescent Meadow Road and drive 1.2 miles to the junction with the road to Moro Rock. Continue on the Crescent Meadow Road another 1.3 miles to the end of the road at the Crescent Meadow parking lot.

DESCRIPTION: Follow directions in Trip 30 to the junction between the High Sierra Trail and the Wolverton Cutoff, 2.5 miles from the Crescent Meadow trailhead.

Leaving the High Sierra Trail behind, you begin a 1.25-mile, 800-foot switchbacking climb to the top of a ridge through

Alta Peak and the Great Western Divide

a forest of white and red firs. As you near the crest, the trees part enough to allow good views of Alta Peak, the Great Western Divide, and Castle Rocks. Just past granite humps at the crest, the trail descends across the edge of the Giant Forest Grove and into the presence of the noble monarchs. On a gently descending trail, you pass many fine examples of the giant sequoia as well as a pair of tiny seasonal streams. Near the 5-mile mark, you curve around a meadow and cross Crescent Creek on a log footbridge.

For the next mile, you arc around peak 7758-T, as shown on the *Lodgepole* quad map, passing more interesting sequoia specimens and crossing more diminutive brooks. A short descent brings you to a junction with the Alta Trail near a pocket meadow carpeted with ferns and lupine, 6.2 miles from the parking lot.

Turn southwest onto the Alta Trail and make a moderate 0.4-mile descent past more splendid sequoias to the highly popular Congress Trail. Although it would add an extra 0.4 mile to your trip, a jaunt around the southern end of the Congress Trail loop exposes you to a handful of noteworthy sequoia landmarks, including the Senate and House groups and the President Tree, fourth largest in the world. However you choose to continue, 0.2 mile west of the first intersection, the Congress and Alta trails meet again near the McKinley Tree at a five-way junction, 6.8 miles from the trailhead.

Leaving the Alta Trail, you turn south and quickly reach a series of interesting features. The first is the Room Tree, a large sequoia with a small opening into a roomy, fire-hollowed base. Just beyond is the Founders Group, an attractive collection of

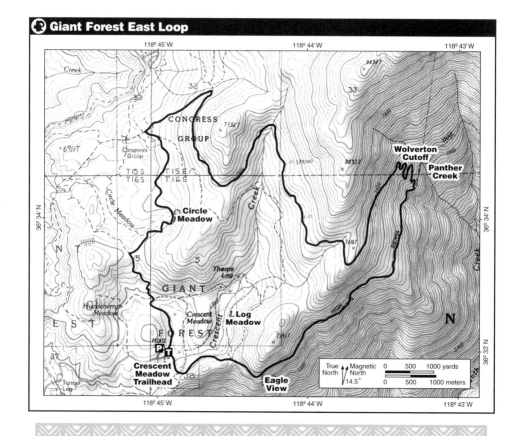

a dozen impressive sequoias named in honor of those who were instrumental in the establishment of Sequoia National Park. Next you step over a rivulet that courses through the narrow swath of Circle Meadow, which in actuality more closely resembles a horseshoe than a true circle. On the far side of the meadow is Cattle Cabin, originally used by ranchers who grazed their cattle in the meadows of Giant Forest.

Your trail arcs around the east edge of Circle Meadow, passing an unsigned lateral heading northwest. Soon, you encounter the Pillars of Hercules, a pair of massive sequoias that the trail passes between. Just beyond is the Black Arch, a huge, scorched sequoia. A short descent leads to another thin ribbon of Circle Meadow and a junction on the far side with the Trail of the Sequoias, at 7.6 miles. Continue south a short distance to the next intersection, with the Huckleberry Meadow Trail, and proceed southeast for 0.4 mile to connections with the Crescent Meadow Trail. A half mile stroll along the west edge of Crescent Meadow takes you back to trailhead at the parking lot.

O Stronger hikers can opt for a longer loop, a more strenuous 14-mile trek, continuing east on the High Sierra Trail to a junction with the Seven Mile Hill Trail, 0.4 mile past Mehrten Creek. This trail can be a blistering 2-mile, 1400-foot climb to a connection with the Alta Trail, west of Mehrten Meadow. From there, head west past Panther Gap and Red Fir Meadow to join the previous route at the junction with the Wolverton Cutoff.

Depending on the status of the Giant Forest shuttle bus, trips that terminate at trailheads other than Crescent Meadow can be made without the use of an additional vehicle. Contact the Park Service for information on the shuttle-bus program.

CRESCENT MEADOW TRAILHEAD

TRIP **32**

Bearpaw Meadow, Hamilton Lakes, and Nine Lakes Basin

(M) ↗ BP/BPx/X

DISTANCE: 10.5 miles to Bearpaw Meadow; 14.0 miles to Upper Hamilton Lake; 17.75 miles to Nine Lakes Basin

ELEVATION: 6720/7650, +4085'/-3155' 6720/8235, +5730'/-4215' 6720/10,600, +7270'/-3390'

SEASON: Late May to November

Late June to mid-October

Mid-July to early October

USE: Moderate

MAPS: *Lodgepole, Triple Divide Peak*

TRAIL LOG:

5.5	Mehrten Creek
9.5	Buck Creek
10.5	Bearpaw Meadow Camp
12.2	Elizabeth Pass Trail Jct.
14.0	Upper Hamilton Lake
17.25	Kaweah Gap
17.75	Nine Lakes Basin

INTRODUCTION: For backpackers unable to commit to the entire 70-mile trip on the High Sierra Trail (HST) from Crescent Meadow to Mt. Whitney, this trip along the initial segment offers a representative sample, with terrain ranging from giant sequoia groves to the alpine zone. Even a weekend trip along the mildly graded trail to Bearpaw Meadow offers plenty of pleasant scenery. Beyond the meadow, you'll encounter impressive mountainous terrain

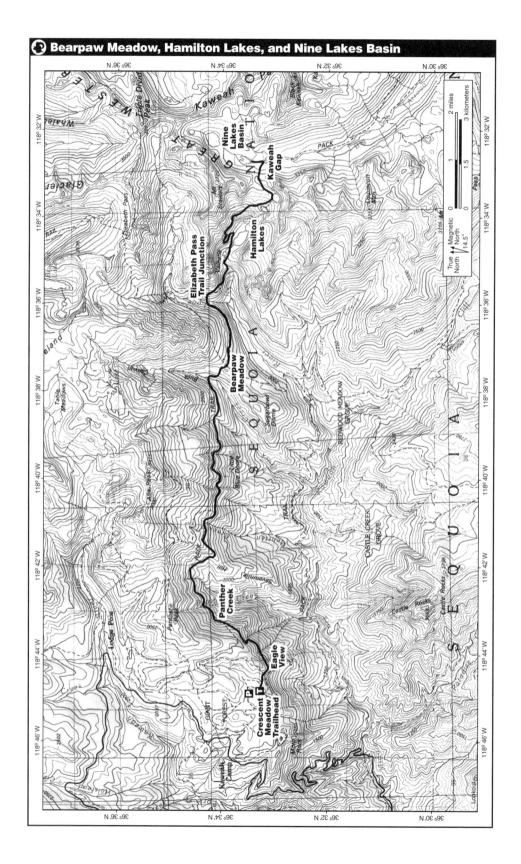

and stunning views of Angel Wings, Sequoia's largest rock wall.

The relatively low elevation, southern exposure, and mostly open terrain for the first several miles through the canyon of the Middle Fork Kaweah River can make for a scorching trip on a typical summer day, so an early start is highly recommended. Beyond Bearpaw Meadow the trail starts climbing in earnest, passing through the glacier-carved granite basin of Hamilton Lakes on the way over Kaweah Gap to Nine Lakes Basin. The scenery around Hamilton Lakes is as dramatically rugged as any in the Sierra, comparable to the alpine Nine Lakes Basin, where off-trail enthusiasts may roam amongst picturesque lakes backdropped by the towering summits of the Great Western Divide and the Kaweah Peaks.

DIRECTIONS TO THE TRAILHEAD: From the Generals Highway near the Giant Forest Museum, turn onto the narrow Crescent Meadow Road and drive 1.2 miles to the junction with the road to Moro Rock. Continue on the Crescent Meadow Road another 1.3 miles to the end of the road at the Crescent Meadow parking lot.

DESCRIPTION: The High Sierra Trail begins at the east end of the parking area near the restroom building. Follow the paved trail across a pair of wooden bridges over Crescent Creek and past junctions with the Crescent Meadow and Bobcat Point trails. Beyond the second junction, the trail turns to dirt as you make a mild ascent across the north side of a low hill. You arrive at a fork in a forested saddle near the Burial Tree, a half mile from the parking lot.

Continue east as the trail swings across an open hillside high above the Middle Fork Kaweah River.

Nearly level hiking brings you to Eagle View at 0.75 mile. You then traverse the south-facing hillside, where open areas alternate with stretches of light, mixed forest. A series of four switchbacks interrupts the gentle trail, beyond which you continue toward a high point, near the 2-mile mark.

You then make a general descent through light forest, past a short rock wall to the signed junction with the Wolverton Cutoff at 2.5 miles. From the junction, a short walk brings you to the banks of refreshing Panther Creek.

For the next couple of miles beyond Panther Creek you follow the mildly undulating trail in and out of the seams of the creek's tributaries. Beyond the final branch, you climb over Sevenmile Hill and continue the 0.75-mile ascent to the crossing of Mehrten Creek (7600´±), 5.5 miles from the trailhead. On the west side of the creek, a use-trail leads steeply up the hillside to the first legal campsites along the HST, with bear box.

One-third mile beyond Mehrten Creek, you pass the junction with the Sevenmile Trail, which provides a steep, 2.2-mile connection with the Alta Trail. From the junction, make a short traverse through light forest to the crossing of a tiny branch of Mehrten Creek, followed by a pronounced descent to the twin-channeled crossing of the first tributary of Buck Creek. Periodic breaks in the mixed forest allow fine views of Castle Rocks, Middle Fork canyon, Sugarbowl Dome, and Little Blue Dome as you continue up the trail, stepping across more refreshing brooks along the way. The next developed campsite with bear box is at 8.25 miles, near the first branch of the twin-branched tributary prior to the main channel of Buck Creek. Beyond the streams, the trail bends around the mostly open slope of Buck Canyon and descends to a bridge over Buck Creek (7200´±), 9.5 miles from the parking lot.

You make the switchbacking climb up the east wall of Buck Canyon, amid dense sugar pine and fir forest to the top of a low ridge and the signed 200-yard lateral to Bearpaw Meadow Campground (7650´±), 10.5 miles from the trailhead. The overused campground has numbered sites sheltered by dense timber, with bear boxes, pit toilets, and a spigot with treated water. Open fires are not allowed. Approximately 0.2 mile east of the camp and the HST junction

Eagle Scout Peak and vicinity

are the A-framed ranger station and Bearpaw High Sierra Camp, near the lip of the Middle Fork canyon. Similar to arrangements at the famed High Sierra Camps of Yosemite, guests sleep in tent cabins and enjoy hot meals for breakfast and dinner (by reservation only). Unlike the claustrophobic backpackers' campground, Bearpaw Camp has excellent views of the glacier-scoured surroundings over the canyon, including Eagle Scout Peak and Mt. Stewart on the Great Western Divide, the Yosemite-esque cleft of Hamilton Creek, and Black Kaweah above Kaweah Gap.

From the ranger station, you follow a descending traverse across the precipitous north wall of River Valley with excellent views across the canyon. At the bottom of the canyon, a concrete culvert spans rowdy Lone Pine Creek. A short climb away from the creek leads to a small bench and a junction with the Elizabeth Pass Trail (7400′±) at 12.2 miles. Decent campsites are near the junction.

A stiff, switchbacking climb ensues, through sagebrush, manzanita, and scat-tered black oaks, that takes you around a corner and into the canyon of Hamilton Creek. The view-packed topography in this granite sanctuary is absolutely stunning. North of the trail is the towering wall of Angel Wings, a rival to the better known climbing walls of Yosemite Valley. The white domes of Hamilton Towers top the ridge on the opposite side of the canyon. Soon, you ford the tumbling creek and climb above Lower Hamilton Lake over shards of rock to the outlet of Upper Hamilton Lake (8235′), 14.0 miles from the trailhead.

You'll find excellent campsites above the northwest shore of Upper Hamilton Lake, but the basin is a very popular overnight destination, so don't expect solitude. The Park Service has instituted a two-night limit, banned campfires, and built pit toilets to try to mitigate the effects of overuse. The scenery is magnificent, and anglers will enjoy the challenge of trying to land brook, rainbow, and golden trout. Glacier-polished slabs around the shoreline provide ideal spots for sunbathers.

Now you face the 2500-foot climb to Kaweah Gap. The trail itself is something of an engineering feat, blasted right out of the rock in many spots. From the outlet of Upper Hamilton Lake, you zigzag up the north wall of the enormous cirque and then veer south past a tarn on the way to Precipice Lake (10,310´±), 2.6 miles from Upper Hamilton Lake.

The frigid lake reposes at the base of the impressive north face of Eagle Scout Peak. A final 0.75-mile climb past a smattering of miniature tarns leads to Kaweah Gap (10,700´±), 17.25 miles from Crescent Meadow, where you have a grand view of the Kaweah Peaks, Nine Lakes Basin, and Big Arroyo.

To visit Nine Lakes Basin, descend a few switchbacks and head north from the High Sierra Trail cross-country to the first lake (10,455´±). Off-trail travel north to the upper two lakes is easy. The set of lakes to the east is reached over more difficult terrain requiring more advanced route-finding skills. Whichever lake you decide to visit, the U-shaped basin at the convergence of the Great Western Divide and Kaweah Peaks Ridge, culminating at Triple Divide Peak, presents unparalleled alpine scenery.

⊡ A base camp at Bearpaw Meadow allows hikers to make short forays to Hamilton Lakes and Tamarack Lake sans backpacks. A scenic 4.4-mile loop combines the HST with a portion of the Elizabeth Pass Trail and the Over the Hill Trail.

Backpackers in search of more solitude than what's potentially available at Hamilton Lakes can take the short detour via the 2.2-mile maintained trail to Tamarack Lake (9215´±), where lonely campsites nestle in a grove of lodgepole pines, and Lion Rock, and Mt. Stewart provide pleasant alpine scenery.

A 2-mile, steep off-trail ascent from Tamarack Lake leads to austere Lion Lake, where a pair of class 2 passes provide access north to Cloud Canyon over Lion Lake

Pass (11,600´±), or south to Nine Lakes Basin via Lion Rock Pass (11,760´±).

From Nine Lakes Basin, a difficult cross-country route travels over Pants Pass (12,000´±) (class 2) on the way to the Kern-Kaweah River country.

Mountaineers have plenty of choices for intermediate and advanced climbs once they get within striking distance of the Great Western Divide and Kaweah Peaks Ridge. From Tamarack Lake, Lion Rock is class 2–3 from the bowl on the southwest side of the peak. The southwest face of Triple Divide Peak is also class 2–3, from Lion Lake. Nine Lakes Basin is a fine base camp for class 2 routes up the southwest slope of Lawson Peak or the east side of Mt. Stewart. The Kaweah Peaks provide more difficult routes.

R **PERMITS:** Wilderness permit required for overnight stays. (Quota: 30 per day)

CAMPFIRES: Prohibited at Bearpaw Meadow, Hamilton Lakes basin, and above.

CAMPING: Designated sites only at Bearpaw Meadow. Two-night limit at Hamilton Lakes.

CRESCENT MEADOW TRAILHEAD

TRIP **33**

High Sierra Trail: Crescent Meadow to Mt. Whitney

Ⓜ️Ⓢ / BPx

DISTANCE: 62 miles one way

ELEVATION: 6720/10,700/6720/
13,580/8360,
+18,475´±/-16,835´±

SEASON: Mid-July to early October

USE: Light (Heavy near Crescent Meadow & Mt. Whitney)

MAPS: *Lodgepole, Triple Divide Peak, Mt. Kaweah, Chagoopa Falls, Mt. Whitney, Mount Langley*

TRAIL LOG:

5.5	Mehrten Creek
10.5	Bearpaw Meadow
17.25	Kaweah Gap
20.0	Little Five Lakes Jct.
27.25	Moraine Lake
32.25	Kern River Trail Jct.
34.0	Kern Hot Spring
41.25	Junction Meadow/ Colby Pass Trail
45.5	John Muir Trail Jct.
49.0	JMT/PCT Jct.
53.25	Mt. Whitney Trail Jct./Trail Crest
55.25	Trail Camp

INTRODUCTION: Although less traveled than the more famous John Muir Trail (JMT), the High Sierra Trail (HST) is perhaps the next most significant jewel in the backpacker's crown. Built by the CCC in the early 1930s, the trail was the grand scheme of Park Superintendent Colonel John White, who fancied a link between the park's two most enchanting features, Giant Forest and Mt. Whitney. Grand in scope, the trail passes through some of Sequoia's most majestic scenery—the beauty of Hamilton Lakes, an awesome view from Kaweah Gap, the splendor of Big Arroyo, the remote Chagoopa Plateau, the serenity of Moraine Lake, the glacier-carved, U-shaped Kern Trench—and reaches a climax at dramatic Mt. Whitney.

Starting and ending on some of the region's most heavily traveled sections of trail, the HST in its middle portion is quite remote, offering backpackers a high probability of solitude. The sections near Crescent Meadow and Whitney Portal are a different matter entirely, as hordes of tourists fill the trail at the beginning and an equal number of Mt. Whitney hopefuls clog the route at the end. Between those areas, peace and quiet reign, except possibly around Kern Hot Springs, where backpackers are drawn to the soothing waters, despite their remoteness.

As with every long-distance backpack, logistics are important. The greatest obstacle to overcome on the HST is the tremendously long shuttle between the two trailheads—a driver willing to drop you off at one end and pick you up at the other is certainly a friend worth keeping. Although conquering the HST in a week is within most backpackers' capabilities, more time is required to adequately savor all the trail has to offer. Nine Lakes Basin and the Wallace Lake area are certainly worthy of extra days for exploration.

DIRECTIONS TO THE TRAILHEAD:
START: From the Generals Highway near the Giant Forest Museum, turn onto the narrow Crescent Meadow Road and drive 1.2 miles to the junction with the road to Moro Rock. Continue on the Crescent Meadow Road another 1.3 miles to the end of the road at the Crescent Meadow parking lot.

END: In the heart of Lone Pine, turn west from U.S. 395 onto Whitney Portal Road and drive 13 miles to the parking lots at Whitney Portal. You'll find camp-grounds, restrooms, and a small store with a cafe nearby.

DESCRIPTION: The High Sierra Trail begins at the east end of the parking area near the restroom building. Follow the paved trail across a pair of wooden bridges over Crescent Creek and past junctions with the Crescent Meadow and Bobcat Point trails. You arrive at a fork in a forested saddle near the Burial Tree, a half mile from the parking lot.

Continue east as the trail swings across an open hillside high above the Middle Fork Kaweah River.

Nearly level hiking brings you to Eagle View at 0.75 mile. You then traverse the south-facing hillside, continuing to the signed junction with the Wolverton Cutoff at 2.5 miles. From the junction, a short walk brings you to Panther Creek.

For the next couple of miles beyond Panther Creek you follow the mildly undu-lating trail in and out of the seams of the creek's tributaries. Beyond the final branch, you climb over Sevenmile Hill and continue the 0.75-mile ascent to the crossing of Mehrten Creek (7600′±), 5.5 miles from the trailhead. On the west side of the creek, a use-trail leads steeply up the hillside to the first legal campsites along the HST, with bear box.

One-third mile beyond Mehrten Creek, you pass the junction with the Sevenmile Trail, which provides a 2.2-mile connection with the Alta Trail. From the junction, you make a short traverse through light forest to the crossing of a tiny branch of Mehrten Creek, followed by a pronounced descent to the twin-channeled crossing of the first tributary of Buck Creek. The next devel-oped campsite with a bear box is at 8.25 miles, near the first branch of the twin-branched tributary prior to the main chan-nel of Buck Creek. Beyond the streams, the trail bends around the mostly open slope of Buck Canyon and descends to a bridge over Buck Creek (7200′±), 9.5 miles from the parking lot.

You make the switchbacking climb up the east wall of Buck Canyon, to the top of a low ridge and the signed 200-yard lateral leading to Bearpaw Meadow Campground (7650′±), 10.5 miles from the trailhead. Approximately 0.2 mile east of the camp and the HST junction are the A-framed ranger station and Bearpaw High Sierra Camp, near the lip of the Middle Fork canyon. Bearpaw Camp has excellent views of the glacier-scoured surroundings over the canyon.

From the ranger station, you follow a descending traverse across the precipitous north wall of River Valley. At the bottom of the canyon, a concrete culvert spans rowdy Lone Pine Creek. A short climb away from the creek leads to a small bench and a junc-tion with the Elizabeth Pass Trail (7400′±) at 12.2 miles. Decent campsites are near the junction.

A stiff, switchbacking climb that takes you around a corner and into the canyon of Hamilton Creek ensues. The view-packed topography in this granite sanctuary is absolutely stunning. Soon, you ford the tumbling creek and climb above Lower Hamilton Lake over shards of rock to the outlet of Upper Hamilton Lake (8235′), 14.0 miles from the trailhead.

You'll find excellent campsites above the northwest shore of Upper Hamilton Lake, but the basin is a very popular overnight destination.

Now you face the 2500-foot climb to Kaweah Gap. From the outlet of Upper Hamilton Lake, you zigzag up the north wall of the enormous cirque and then veer south past a tarn on the way to Precipice Lake (10,310′±), 2.6 miles from Upper Hamilton Lake. A final three-quarter-mile climb past a smattering of miniature tarns leads to Kaweah Gap (10,700′±), 17.25 miles from Crescent Meadow.

From the gap, you make a continuous, steady descent down the west side of Big Arroyo Creek. Halfway down the canyon you cross the stream and proceed on the east side of the canyon through alternating pockets of meadow and granite, crossing

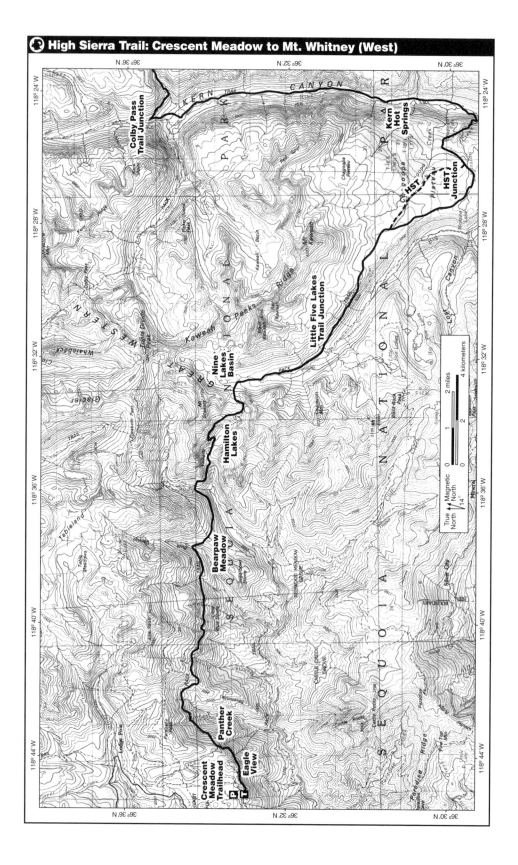

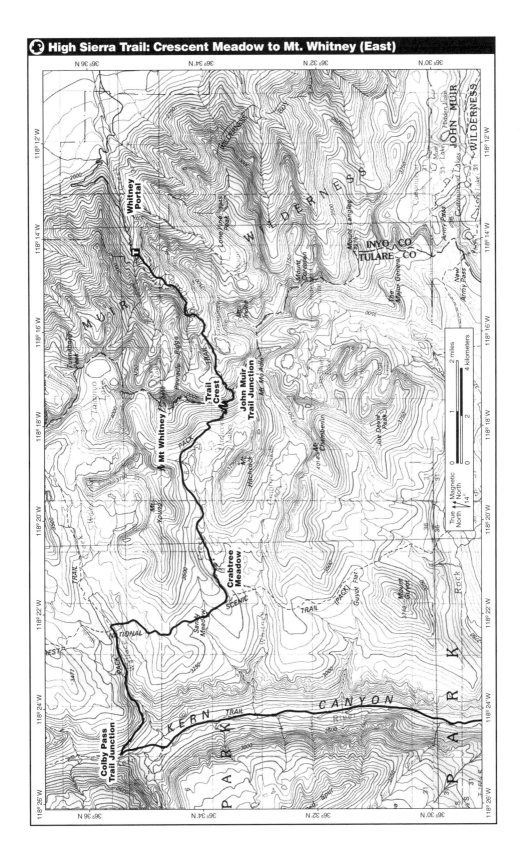

Lone Pine Lake on the Mt. Whitney Trail

numerous side streams along the way. The open terrain allows fine views of the canyon and the multi-hued Kaweah Peaks to the north. Near a tributary draining an unnamed tarn, you encounter some campsites and then shortly reach a junction with the trail to Little Five Lakes, 3.0 miles from the gap.

You begin a long, sustained climb on a traverse across the canyon of Big Arroyo, quickly hopping over a healthy stream. The timber along this section of the canyon is sparse, and much of the hillside is covered with sage, manzanita, and chinquapin, splashed with touches of color from a bevy of wildflowers, including paintbrush, lupine, and columbine. After crossing several tributary streams, you come to a small tarn and then start a mild descent that leads away from the lip of the canyon. Through alternating sections of meadow and lodgepole and foxtail forest, you reach a junction in a large meadow, 7.4 miles from Kaweah Gap, with a lateral to Moraine Lake.

Although the designated HST continues across Chagoopa Plateau, you'll find better scenery on the trail to Moraine Lake, so veer right at the junction. Leave the meadow behind and descend through dense

stands of foxtail and lodgepole pine. As you return to the edge of Big Arroyo canyon, excellent views of the gorge below and of the peaks of the Great Western Divide are quite impressive. The descent intensifies and eventually delivers you to the wooded shore of Moraine Lake (9302′), 10.0 miles from Kaweah Gap. Excellent campsites are scattered around the shoreline; those on the south shore provide the best views of the Kaweah Peaks.

From the lake, you hop across the outlet, traverse the moraine at the east end of the lake, and descend to lovely, flower-filled and grass-covered Sky Parlor Meadow. Across the meadow, you have more excellent views of the Kaweah Peaks and the Great Western Divide. Just beyond the ford of Funston Creek, near the east end of meadow, you rejoin the HST, 1.25 miles from Moraine Lake.

A moderate, then steep descent follows, which leads you toward the deep U-shaped Kern Trench. As you drop toward the canyon, white fir and Jeffrey pine quickly replace lodgepole pine, and farther down, an occasional juniper or black oak extends above shrubs of manzanita and snowbush. Tight, rocky switchbacks follow the tumbling course of Funston Creek. You cross and recross the creek before finally reaching the bottom of the trench, where you meet the Kern Canyon Trail, 5 miles from Moraine Lake and 4000 vertical feet below Kaweah Gap.

Heading north on the Kern Canyon Trail, you drop into a marshy area, make an imperceptible climb across a pair of meadows and then continue upstream through Jeffrey pines and incense cedars. You cross Chagoopa Creek 0.75 mile from the junction, catching glimpses through the trees of the falls high on the west side of the canyon.

The gentle trail leads upstream to the stout bridge across the Kern River. Now on the east side of the canyon, you quickly ford Rock Creek. Shortly beyond the ford, around a point, is Kern Hot Spring (6920′±) near the edge of the rushing river, 1.75 miles from the junction. Hot water fills a crude cement bathtub downstream from the spring, providing a warm oasis which has soothed hikers' tired muscles for many decades. Despite the seemingly remote location, the spring is a magnet for backpackers from far and wide. The designated campground just northeast of the spring is cramped and overused, offering little in the way of a wilderness experience. The campground does have bear boxes, but parties desiring solitude should plan on camping away from the spring.

Away from the spring, you ford the upper branch of Rock Creek and proceed upstream on a gravelly path past some campsites. For the next 7 miles, you follow the trail up the east side of the U-shaped gorge of the Kern River, beneath towering canyon walls. Glacial action has left many hanging valleys on both sides of the gorge, where scenic cascades and falls spill down tributaries to the river. The trail crosses numerous creeks and rivulets as you head north, some of which can be difficult in early season, particularly the creek that drains Guyot Flat, Whitney Creek, and Wallace Creek. The ascent up the canyon is gentle for the most part, making for straight-

forward travel through generally open terrain. Near the ford of Wallace Creek, you enter a moderate forest of mainly Jeffrey pine with a smattering of lodgepole pine and western white pine. Continue through the trees to shaded campsites with bear boxes near Junction Meadow (8035′±), 9 miles from the junction with the Kern Canyon Trail. A short distance up the trail you reach the junction with the Colby Pass Trail, which heads west toward the Kern-Kaweah canyon.

From the junction, climb moderately through alternating stretches of mixed forest and manzanita-and-currant-covered clearings, with excellent views of the Kern-Kaweah canyon and the Kern River trench. At 1.2 miles from Junction Meadow, the HST leaves the Kern on an ascending traverse toward Wallace Creek. A mile farther, the path veers northeast to follow the Wallace Creek canyon toward an intersection with the JMT. Another mile of moderate ascent brings you to the ford of Wright Creek, followed by a 1.1-mile climb to the John Muir Trail (10,400′±) junction, 4.2 miles from Junction Meadow.

Follow the JMT south 3.4 miles to the junction with the Pacific Crest Trail. From there, continue east on the JMT to the junction with the 2-mile trail to Mt. Whitney. From that junction, travel 9 miles east to the Whitney Portal trailhead.

Ⓞ Options are too numerous to list in the vicinity of the HST. Consult Trip 32 for options in the Kaweah Gap area, and Trip 59 for side trips near Mt. Whitney.

Ⓡ **PERMITS:** Wilderness permit required for overnight stays. (Quota: 30 per day)

CAMPFIRES: Prohibited at Bearpaw Meadow, Hamilton Lakes basin, Nine Lakes Basin, and Big Arroyo above 10,000 feet.

CAMPING: Designated sites only at Bearpaw Meadow.

Two-night limit at Hamilton Lakes.

No camping at Mirror Lake or Trailside Meadow.

GIANT FOREST TRAILHEADS

TRIP **34**

Moro Rock:
Soldiers Trail and
Moro Rock Trail Loop

Ⓜ ↻ DH

DISTANCE: 4.4 miles

ELEVATION: 6395/6725/6395,
+1475′±/-1475′±

SEASON: Late May to November

USE: Moderate (High at Moro
Rock)

MAPS: *Giant Forest,*
Giant Forest, SNHA

INTRODUCTION: This 4-mile loop across
the Giant Forest plateau is definitely the
long way to the extraordinary view from
the top of the exfoliated granite dome of
Moro Rock, but hikers will enjoy a modicum of serenity before reaching the tourist
mecca near the mid-point. Each summer
day, tourists drive the narrow Crescent
Meadow Road to the parking lot and huff
and puff up the quarter of a mile stairway
climb to the top of Moro Rock. Restrooms,
interpretive displays and steel railings lend
a decidedly civilized feel to the otherwise
rugged surroundings. Spring and fall are
the best times to enjoy the view from the
dome sans crowds.

DIRECTIONS TO THE TRAILHEAD: Follow
the Generals Highway to the large parking
area near the Giant Forest Museum.

DESCRIPTION: From the Giant Forest
Museum, follow the crosswalk over
Crescent Meadow Road to the well-signed
trailhead. You make a mild ascent across
the hillside through mixed forest along the
west edge of the Giant Forest plateau, passing a sprinkling of giant sequoias along the

way. At 1.2 miles, as you near the Moro
Rock Road, you meet the Bear Hill Trail,
which parallels the Moro Rock and
Soldiers trails between the museum and the
rock. About 0.2 mile farther, your trail
once again nears the road, and you encounter a signed lateral to Hanging Rock.

If you make the short climb to Hanging
Rock, it takes you up to an exposed granite
slab, where you have fine views to the
Middle Fork Kaweah River and west to
Ash Peaks Ridge. A short scramble up the
nearby rock knob provides the added 👁
bonus of a close-up look at Moro Rock,
backdropped nicely by the crags of Castle
Rocks.

From the lateral to Hanging Rock, you
quickly cross the road and proceed 0.2 mile
to the junction with the Soldiers Trail,
where a short descent leads away from the
serenity of the forest to the hustle and bus-
tle of the Moro Rock parking lot. Across
the pavement, the popular quarter-mile
Moro Rock Trail leads to the top of the
granite dome.

MORO ROCK

In 1861, Hale Tharp and his stepson
were the first settlers to climb Moro
Rock. Nearly a century and a half
later, hundreds attempt the journey
every summer day, ascending 300 vertical feet in a quarter mile, with the
aid of almost 350 steps. Interpretive
displays along the way give out-of-
shape tourists opportunities to catch
their breath, and railings at the top
keep them safely corralled. The steps
were constructed in 1931, and subsequently placed in the National
Register of Historic Places. The rock
was named Moro after the Spanish
word for the color of a blue roan
mustang belonging to a neighbor of
Tharp's. History tells us the horse
was often seen roaming beneath the
large granite dome.

As billed, the view from the top of Moro Rock, jutting out into the canyon, is breathtaking. The Giant Forest plateau spreads out in the northern foreground, the characteristic crowns of the Big Trees rising above the rest of the conifers. The sculpted summits of the Great Western Divide scrape the sky to the east. The deep canyon of the Middle Fork Kaweah River 4000 feet below is equally impressive, with the multi-spired Castle Crags dominating the far wall. Miniature-looking cars wind down the Generals Highway, and the community of Three Rivers is visible farther downstream. On clear days vistas extend across the San Joaquin Valley to the Coast Range; unfortunately, clear days are the exception, and smoggy days the rule. In fact, air pollution from urban areas in southern California remains the biggest threat to the health of both Sequoia and Kings Canyon parks. Common sense dictates that visitors should avoid the dome during thunderstorms and stay off the glacier-polished rock when it's slick from snow or ice.

To resume the loop trip, return to the junction of the Moro Rock and Soldiers trails above the parking lot. A short, moderate climb up the Soldiers Trail brings you to another junction, this one with the Bear Hill Trail, near the symmetrical Roosevelt Tree (named for Teddy, not FDR). Beyond the junction, you curve around to a diagonal crossing of the Moro Rock Road. On the far side you pass near the base of the Triple Tree, an unusual sight where three giant sequoias have merged together over time. Then, a half-mile of easy hiking brings you to the crossing of Crescent Meadow Road near the Tunnel Log, a massive, unnamed sequoia that fell across the Crescent Meadow Road on December 4, 1937. The next summer, a CCC crew cut a 17-foot-wide by 8-foot-high hole, allowing

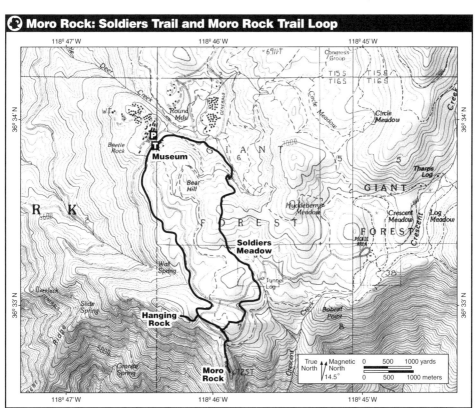

modern-day motorists the chance to drive through the downed tree.

Beyond the road, you stroll along the edge of picturesque Soldiers Meadow, a lush swath of vegetation, well-watered by a tributary of Crescent Creek.

SOLDIERS MEADOW

U.S. Calvary soldiers camped on the knoll above Soldiers Meadow between 1891 and 1913, while charged with protecting the sequoias from loggers and the wildlife from poachers. In addition to these duties, they extended Colony Mill Road from the mill site to Giant Forest, completing the project in 1903.

Leaving the meadow behind, you climb toward the crest of a ridge, passing the Broken Arrow, a burned, topless sequoia. A winding descent from the ridge leads to a junction with the Alta Trail, shortly followed by a junction with the Hazelwood Nature Trail. Proceed on the west loop of the nature trail to the paved path that parallels the Generals Highway and head back to the museum.

GIANT FOREST TRAILHEADS

TRIP 35

Sunset Rock

E ↗ DH

DISTANCE: 0.8 mile one way

ELEVATION: 6370/6472, +215′±/-115′±

SEASON: May to November

USE: Moderate

MAPS: *Giant Forest,*
Giant Forest, SNHA

INTRODUCTION: An easy trail with a negligible elevation gain leads hikers to a vista point atop the summit of one of Sequoia's numerous granite domes. Despite the short distance, you'll find relative peace and quiet on the trail and great views from the top.

DIRECTIONS TO THE TRAILHEAD: Follow the Generals Highway to the large parking area at the Giant Forest Museum.

DESCRIPTION: The well-signed Sunset Rock Trail begins across the Generals Highway at the north end of the Giant Forest Museum. Follow the paved trail on a short descent through a dense forest of white firs and sugar pines to a wooden bridge over Little Deer Creek. Immediately beyond the bridge, you veer left at a junction with a connecting trail to Round Meadow. Your trail proceeds above the creek for a ways and then leaves the stream on a mild ascent across the hillside, passing the tiny meadow named Eli's Paradise. Incense cedars, ponderosa pines, and black oaks join the mixed forest as you climb up the paved trail to a saddle, where the main trail continues on a seldom-used route that descends to the Marble Fork Bridge (see Trip 25). From the saddle, you venture a short distance out onto the top of the broad, exposed granite dome of Sunset Rock.

The view from the top of Sunset Rock is certainly not as dramatic as the one from nearby Moro Rock, but is quite fine nonetheless, including the precipitous canyon of the Marble Fork Kaweah River, Ash Peaks Ridge, Colony Mill, and the companion dome of Little Baldy to the north. When the dome first received its name, the sunsets were probably quite eye-catching. Nowadays, excessive valley smog has unarguably diminished the experience considerably.

Granite gilia

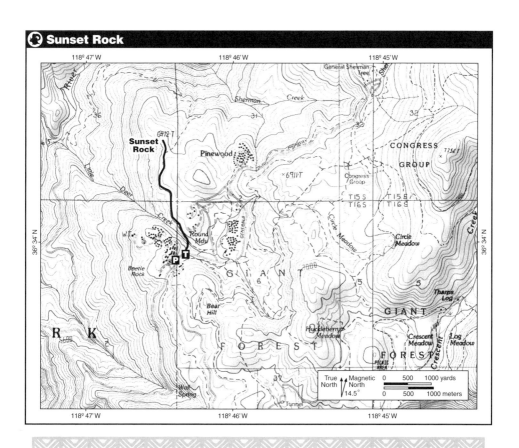

TRIP **36**

Big Trees Trail
(Trail for All People)

Ⓔ ↻ DH/WC

DISTANCE: 1.3 miles

ELEVATION: 6360, +90´/-90´

SEASON: May to November

USE: Heavy

MAPS: *Giant Forest,*
Giant Forest, SNHA

INTRODUCTION: Fresh paving, park benches, and new interpretive signs are among the improvements to the Big Trees Trail, made in conjunction with the restoration of the Giant Forest Area. Formerly the Round Meadow Nature Trail, the Big Trees Trail is a must-see experience for all those who enjoy the giant sequoias and appreciate the picturesque meadows sprinkled throughout Giant Forest. The signs along the 0.6-mile loop around Round Meadow are an excellent way to learn about giant sequoia ecology. The paved, well-graded trail is now completely wheelchair-accessible and provides an easy hike for families with young children.

DIRECTIONS TO THE TRAILHEAD: Follow the Generals Highway to the large parking area at the Giant Forest Museum.

DESCRIPTION: From the museum, follow a sign marked BIG TREES TRAIL through mixed forest, heading east on a paved trail that roughly parallels the Generals Highway.

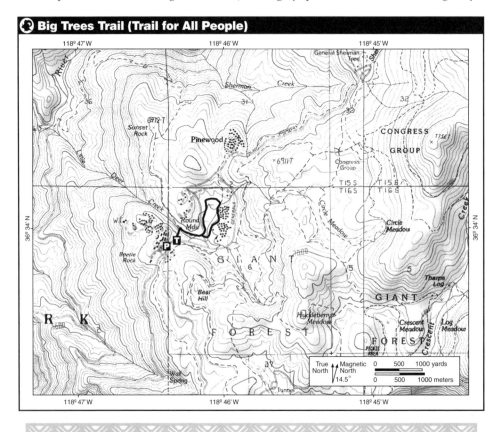

Big Trees Trail (Trail for All People)

After a quarter mile, cross the highway and go north. The loop divides at a junction just beyond a crossing of Little Deer Creek, and a 0.3-mile connector trail goes west past the Clara Barton Tree to the intersection with the Sunset Rock Trail. Follow the loop clockwise around picturesque Round Meadow back to the junction, and then retrace your steps to the museum. Midway around the meadow, you pass another junction with a trail that follows the route of Generals Highway 1.5 miles northeast to the General Sherman tree.

GIANT FOREST TRAILHEADS

TRIP 37

Hazelwood Nature Trail

E ◯ **DH**

DISTANCE: 0.5 mile

ELEVATION: 6450, +50′/-50′

SEASON: May to November

USE: Heavy

MAPS: *Giant Forest,*
Giant Forest, SNHA

INTRODUCTION: An easy loop, the Hazelwood Nature Trail provides a good introduction to the sequoias of the Giant Forest. Interpretive trailside displays inform

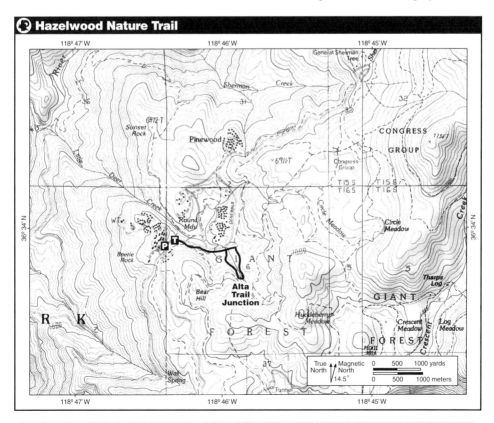

walkers about historical figures and their impact on the forest, as well as giant sequoia ecology. The nearly level loop takes unwitting admirers of the Big Trees past the 18th largest sequoia in the world.

DIRECTIONS TO THE TRAILHEAD: Find the small, unsigned parking lot on the shoulder of the Generals Highway, 0.4 mile north-bound from the Giant Forest Museum. If parking is not available here, park in the large lot near the museum and walk the path signed BIG TREES TRAIL along the road to the start of the trail.

DESCRIPTION: Heading away from the Generals Highway on paved path, you come to a large fallen sequoia and pass through a notch in the tree and reach a junction where the loop divides. Follow the right-hand fork and proceed counterclock-wise through a mixed forest. The mighty sequoias dwarf the other conifers and the dogwoods that provide splashes of color, from creamy white blossoms in early sum-mer to blazing orange leaves in autumn. Patches of azalea and thimbleberry appear along the trail, while a thick tangle of ferns, flowers, and plants carpets the drainage. At a signed junction with the Alta Trail, the Hazelwood trail bends left, then crosses a tiny rivulet and continues the loop, heading north through the forested dell. Eventually, you veer west to cross a tributary of Little Deer Creek on a wooden bridge and close the loop at the first junction, From there, retrace your steps to the car.

<table>
<tr><td colspan="2">**GIANT FOREST TRAILHEADS**</td></tr>
</table>

TRIP **38**

Congress Trail

E ↻ DH / WC

DISTANCE: 2 miles

ELEVATION: 6830/7045, +550′/-550′

SEASON: May to November

USE: High

MAPS: *Giant Forest, Lodgepole, Giant Forest, SNHA*

INTRODUCTION: Predictably, the most pop-ular trail in Giant Forest takes visitors to some of the most significant giant sequoia landmarks. Starting at the world's largest tree — General Sherman — the paved, wheelchair-accessible, 2-mile trail passes the fourth, fifth, and 29th biggest trees. You can also visit two of the most majestic stands of giant sequoias, the Senate and House groups. Short side trips offer even more possibilities for viewing dramatic stands of Big Trees. Don't expect to see these trees in reverent solitude, as the pop-ularity of this hike dictates otherwise. The park has recently repaved the trail and made other improvements, which will very likely make it even more popular.

DIRECTIONS TO THE TRAILHEAD: When park improvements have been completed, probably by the time you read this book, parking for the General Sherman Tree and the Congress Trail will have been moved to a more environmentally friendly location, north of the old site. Access to the lot is via the road to Wolverton. By 2005 hikers should have the choice of riding a shuttle bus or walking a connecting trail from the parking lot to the old trailhead near the General Sherman Tree. For the old parking area, follow signs from the Generals Highway to the parking area for General

Sherman, 2.2 miles northeast of the Giant Forest Museum.

DESCRIPTION: Any hike on the Congress Trail should begin with the obligatory short stroll around the General Sherman Tree. At 275 feet-high, 103 feet-around (at the base), and with a volume of 52,508 cubic feet, this giant sequoia has been declared not only the biggest tree in existence but also the largest living thing in the world. The diameter of the largest branch is nearly 7 feet, larger than the diameter of the trunk of most mature trees. Naming such a distinguished tree after a Union officer in the Civil War whose most notable accomplishment was "Sherman's March to the Sea" may seem a bit unusual, but James Wolverton, a pioneer cattleman who served under General William Tecumseh Sherman, did exactly that in 1879. Even more dubi-

ous was the name the Kaweah Colonists applied to the tree, Karl Marx.

From the Sherman tree, walk to the signed trailhead for the Congress Trail and then downhill, to the Leaning Tree. Follow a pair of footbridges over branches of Sherman Creek, passing a number of stately sequoias along the way. After the second bridge, you encounter a lateral trail to the right that provides a shorter loop back to the trailhead. A winding quarter-mile climb leads to a four-way intersection with the Alta Trail. Beyond the junction, near the bottom of the loop, you encounter many notable sequoias, including the Chief Sequoyah and the President (29th and fourth largest, respectively), the Senate and House groups, the General Lee, and the McKinley. Amid the staid Senate Group, the Trail of the Sequoias branches south at 0.8 miles from the trailhead. Near the

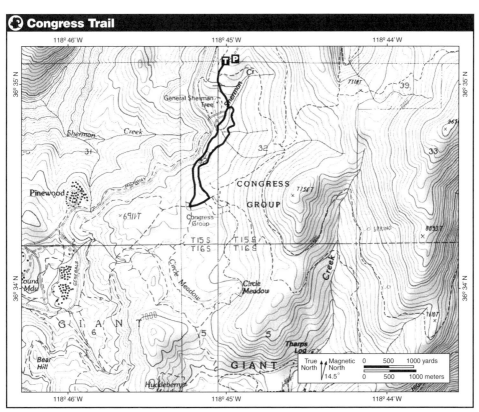

Congress Trail

McKinley Tree is a five-way junction with the Alta and Circle Meadow trails.

If you have extra time, you can visit additional sequoia landmarks on easy side trips from the junction. The Cloister and the Lincoln Tree (fifth largest) are just a short jaunt west on the Alta Trail. A longer, 0.9-mile excursion leads to the Washington Tree (second largest) via the Alta and Huckleberry Meadow trails. Southbound, the Circle Meadow Trail takes you quickly to the Room Tree, the Founders Group, and Cattle Cabin.

From the five-way junction with the Alta and Circle Meadow trails, head north on a mild descent, weaving your way back through the grove toward the General Sherman.

GIANT FOREST TRAILHEADS

TRIP **39**

Trail of the Sequoias

Ⓜ Ↄ DH

DISTANCE: 6.1 miles

ELEVATION: 6830/7325, +1770′/-1770′

SEASON: May to November

USE: Heavy/Moderate

MAPS: *Giant Forest, Lodgepole, Giant Forest, SNHA*

INTRODUCTION: The Trail of the Sequoias offers hikers the chance to explore the heart of the Giant Forest plateau in solitude and serenity, away from the crowds on the

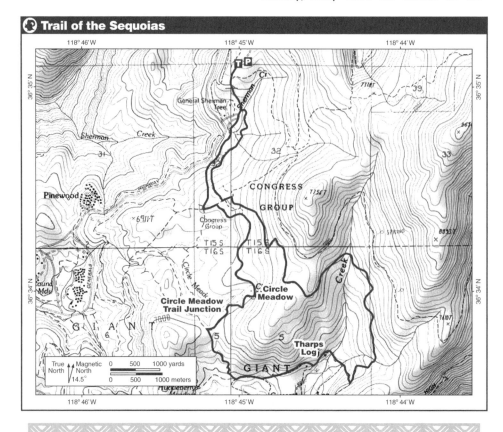

Congress and Crescent Meadows trails. You'll pass plenty of notable sequoia landmarks on this loop, many fine unnamed specimens, and portions of three picturesque meadows.

DIRECTIONS TO THE TRAILHEAD: When park improvements have been completed, very likely by the time you read this book, parking for the General Sherman Tree and the Congress Trail will have been relocated to a more environmentally friendly location, north of the old site. Access to the lot is via the road to Wolverton. Hikers should have the choice of riding a shuttle bus or walking a connecting trail from the parking lot to the old trailhead near the General Sherman Tree. For the old parking area, follow signs from the Generals Highway to the parking area for General Sherman, 2.2 miles northeast of the Giant Forest Museum.

DESCRIPTION: From the Sherman tree, walk to the signed trailhead for the Congress Trail and then downhill, to the Leaning Tree. Follow a pair of footbridges over branches of Sherman Creek. After the second bridge, you encounter a lateral trail to the right that provides a shorter loop back to the trailhead. A winding quarter-mile climb leads to a four-way intersection with the Alta Trail. Beyond the junction, near the bottom of the loop, you encounter many notable sequoias, including the Senate and House groups. Amid the staid Senate Group, the Trail of the Sequoias branches south at 0.8 miles from the trailhead.

Head south from the junction on the Trail of the Sequoias, through the mature sequoias in the Senate Group. On a general descent, you pass a couple of scorched giants that at first glance appear to be dead, but under further examination are, amazingly, still alive. You cross a tiny rivulet trickling into the southeast end of Circle Meadow and follow the trail across the hillside above the verdant clearing. Pass the unsigned fork of a use-trail heading out into the meadow, and a short distance far-

Giant Forest, Trail of the Sequoias

ther you reach a junction with the Circle Meadow Trail, 1.6 miles from trailhead.

A short distance beyond the Circle Meadow Trail is another junction, where for the next 0.4 mile your trail merges with the Huckleberry Meadow Trail. Head southeast and descend through moderate forest cover to a pair of Y-junctions, separated by approximately 25 yards. Continue southeast at both junctions, following signs for CRESCENT MEADOW at the first and THARPS LOG at the second. You skirt the north end of verdant Crescent Meadow for 0.2 mile to yet another pair of junctions, separated by a mere 10 yards. The Chimney Tree, a fire-hollowed giant sequoia monarch, is just up the hill past the second junction. After pondering the effects of fire on the Big Tree, turn right from the second junction and proceed toward Tharps Log. A short, winding climb takes you to the crest of a low ridge, followed by a short descent to the log at the north end of Log Meadow at 2.8 miles.

From a signed junction near Tharps Log, you head east around the tip of Log Meadow. You cross Crescent Creek on a wood-plank bridge and shortly step over a smaller tributary, soon arriving at a junction with the trail continuing along the east side of Log Meadow. Turn left and make a 0.2-mile climb up a fern-covered hillside to a seldom-used connecting trail.

Remain on the Trail of the Sequoias and make a lengthy traverse across the hillside, stepping over a couple of small streams along the way. On the traverse, you pass many fine sequoia specimens and even pass through a break in the trunk of one fallen giant. Follow the path as it arcs across the drainage of Crescent Creek and then climbs to the top of a ridge, where you have limited views of the surrounding woodland. Gazing across the mixed coniferous forest, you can see the characteristic sequoia crowns overshadowing the tops of lesser pines and firs. A half-mile descent leads past more sequoias to an abandoned junction. Before trail improvements to the Congress Trail, a short lateral trail to the right went past the Chief Sequoyah Tree and connected with the Alta Trail, but this path has been discontinued. Therefore, turn left and quickly come to the junction with the Congress Trail near the President Tree.

From the junction turn left and, from the five-way junction with the Alta and Circle Meadow trails, head north on a mild descent, weaving your way back through the grove toward the General Sherman.

GIANT FOREST TRAILHEADS

TRIP **40**

Circle Meadow Loop

E ↻ DH

DISTANCE: 3.8 miles

ELEVATION: 6830/7045, +740′/-740′

SEASON: May to November

USE: Heavy/Light

MAPS: *Giant Forest, Lodgepole, Giant Forest, SNHA*

INTRODUCTION: This trip is a journey of contrasts, beginning and ending on the heavily used, paved Congress Trail, and passing a number of notable sequoia landmarks along the way. The middle portion of the trip travels a portion of the Trail of the Sequoias and the Circle Meadow Trail to visit such Giant Forest attractions as Black Arch, Pillars of Hercules, Cattle Cabin, Founders Group, and the Room Tree. Most users of the Congress Trail

Pillars of Hercules

don't deviate from the overly popular loop, but by venturing farther into Giant Forest, you will almost surely have a serene encounter with the majestic giants. Verdant Circle Meadow delights visitors with a slender flower-filled clearing rimmed by statuesque trees.

DIRECTIONS TO THE TRAILHEAD: Follow directions in Trip 38 to the parking area for General Sherman/Congress Trail.

DESCRIPTION: Follow directions in Trip 38 and 39 to the junction between Circle Meadow Trail and Trail of the Sequoias.

Turn right and head northwest on the Circle Meadow Trail, immediately crossing the thin ribbon of Circle Meadow. Climbing a low hill, you encounter the Black Arch, another interesting scorched giant, and Pillars of Hercules, where the trail passes between two massive sequoias.

Follow the path along the fringe of Circle Meadow past a junction with an infrequently used connecting trail and continue to Cattle Cabin. The structure was built by cattlemen who pastured their stock in the nearby meadows. Just beyond the cabin, you step over another little rivulet that courses through the north swath of Circle Meadow. Then the trail bisects the Founders Group, a stand of a dozen stately sequoias named in honor of citizens who assisted in the establishment of Sequoia National Park. Next, you approach the Room Tree, which is a sequoia with a small passageway in the trunk leading into a large hollowed-out section at the base of the tree. A short way farther, you reach the junction of the Circle Meadow, Alta and Congress trails.

From the junction, follow directions in Trip 38 back to the trailhead via the Congress Trail.

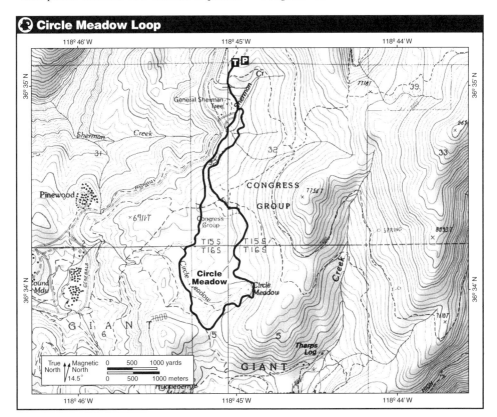

Circle Meadow Loop

Introduction to Wolverton, Lodgepole, and Wuksachi

Wolverton, Lodgepole, and Wuksachi were of little interest to Native Americans, who favored more temperate areas nearby, such as Giant Forest. Nowadays, these areas of Sequoia National Park are bustling hubs of activity for a wide range of visitors, as the Park Service has wisely moved infrastructure away from Giant Forest. While Lodgepole serves as the center for commercial activity and camping, and Wuksachi Village is the focal point for lodging, Wolverton is the main trailhead for hikers, backpackers and equestrians bound for the western backcountry of Sequoia National Park.

The large Wolverton trailhead parking lot is near flower-bedecked and forest-rimmed Long Meadow, with trails headed into the mid-elevation forests common to the western side of the park. Lodgepole is located in the picturesque, glacier-scoured Tokopah Valley, near the banks of the Marble Fork Kaweah River, where steep cliffs rise out of the valley up to granite ridges and peaks characteristic of the Sierra Nevada. Wuksachi Village is tucked quietly away from Generals Highway in serene forest along Clover Creek.

Several of the park's more popular trails begin from Wolverton and Lodgepole, as do more remote routes into lightly used areas of the backcountry. Many trails climb to high elevations that may leave hikers and backpackers who are unaccustomed to such heights short of breath. Whether you're looking for quiet forest strolls, grand views, wildflower-covered meadows, or

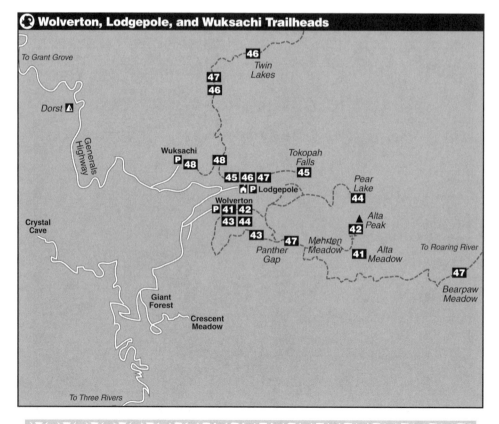

Campgrounds							
Campground	Fee	Elevation	Season	Restrooms	Running Water	Bear Boxes	Phone
LODGEPOLE	$16*	6700´	Open all year	Flush Toilets	Yes	Yes	Yes

Free when snow-covered

alpine lakes cradled in rugged cirques, this area has plenty of options. You'll find short day hikes, overnight backpacks, and extended journeys into the heart of the wilderness.

ACCESS: *(Open all year)* All three trailheads in this group are easily accessed by turnoffs from the Generals Highway, which the Park Service keeps open all year from the Ash Mountain Entrance. Access from the north via the Generals Highway is subject to storm closures during winter. Wolverton, Lodgepole, and Wuksachi are 19.5, 25.4, and 26.9 miles respectively from the Ash Mountain Entrance, and 26.9, 25.4, and 23.9 miles respectively from the Y-intersection with Highway 180, near the Big Stump Entrance.

AMENITIES: Lodgepole is the center of much of the activity on the western side of Sequoia National Park. Facilities include a visitor center, market, gift shop, snack bar and deli, laundry, public showers (closed in winter), post office, picnic areas, and the Walter Fry Nature Center (also closed in winter).

Upscale lodging is available all year at Wuksachi Village, which was recently constructed to replace the environmentally damaging facilities at Giant Forest. The village consists of the lodge center, housing

guest registration, gift shop, restaurant, lounge, and conference facilities, and three detached structures with 102 guest rooms. Rates from May through October are $150–219. Winter rates are from $86–123. Call (888) 252-5757 for reservations or more information.

Aside from being primarily a backcountry trailhead, Wolverton Corrals offers visitors horseback riding and pack trips during the summer. In winter, Wolverton is the snow-play center for Sequoia National Park, with a snow-covered meadow and two sledding hills. Ski and snowshoe rentals are available at Lodgepole.

RANGER STATION: Wilderness permits and backcountry information are available in the office next to the Lodgepole visitor center. A parking permit is also necessary if you're planning on leaving a vehicle overnight at the Lodgepole trailhead parking lot. General information is available at the visitor center.

GOOD TO KNOW BEFORE YOU GO:

1. If you plan on staying at Lodgepole the night before your backpack, be forewarned that this is one of the more popular campgrounds in either of the parks. Advance reservations are recommended during the height of summer.

2. Since the Lodgepole trailhead lies inside the entrance to the campground, you must obtain a parking permit and display it on the dashboard of your vehicle (available at the wilderness permit office near the visitor center).

3. Bear boxes are provided at the trailheads, but they are often full during the height of summer at the Wolverton trailhead. Minimize the amount of food and scented items that you bring to the trailhead.

View from the Hump Route

WOLVERTON TRAILHEAD

TRIP **41**

Mehrten and Alta Meadows

Ⓜ ↗ DH/BP

DISTANCE: 5.9 miles one way to Alta
Meadow

ELEVATION: 7270/9300, +2600´/-570´

SEASON: July to mid-October

USE: Moderate

MAP: *Lodgepole*

TRAIL LOG:

4.0   Mehrten Meadow
4.7   Alta Peak Trail Jct.
6.0   Alta Meadow

INTRODUCTION: Journey through the
serenity of a red-fir forest to the magnifi-
cence of a flower-bedecked meadow graced
with wonderful views of impressive peaks
near and far. The 12-mile round trip is
within the range of day hikers in good
shape, while excellent campsites provide a
fine opportunity for backpackers to linger
and enjoy the surroundings. The first clus-
ter of campsites, which you'll find near
Mehrten Meadow, reposes in the cool
shade of the forest, a mere 4 miles from the
trailhead. The second set is found along the
fringe of Alta Meadow beneath the ramparts of Tharps Rock and Alta Peak. A
route to alpine Moose Lake will tantalize
off-trail buffs.

Although it officially begins near the
Giant Forest Museum, most trail users will
want to access the Alta Trail from Wolverton, saving considerable mileage and elevation.

DIRECTIONS TO THE TRAILHEAD: From the
Generals Highway, 1.75 miles southeast of
the Lodgepole turnoff, turn east at the
signed Wolverton junction and follow

paved road 1.5 miles to the large trailhead
parking area. Restrooms, running water,
and bear boxes are nearby.

DESCRIPTION: Near a plethora of signs in
the parking lot, concrete steps lead to a
wide, single-track trail that quickly takes
you up the hillside to the crest of a ridge
and a junction with a trail from Lodgepole.
Turn right and follow the Lakes Trail,
quickly passing another junction with the
path around Long Meadow on your right.
After the initial ascent, the grade eases to a
mild-to-moderate climb, as you stroll
through light, red-fir forest. The ascent
continues along the course of Wolverton
Creek, trickling melodically through a strip
of verdant, wildflower-filled meadow.
Eventually, you cross a spring-fed tributary
lined with an array of flowers, including
columbine, lupine, monkey flower, leopard
lily, aster, and cow parsnip. At 1.75 miles,
you reach a signed junction of the Lakes
Trail and your route to Panther Gap.

Turn south, to your right, and follow
the well-maintained trail through moderate
forest cover on a course roughly paralleling
Wolverton Creek, crossing numerous lush-
banked tributaries along the way. Eventually, you leave the delightful streams and
lush foliage behind and climb out of the
drainage to a T-junction with the Alta Trail
at Panther Gap (8520´±), 2.7 miles from
the parking lot. A short stroll toward the
edge of the canyon reveals a commanding
view of the Middle Fork Kaweah River
canyon, Castle Peaks, and summits of the
Great Western Divide.

Head east on the Alta Trail, initially
along the crest, through distinctly drier vegetation composed of manzanita, ceanothus,
and Jeffrey and sugar pines. Soon, the path
veers onto the open, south-facing hillside,
which allows more excellent views. You
step across a spring-fed rivulet and then follow a short series of switchbacks up to a
junction with the Sevenmile Trail, at 3.7
miles, which provides a connection to the
High Sierra Trail. From the junction, you
head into forest cover and down to a ford

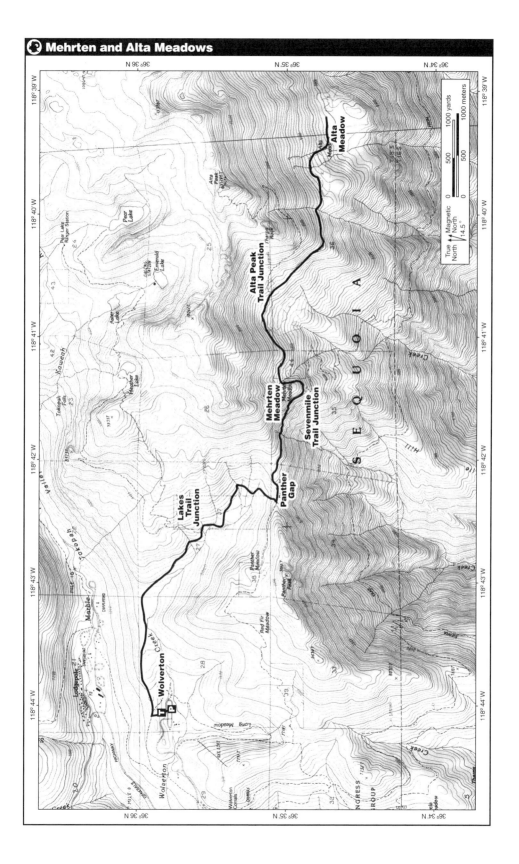

California cow parsnip

of Mehrten Creek, 3.9 miles from the parking lot. Near the stream is the Mehrten Meadows Camp (9100′±), where a few campsites with bear box are sheltered by red firs. Mehrten Meadow itself is a narrow, sloping, flower-packed glade well below the trail.

You leave Mehrten Creek behind and make a mildly ascending traverse across the hillside through patchy fir cover. Tharps Rock makes appearances through the breaks in the forest. At 0.8 mile from Mehrten Creek (4.7 miles from the trailhead), you reach a junction with the Alta Peak Trail. Backpackers with base camps at either Mehrten Creek or Alta Meadows should consider climbing Alta Peak (see Trip 42).

From the junction, you make a mild ascent around the forested base of Tharps Rock until you break out of the trees to a wide-ranging view up the canyon. Beyond a stream crossing, you encounter the verdant and extensive flower garden of Alta Meadow (9300′±). The beauty of the meadow is complemented exquisitely by views of Tharps Rock, Alta Peak, and the Great Western Divide. Fine campsites nestle beneath red firs on a low ridge south of the

trail. An unmaintained section of trail continues a short distance over vales and rivulets to Last Chance Meadow and additional campsites.

Ⓞ From Last Chance Meadow, a fairly well-known cross-country route connects to Moose Lake. You can follow an obscure path (unmaintained) most of the way. From Last Chance Meadow, head northeast to an open ridge above Buck Canyon. Follow the ridge northwest to the last of the stunted pines and descend boulder-filled slopes north toward the lake. You continue north over rocky terrain to a grassy swale that leads to a series of ramps. Climb up the ramp system to a saddle overlooking the south shore, where you'll find campsites. A short drop to Moose Lake (10,530′) leads to additional campsites near the shoreline. Brook trout will entice the angler. Experienced cross-country types can follow a more difficult route from Moose Lake west over the ridge to Pear Lake and a connection with the Lakes Trail (see Trip 44).

Ⓡ **PERMITS:** Wilderness permit required for overnight stay. (Quota: 25 per day)

CAMPFIRES: Permitted at Mehrten Meadow.

TRIP **42**

Alta Peak

S / DH

DISTANCE: 6.7 miles one way

ELEVATION: 7270/11,204,
+4265′±/-330′±

SEASON: Mid-July to mid-October

USE: Moderate

MAPS: *Lodgepole*

INTRODUCTION: The airy summit of Alta Peak is blessed with one of the best views you can reach from the western side of the park via a maintained trail. A one-day ascent is a viable option for strong hikers who are well acclimatized, but lesser mor-

tals can make a two-day summit bid from a base camp at either Mehrten or Alta meadows. However many days you need, the supreme vista is just too good to pass up. Technically, the Alta Trail begins near the Giant Forest museum, but a start at the Wolverton trailhead will save you approximately 3 miles and 1000 feet of elevation.

DIRECTIONS TO THE TRAILHEAD: From the Generals Highway, 1.75 miles southeast of the Lodgepole turnoff, turn east at the signed Wolverton junction and follow paved road 1.5 miles to the large trailhead parking area.

DESCRIPTION: Near a plethora of signs in the parking lot, concrete steps lead to a wide, single-track trail that quickly takes you up the hillside to the crest of a ridge and a junction with a trail from Lodgepole. Turn right and follow the Lakes Trail, quickly passing another junction with the path around Long Meadow on your right.

The Great Western Divide from the Alta Peak Trail

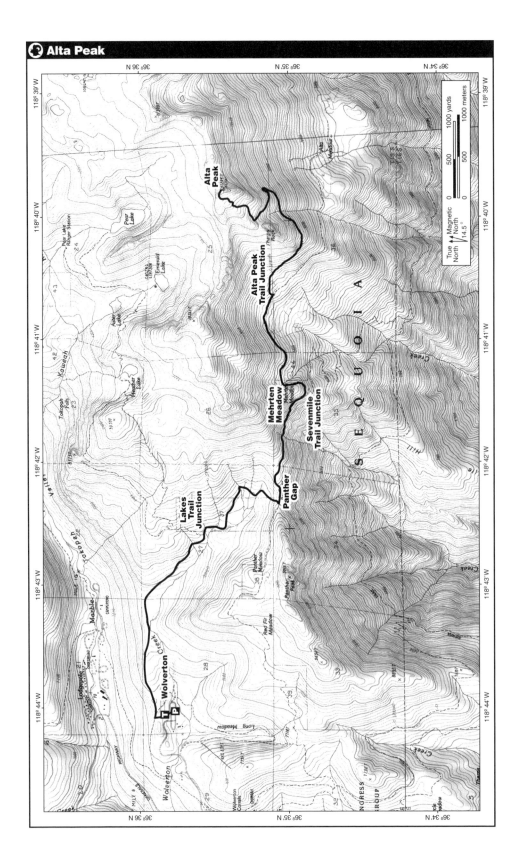

Alta Peak

Pear Lake Ranger Station

Pear Lake

Emerald Lake

Aster Lake

Heather Lake

Tokopah Falls

Alta Peak Trail Junction

Mehrten Meadow

Sevenmile Trail Junction

Panther Gap

Lakes Trail Junction

Panther Meadow

Panther Peak

Red Fir Meadow

Long Meadow

Wolverton Creek

Wolverton

Lodgepole

S E Q U O I A

True North / Magnetic North 14.5°

0   500   1000 yards
0   500   1000 meters

After the initial ascent, the grade eases to a mild-to-moderate climb. The ascent continues along the course of Wolverton Creek, Eventually, you cross a spring-fed tributary. At 1.75 miles, you reach a signed junction of the Lakes Trail and your route to Panther Gap.

Turn south, to your right, and follow the well-maintained trail, through moderate forest cover on a course roughly paralleling Wolverton Creek, crossing numerous tributaries along the way. Eventually, you leave the delightful streams and lush foliage behind and climb out of the drainage to a T-junction with the Alta Trail at Panther Gap (8520´±), 2.7 miles from the trailhead parking lot.

Head east on the Alta Trail. Soon, the path veers onto the open, south-facing hillside, which allows more excellent views. You step across a rivulet and then follow a short series of switchbacks up to a junction with the Sevenmile Trail, at 3.7 miles, which provides a connection to the High Sierra Trail. From the junction, you head into forest cover and down to a ford of Mehrten Creek, 3.9 miles from the parking lot. Near the stream is the Mehrten Meadows Camp (9100´±), where a few campsites with bear box are sheltered by red firs. Mehrten Meadow itself is a narrow glade, well below the trail.

You leave Mehrten Creek behind and make a mildly ascending traverse across the hillside. At 0.8 mile from Mehrten Creek (4.7 miles from the trailhead), you reach a junction with the Alta Peak Trail.

From the junction, the trail zigzags up the hillside through the intermittent shade of a grove of scattered red firs. You quickly leave the trees behind and continue the ascent to a refreshing, spring-fed, willow-and-wildflower-lined creek, where a small campsite is nestled above the far bank. After fording the creek, you make a long ascending traverse across the face of Tharps Rock through more scattered firs and patches of chinquapin. Excellent views abound across the Middle Fork Kaweah River to the terrain of the southwestern part of the park, as well the verdant swath of Alta Meadow below, and Tharps Rock and Alta Peak above. Nearing the end of the traverse, you reach the last reliable water below the summit at a pretty arroyo, filled with heather and wildflowers.

Beyond a switchback, you make a stiff climb, zigzagging and winding up the rocky slope above Tharps Rock. A few stunted foxtail pines herald your arrival into the alpine zone, where tufts of ground-hugging flowers and plants cling to the nearly barren slopes. Over decomposed granite and through boulders, the ascent follows just below the southwest ridge of the peak to the crest of the summit ridge. A short climb leads to the summit block and a final scramble to the top.

To say that the view from Alta Peak is awesome is an understatement. The body of water directly north is Pear Lake, backdropped by a sea of granite rising toward the Tableland. You can see numerous park landmarks, including the crest of Sierra peaks stretching out across the eastern horizon. Make sure you carry a map to help you identify them. You will be truly blessed if the normal western haze abates enough to see beyond the foothills to the patchwork farmland of the San Joaquin Valley. Nearly forgotten in our day is the view all the way across the plain to the Coastal Range.

WOLVERTON TRAILHEAD

TRIP 43

Panther Gap Loop

M **Q** DH

DISTANCE: 7.0 miles

ELEVATION: 7270/8645, +1720'/-1720'

SEASON: Early July to mid-October

USE: Light to moderate

MAP: *Lodgepole*

INTRODUCTION: Grand views, flower-packed meadows, and quiet forests greet you on this day-hike loop. The route starts by following the popular Lakes Trail and the almost-as-popular lateral to the Alta

Trail, but beyond Panther Gap it veers away from the crowds. As you stroll past serene Panther and Red Fir meadows, you should have the area to yourself. The last leg of the loop, around picturesque Long Meadow, follows a trail where you'll see few people on foot, but plenty on horseback from the nearby Wolverton Corrals.

DIRECTIONS TO THE TRAILHEAD: From the Generals Highway, 1.75 miles southeast of the Lodgepole turnoff, turn east at the signed Wolverton junction and follow paved road 1.5 miles to the large trailhead parking area.

DESCRIPTION: Near a plethora of signs in the parking lot, concrete steps lead to a wide, single-track trail that quickly takes you up the hillside to the crest of a ridge and a junction with a trail from Lodgepole. Turn right and follow the Lakes Trail,

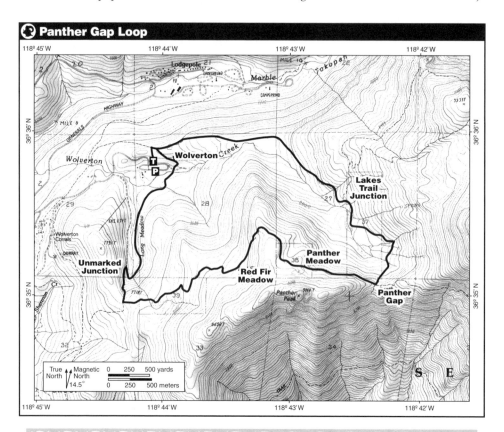

Castle Rocks from Panther Gap

descent to Red Fir Meadow, 4.1 miles from the trailhead. The serene meadow is lined with willows and edged by forest, and is a good place for wildlife viewing. Continue the descent from Red Fir Meadow to a saddle and a junction at 5.1 miles.

Leave the Alta Trail and turn north toward Long Meadow. A steep descent via switchbacks brings you quickly to another junction after 0.3 mile. A paucity of signed directions leaves you with little helpful information, as the only marking is for the Alta Trail behind you. Nevertheless, turn right at the junction and follow a dusty path around the south and east sides of Long Meadow, through lush foliage and across tiny rivulets. Eventually the trail veers away from the meadow and crosses a grassy slope to a pair of crossings of Wolverton Creek amid pockets of fir. You then cross an old road, climb up a forested hillside, and meet the Lakes Trail at 6.75 miles. Turn left, walk a short distance to the trail from the parking lot, and follow it back to the car.

quickly passing another junction with the path around Long Meadow on your right. After the initial ascent, the grade eases to a mild-to-moderate climb. The ascent continues along the course of Wolverton Creek, Eventually, you cross a spring-fed tributary. At 1.75 miles, you reach a signed junction of the Lakes Trail and your route to Panther Gap.

Turn south, to your right, and follow the well-maintained trail, through moderate forest cover on a course roughly paralleling Wolverton Creek, crossing numerous tributaries along the way. Eventually, you leave the delightful streams and lush foliage behind and climb out of the drainage to a T-junction with the Alta Trail at Panther Gap (8520′±), 2.7 miles from the parking lot.

From Panther Gap, turn west and follow the Alta Trail around the north side of Panther Peak, rising slightly through pine forest to reach diminutive Panther Meadow. You traverse over to the high point of your trip and then begin a steep 0.4-mile

WOLVERTON TRAILHEAD

TRIP **44**

Lakes Trail: Heather, Aster, Emerald, and Pear Lakes

Ⓔ ♤ DH/BP

DISTANCE: 5.75 miles one way to Pear Lake

ELEVATION: 7270/9530, +2795′/-535′

SEASON: Mid-June to mid-October

USE: Heavy

MAP: *Lodgepole*

TRAIL LOG:

1.75	Panther Gap
2.1	Hump/Watchtower Jct.
3.75	Heather Lake
4.7	Aster & Emerald Lakes
5.75	Pear Lake

INTRODUCTION: Easy access and spectacular alpine scenery combine to make this trip one of the most popular hikes and backpacks in Sequoia National Park. In an attempt to mitigate this popularity and to minimize human impact on the area, the Park Service has instituted camping bans and restrictions, as well as backcountry toilets. If you're planning an overnight visit, bear in mind that permits are at a premium. Such concerns aside, all four lakes are quite picturesque and plenty of views are to be had along the way, including spectacular vistas from the Watchtower, a narrow ledge dynamited out of a sheer cliff nearly 2000 feet above Tokopah Valley. An early start should allow most hikers in reasonable shape to complete the 12-mile loop during daylight hours.

DIRECTIONS TO THE TRAILHEAD: From the Generals Highway, 1.75 miles southeast of the Lodgepole turnoff, turn east at the signed Wolverton junction and follow paved road 1.5 miles to the large trailhead parking area.

DESCRIPTION: Near a plethora of signs in the parking lot, concrete steps lead to a wide, single-track trail that quickly takes you up the hillside to the crest of a ridge and a junction with a trail from Lodgepole. Turn right and follow the Lakes Trail, quickly passing another junction with the path around Long Meadow on your right. After the initial ascent, the grade eases to a mild-to-moderate climb. The ascent continues along the course of Wolverton Creek and eventually, you cross a spring-fed tributary. At 1.75 miles, you reach a signed junction of the Lakes Trail and the route to Panther Gap.

Remaining on the Lakes Trail, weave up the hillside and then drop briefly to a crossing of another flower-and-fern-lined tributary of Wolverton Creek. A moderate climb leads to the next junction at 2.1 miles, where you have two options for travel to Heather Lake. The Watchtower is by far the more scenic path, granting dramatic views into the deep gorge of Tokopah Valley. However, acrophobes may feel safer on the Hump Route, which is a quarter of a mile shorter, but gains an additional 200 vertical feet. The Hump Route is not completely devoid of fine scenery, as you'll have a nice view of Silliman Crest and the Tableland from the high point. Whichever route you select, you can return on the other one and not miss any of the excellent views.

To take the Hump Route, turn right at the junction and follow switchbacks on a moderate-to-moderately steep climb through red-fir forest. In the midst of the ascent, you step across a tiny stream lined by pockets of flower-dotted meadow. A three-quarter-mile mile climb leads to the fine view from atop the Hump (9485′±), 3.4 miles from the trailhead. The vista is easily improved by strolling onto the open hill past the scattered trees.

A steep descent leads from the saddle down to a small flat, carpeted with pockets of heather and dotted with a smattering of lodgepole pine, where you rejoin the Watchtower route, 3.6 miles from Wolverton. Along a brief, mild descent, you glimpse Heather Lake below, as you pass a lateral to the open-air toilet near the lake. The facility is screened on three sides by wood boards, but affords a spectacular view. A short distance beyond the lateral, you near the heather-laced shore of aptly named Heather Lake (9260′±), 3.75 miles from the trailhead. A few pines used to shelter shoreline campsites around the cliff-rimmed lake, but the area has been closed to camping for a number of years due to overuse.

You proceed up the rocky trail, climbing through boulders and scattered pines on the way out of the Heather Lake basin. The trail then leads across open granite on an easier route, affording fine views across the canyon and up toward Alta Peak. You wrap around the hillside and drop to the floor of the basin that cradles Aster and Emerald Lakes, 4.7 miles from Wolverton.

Located between the lakes, not far from the trail, a completely enclosed three-hole solar toilet provides a much more sophisticated facility than the primitive one at Heather Lake, albeit without the view. Although camping has been banned at Aster Lake (9075′±), 0.2 mile downstream from the trail, granite slabs around the mostly open shoreline afford fine opportunities for sunbathing. Anglers can test their skill on rainbow trout. Between the trail and Emerald Lake, ten designated campsites, with bear boxes, offer backpackers the first opportunity for legal camping between here and the trailhead. Smatterings of pines shelter the campsites, and thin strips of verdant meadow border the nearby outlet. Beyond the campsites, Emerald Lake (9235′±) is beautifully situated below

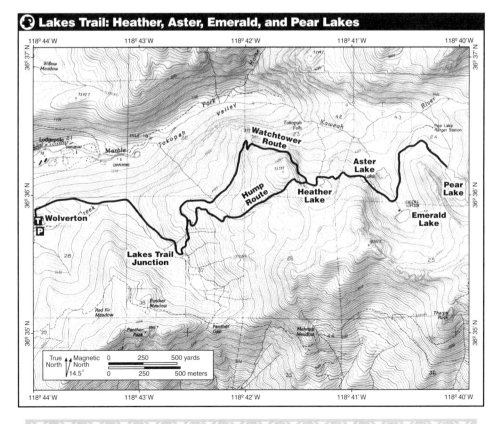

Lakes Trail: Heather, Aster, Emerald, and Pear Lakes

Alta Peak rises above Pear Lake

Alta Peak, backdropped by steep cliffs surrounding the lake on three sides. The inlet cascades dramatically down cliffs above the far shore before gracefully pouring across granite slabs into the lake. Resident brook trout will tempt the angler.

A mildly ascending traverse takes you from the Aster and Emerald lakes basin around a spur ridge and into the Pear Lake basin. Small pockets of wildflowers soften the otherwise rocky terrain. Nice views into the cleft of the Marble Fork Kaweah River and Tokopah Valley capture your attention as you follow the trail around the ridge. At 5.2 miles, you pass the junction with the trail to the ranger station and continue the curving ascent toward the lake a half mile farther. Rockbound Pear Lake (9550′±) is rimmed by craggy ridges and towered over by the lofty summit of Alta Peak. Widely scattered pines and small tufts of grasses find tenuous footholds in the stony basin. Similar to Emerald, Pear Lake boasts a solar toilet, and camping is restricted to the 12 designated sites near the outlet. Brook trout will test the skill of anglers.

Return via Watchtower: For the return trip, find your way back to the junction between the two routes, a quarter of a mile west of Heather Lake. From that junction, bear right and follow the trail on a gentle descent. Soon the trail begins to cling to the side of a near-vertical cliff. Views are staggering as you peer straight down to the Marble Fork churning and careening through Tokopah Valley. The thunderous sound of the river reverberates all the way up to the trail. With all the drama below, don't forget to experience the view behind you of the Silliman Crest.

As you proceed down the trail, a more moderate descent ensues, leading along a wedge of rock that protrudes into the canyon, shown as point *8973T* on the *Lodgepole* quad. An unofficial scramble route leads bold adventurers to the extraordinary views from the top. A few switchbacks take you across less precipitous slopes and into a light forest. At 1.4 miles from the junction, you step over a vigorous creek lined with lush foliage and continue the moderate descent another 0.4 mile to the junction at the convergence of the Watchtower and Hump trails.

O While the maintained trail ends at Pear Lake, experienced cross-country enthusiasts have the option of visiting remote Moose Lake or the Tablelands.

R **PERMITS:** Wilderness permit required for overnight stays. (Quota: 25 per day)

CAMPING: Restricted to designated sites at Emerald and Pear lakes. No camping at Heather and Aster lakes.

CAMPFIRES: Not allowed.

TRIP **45**

Tokopah Falls

ⓔ ↗ **DH**

DISTANCE: 1.9 miles one way

ELEVATION: 6735/7335, +700′/-0′

SEASON: April to late October

USE: Heavy

MAP: *Lodgepole*

INTRODUCTION: The Tokopah Falls Trail provides an easy 2-mile hike to a viewpoint along the Marble Fork Kaweah River, where a stunning waterfall plunges down a steep-walled canyon (Tokopah is a Yokut Indian word meaning high mountain valley). Early season is the best time to view the falls, when snowmelt pushes the river toward its peak flow, but this straightforward route also makes for a short, pleasant hike in summer and fall.

DIRECTIONS TO THE TRAILHEAD: From the Generals Highway, turn east at the Lodgepole junction and drive past the campground entrance station to the hiker/backpacker parking area. Walk along the campground access road, past the Walter Fry Nature Center and restrooms, to a fork in the road. Veer left at the fork and cross the log bridge over the Marble Fork Kaweah River to the beginning of the Tokopah Falls Trail on the north bank.

DESCRIPTION: You follow the Tokopah Falls Trail away from the road on a mild climb through a mixed forest of red and

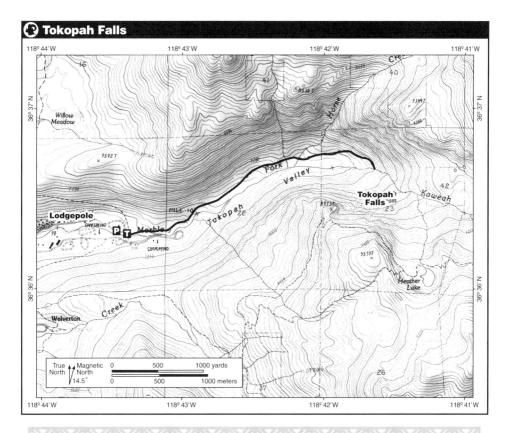

white firs, incense cedars, and ponderosa and Jeffrey pines. The river is lined with willow, aspen, and chokecherry. You proceed up the trail along the north bank, sometimes right alongside the churning stream and sometimes a fair distance away. Between the trees, you climb over low granite outcrops and pass small pockets of grassy meadow, where wildflowers put on a showy display in early season. Along the way you cross several bridges over stream channels.

Depending on the season, you may hear Tokopah Falls well before you actually see the mighty cascade. Early in the year, the roar of the falls can be deafening, as the snowmelt-filled torrent pours over the canyon headwall. Eventually, the forest gives way to elderberry, oak, and manzanita growing amid piles of boulders and large blocks of granite, allowing views of the falls and the surrounding terrain. Across the canyon looms the mighty wall of rock known as the Watchtower, soaring nearly 2000 feet above the valley floor. The trail continues climbing through the boulders and granite piles, more steeply now, before ending at a boulder-rimmed bench near the base of steep cliffs. A sign advises against proceeding any farther up the canyon, where slippery and unstable slopes have contributed to a number of fatalities. Ahead, Tokopah Falls creates a majestic display as it plummets down the steep wall of the upper canyon.

Tokopah Falls

WOLVERTON TRAILHEAD

TRIP 46

Twin Lakes

Ⓜ ↗ DH / BP

DISTANCE: 6.75 miles one way

ELEVATION: 6735/9420, +3030´/-285´

SEASON: Late June to mid-October

USE: Moderate

MAP: *Lodgepole, Mt. Silliman*

INTRODUCTION: The Twin Lakes Trail climbs through mixed forest, past flower-laden meadows, and over gurgling streams to a pair of popular lakes. Despite the name, these two lakes have little in common other than their proximity to one another, but they do provide a pleasant and picturesque destination for a two-day backpack. Permits are often at a premium on weekends, and the first mile of the trail is a scorcher in full sun, so both an early acquisition of your wilderness permit and an early start up the trail are recommended. Day hikers who don't feel up to the task of going all the way to the lakes will find the 2.6-mile trip to lush Cahoon Meadow a worthy alternative.

DIRECTIONS TO THE TRAILHEAD: From the Generals Highway, turn east at the Lodgepole junction and drive past the campground entrance to the hiker parking area. Walk on the camping access road, past the nature center to a fork in the road. Go left, crossing the bridge over the Marble Fork Kaweah River to the Tokopah Falls trailhead. Just beyond the Tokopah Falls trailhead is the Twin Lakes trailhead.

DESCRIPTION: The signed Twin Lakes Trail begins immediately past the Tokopah Falls Trail. You pass through the Lodgepole Campground on a nearly level, rock-lined trail amid a covering of mixed forest. Soon,

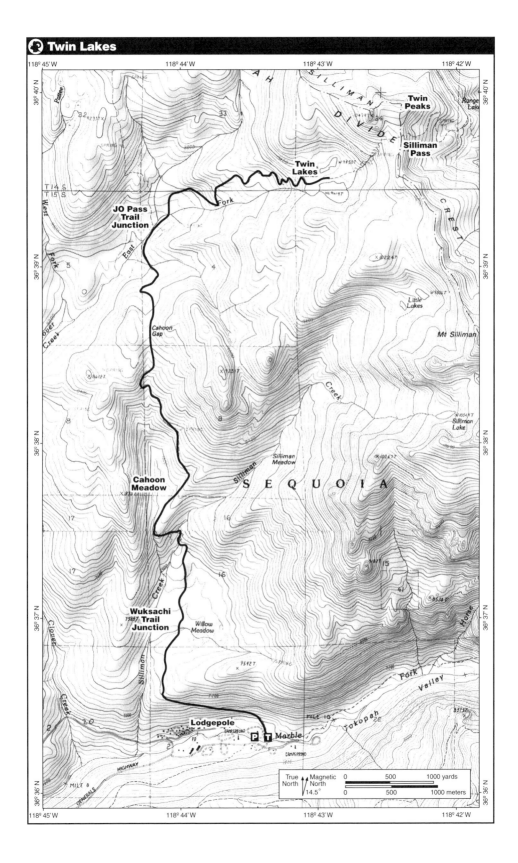

The larger of the Twin Lakes

the grade increases as the trail attacks the hillside above the campground. A mile from the parking area, you enter thicker forest of red firs and lodgepole pines as the trail bends north into the Silliman Creek drainage. At 1.5 miles, you cross a tiny, spring-fed brook and quickly encounter a T-junction with the Wuksachi Trail.

Cross a rock-filled wash, the former bed of Silliman Creek, which now follows a newer course, just over the low ridge to your left. A moderate climb, incorporating rocky switchbacks, leads to the crossing of the main channel of Silliman Creek at 2.25 miles. The ford may be difficult in early season. Silliman Creek is the domestic water supply for Lodgepole, so camping, swimming, fishing, and picnicking are not permitted.

Away from the creek, you continue to climb around the nose of a south-facing spur and then northeast to Cahoon Meadow (7755′±), 2.6 miles from Lodgepole. The pleasant clearing, carpeted with tall grass and wildflowers, is a favorite haunt of the local deer herd. A handful of campsites nestle beneath tall firs along the fringe of the meadow.

More stiff climbing leads to a lush, spring-fed stream, where lupine, tiger lily, monkey flower, and aster lend a splash of color to the greenery. You ascend to a clearing with fine views across Cahoon Meadow and continue up-slope, stepping across numerous rivulets lined with brilliantly colored swaths of wildflowers. The uppermost brook drains a fair-sized, sloping meadow that you pass on the way to Cahoon Gap (8645′), 4 miles from the trailhead.

A mild-to-moderate 0.6-mile descent from the gap leads alongside East Fork Clover Creek and then crosses a tributary on an easy boulder-hop. You'll find campsites with a bear box on the other side. Proceed through firs for another 0.3 mile to a junction with the trail to JO Pass, 4.9 miles from Lodgepole. Firs shelter a few scattered campsites near the junction.

Bear right at the junction and continue a mild-to-moderate ascent that follows the East Fork Clover Creek to a ford where leopard lily, shooting star, and aster liven the banks. The grade increases as you veer away from the stream and head up the steep hillside, traveling through alternating pockets of forest and clearing. Wildflowers blanket an expansive slope, including leopard lily, shooting star, aster, lupine, corn lily, larkspur, cinquefoil, wallflower, golden senecio, and Mariposa lily. Beyond a series of switchbacks, the grade finally eases, and you pass an information sign, glimpse the larger lake through the trees, and then make an easy stroll to the lakeshore.

Your first question upon arriving at Twin Lakes might be, "How did these two completely different lakes end up with this name?" Obviously, the southern lake is quite a bit bigger than its neighbor, and they bear no resemblance to each other in shape. The smaller lake is completely ringed by thick lodgepole-pine-and-red-fir forest, and while the larger lake is similarly treed on the north side; its opposite shore is made up of talus and cliffs that rise 600 feet above the lake. The rugged towers of Twin Peaks are also visible from places along the shore of the larger lake. A pair of bear boxes is located on the strip of forest between the lakes, near a number of overused campsites. Slightly less used campsites are spread around the shorelines of both lake, and a pit toilet is located west of the smaller lake. Fishing is fair for brook trout, and swimming in the shallow lakes can be quite pleasant on hot afternoons.

[O] Using the trail system in the Jennie Lakes Wilderness and the southwestern section of Kings Canyon National Park you can easily create extended backpacks.

From Silliman Pass, rock climbers can tackle short routes on Twin Peaks. Mountaineers may accept the challenge of a class 2 climb of Mt. Silliman by traversing from the pass to the east ridge and following the ridge to the summit.

[R] **PERMITS:** Wilderness permit required for overnight stays. (Quota: 30 per day)

CAMPFIRES: Not permitted at Twin Lakes.

WOLVERTON TRAILHEAD

TRIP 47

Kings – Kaweah Divide Loop

Ⓜ ↻ BPx

DISTANCE: 52 mile loop

ELEVATION: 6735/10,185/7095/
11,370/6725,
+14,100′/-14,100′

SEASON: Mid-July to October

USE: Light

MAPS: *Lodgepole, Mt. Silliman, Sphinx Lakes, Triple Divide Peak*

TRAIL LOG:

9.5	Ranger Lake
11.3	Lost Lake Jct.
14.9	Comanche Meadow
16.5	Sugarbowl Meadow Camp
22.0	Roaring River
28.0	Upper Ranger Meadow
31.5	Elizabeth Pass
34.1	Tamarack Lake Jct.
36.25	Bearpaw Meadow
43.0	Alta Trail Jct.

INTRODUCTION: This moderate 50-mile-plus loop allows backpackers to sample a cross-section of the characteristic grandeur of the western side of Sequoia and Kings Canyon national park. Travelers cross a wide range of elevations and environments, including mid-elevation forest, and subalpine and alpine zones. The topography is equally diverse, with a bounty of beautiful lakes, flower-laden meadows, glaciated canyons, and high alpine basins. Views from the trail of soaring peaks, precipitous canyon walls, and airy spires augment the extraordinary scenery. An added bonus to this excursion is the potential for solitude; between Twin Lakes and Bearpaw Meadow you should see very few people.

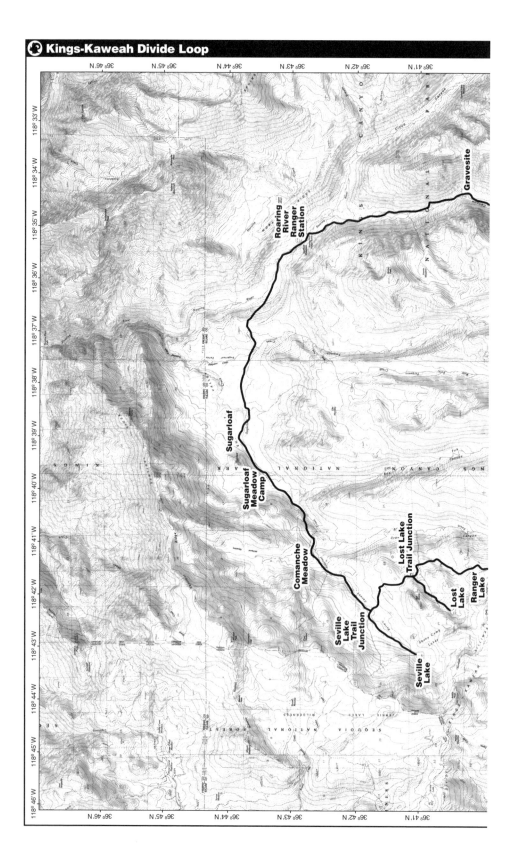

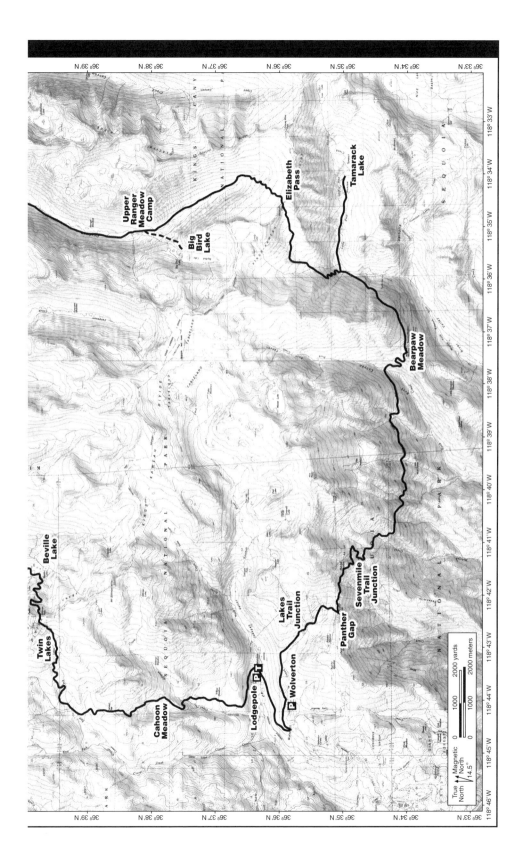

Backpackers will have to exert a hearty effort, as the extended loop crosses the Kings-Kaweah Divide at two significant passes, Silliman and Elizabeth. Most of the trail should be in good condition, although it leaves something to be desired on the south side of Elizabeth Pass. With extra days, forays to other locales are possible.

DIRECTIONS TO THE TRAILHEAD: From the Generals Highway, turn east at the Lodgepole junction and drive past the campground entrance to the hiker parking area. Walk on the camping access road, past the nature center to a fork in the road. Go left, crossing the bridge over the Marble Fork Kaweah River to the Tokopah Falls trailhead. Just beyond the Tokopah Falls trailhead is the Twin Lakes trailhead.

DESCRIPTION: The signed Twin Lakes Trail begins immediately past the Tokopah Falls Trail. You pass through the Lodgepole Campground on a nearly level trail amid a covering of mixed forest. Soon, the grade increases. A mile from the parking area, the trail bends north into the Silliman Creek drainage. At 1.5 miles, you cross a tiny, spring-fed brook and quickly encounter a T-junction with the Wuksachi Trail.

Cross a rock-filled wash and begin a moderate climb that incorporates rocky switchbacks and leads to the crossing of the main channel of Silliman Creek, at 2.25 miles. Camping, swimming, fishing, and picnicking are not permitted in the creek.

Away from the creek, you continue to climb around the nose of a south-facing spur and then northeast to Cahoon Meadow (7755′±), 2.6 miles from Lodgepole. A handful of campsites nestle along the fringe of the meadow.

More stiff climbing leads to a spring-fed stream. You ascend to a clearing with fine views across Cahoon Meadow and continue up-slope. The uppermost brook drains a fair-sized, sloping meadow that you pass on the way to Cahoon Gap (8645′), 4 miles from the trailhead.

A mild-to-moderate 0.6-mile descent from the gap leads alongside East Fork

Clover Creek and then crosses a tributary on an easy boulder-hop. You'll find campsites with a bear box on the other side. Proceed through firs for another 0.3 mile to a junction with the trail to JO Pass, 4.9 miles from Lodgepole. Firs shelter a few scattered campsites near the junction.

Bear right at the junction and continue a mild-to-moderate ascent that follows the East Fork Clover Creek to a ford. The grade increases as you veer away from the stream and head up the steep hillside. Beyond a series of switchbacks, the grade finally eases, and you pass an information sign, glimpse the larger lake through the trees, and then make an easy stroll to the lakeshore.

Twin Lakes aren't very twin-like. The southern lake is bigger than its neighbor, and they bear no resemblance to each other in shape. The rugged towers of Twin Peaks are visible from places along the shore of the larger lake.

A pair of bear boxes is located on the strip of forest between the lakes, near a number of overused campsites. Slightly less used campsites are spread around the shorelines of both lakes, and west of the smaller lake is a pit toilet. Swimming in the shallow lakes can be pleasant on hot afternoons.

From Twin Lakes a series of switchbacks take you up the steep hillside on a winding 700-foot-climb. The trail crosses back and forth over the lakes' diminutive inlet, which provides welcome opportunities to slake your thirst during the stiff ascent. Between sporadic clumps of lodgepole pine, you have improving views of the lakes below and Twin Peaks above. Nearing the crest, the grade eases as you stroll over to Silliman Pass (10,185′±), which marks the boundary between Sequoia and Kings Canyon parks, 7.8 miles from the trailhead. Through the widely scattered trees, you have fine views of Mt. Silliman, the Great Western Divide, the Tableland, and the Sugarloaf Creek drainage below. If not for the ever-present smog, the view west across the San Joaquin Valley would be equally impressive.

Switchbacks descend rather steeply from the pass. Along the way, you have a fine panorama of the Kings River country, including Tehipite Dome and the peaks of the Monarch Divide. Soon, the blue surfaces of Beville and Ranger lakes spring into view. The steep, serpentine descent continues, ultimately leveling as you near the floor of the lakes' basin. In a stand of lodgepole, you reach a signed junction at 9.5 miles, where a faint path branches to the right toward Beville Lake. The grass-rimmed lake offers excellent views of Mt. Silliman, but campsites are marginal. Continuing from the path to Beville Lake, you quickly come to the next junction, where a short lateral heads north over a low rise to the shore of Ranger Lake (9193´). A posted map just before the lake shows the locations of five designated campsites with fire pits, two bear boxes, and a ranger cabin. Anglers can ply the waters in search of rainbow trout around the lodgepole-encircled lake.

From the Ranger Lake junction, you proceed over slabs, around boulders, and beneath widely scattered pines on a general descent, interrupted briefly by a short climb over the crest of a ridge. Just past a verdant pocket meadow and a flower-lined stream, you intersect the trail to Lost Lake, 11.3 miles from Lodgepole. The half a mile trail to Lost Lake follows the fringe of a meadow and then goes up a forested slope to the picturesque lake, backdropped by rugged cliffs of Twin Peaks and the Silliman Crest. Three designated campsites with fire pits are available for backpackers on the north shore, while much of the remaining shoreline is closed for restoration. Anglers should appreciate the relative lack of pressure on the resident brook trout.

From the Lost Lake junction, cross a bridge over the lushly lined outlet and proceed through fir-and-pine forest around the southeast flank of Ball Dome to the top of a ridge. You descend from the ridge, initially down a meadowed vale, to the bottom of Belle Canyon and the broad ford of Sugarloaf Creek. On the far bank is a signed junction with a trail to Seville Lake and Rowell Meadow, 13.1 miles from Lodgepole.

🄾 **SIDE TRIP TO SEVILLE LAKE:** Head east from the junction with the trail to Seville Lake and Rowell Meadow. Step across a tributary of Sugarloaf Creek, and proceed on a gently graded path through mixed forest, following the creek upstream through Belle Canyon. As you continue, the cliffs of the Kings-Kaweah Divide that form the lake's cirque begin to appear over the treetops. Soon, you reach the north shore of lovely Seville Lake (8408´), 1.25 mile from the junction.

Granite cliffs rise above the south shore of the lake, culminating at 10,041-foot Kettle Peak, on the crest of the Kings-Kaweah Divide. Lodgepole pines and red firs rim the marshy shoreline and shade a number of pleasant campsites. Plenty of rainbow and brook trout will tempt the angler. **END OF SIDE TRIP**

Turn right (northeast) at the junction and make a mildly graded descent to a crossing of a tributary stream. Unlike what is shown on the *Mt. Silliman* quad, the trail remains on the north side of Sugarloaf Creek. Just over a mile from the junction, you step across a pleasant side stream that provides a refreshing locale for a rest stop. Continue the easy descent for 0.4 mile to the next junction, 14.6 miles from the trailhead, where another trail heads west out of the park toward Rowell Meadow. You soon encounter aspen-and-willow-lined Comanche Meadow (7800´±), 14.9 miles from the trailhead. Near the far end of the clearing, a path leads to campsites with a bear box and use-trails down to Sugarloaf Creek.

Resume the downhill jaunt through lush foliage to the crossing of the stream that drains Williams Meadow. Beyond the creek, you pass into the markedly drier surroundings of a Jeffrey-pine forest, which still shows clear evidence of an extensive

1974 fire. You go through a drift fence and drop into Sugarloaf Valley, with fine views through scattered trees and over clumps of manzanita of the prominent hump of granite for which the valley is named. A milder trail across the valley floor leads to a side trail marked simply BEAR BOX, at 16.5 miles. The short path heads to a camping area south of wildflower-laden Sugarloaf Meadow (7240´±), where pines shelter a few campsites with a bear box, a hitching post, and a small stream nearby.

Beyond the campsite lateral, you cross a side stream and proceed on gently graded, dusty trail through Sugarloaf Valley along the base of Sugarloaf to a ford of the main channel of the creek, the low point of the journey. Even during low water you should plan on getting your feet wet at this crossing. A couple of primitive campsites can be found above the far shore.

From Sugarloaf Creek, a mild trail takes you through denser forest and across minor rivulets, toward tumbling Ferguson Creek. A stiff, half-mile climb leads to the top of a manzanita-covered and pine-dotted moraine at the lip of Roaring River canyon. The view includes Palmer Mountain, the Sphinx Crest, and summits along the north end of the Great Western Divide. Living up to its name, you can hear the tumultuous sound of Roaring River below.

A three-quarter-mile descent takes you from the crest to the floor of the canyon, through a variety of vegetation. You pass through another drift fence and begin the steady climb up the drainage, sometimes right next to frothy Roaring River tumbling down the boulder-strewn canyon. Just beyond another fence, you cross a side stream and encounter the grassy clearing of fenced Scaffold Meadow, followed by a T-junction near the solar-powered Roaring River Ranger Station, 22 miles from Lodgepole. Up either trail are campsites with bear boxes near the river.

From the ranger station, head up the canyon to a fork in the trail, staying on the west side of Roaring River. From the fork, the more distinct path on the left leads to

additional campsites for backpackers and stock parties; the fainter, right-hand trail is the Deadman Canyon/Elizabeth Pass route. A short, steep climb up this trail leads to milder trail through a light forest of Jeffrey pines, cedars, and red firs, which eventually takes you southbound into Deadman Canyon. After passing through a three-pole gate, you continue upstream on a gentle trail to campsites just before the ford of Deadman Canyon Creek, 1.6 miles from Roaring River.

Beyond the creek, you pass through a pleasant, wildflower-covered meadow with good views of the steep cliffs and granite walls of the canyon. For the next 1.5 miles, the landscape alternates between groves of mixed forest and pockets of clearing, where wildflowers and views of the glacier-carved canyon provide visual delights. Sporadic swaths of young aspen testify to the numerous avalanches that have roared down the hillside.

You encounter a long meadow where the creek glides sinuously through grasses and flowers. A use-trail branches over to some campsites at the near end of the meadow, and a ways beyond is the gravesite from which the canyon received its name.

You ford the creek again, and then continue upstream on a mild ascent through boulders, shrubs, and flowers to a picturesque scene where the creek spills across a series of slabs. Past another drift fence, you ascend through more lush foliage and then the trail eases in a stand of lodgepoles and firs. Soon, you break out of the trees and enter the extensive grasslands of Ranger Meadow. The steep canyon walls and the peaks at the head of the canyon combine to create an awesome view across the flower-bedecked meadow.

At the far end of Ranger Meadow, you make a moderate climb through scattered lodgepole pine to the crossing of a lushly lined tributary stream. The steady ascent continues across rocky slopes dotted with heather to a ford of the vigorous main channel of the creek. A moderate-to-moderately steep climb leads through a rock garden

DEADMAN CANYON

Before the current designation, this area was known as Copper Canyon, for the copper mine near the head. An old sign with the cryptic deteriorating inscription, HERE REPOSES ALFRED MONIERE, SHEEPHERDER, MOUNTAIN MAN, 18–1887, marks the grave. Little else is known about the deceased, which has fueled a variety of interesting tales. One version has the Basque sheepherder murdered, while a less dramatic account has him taking ill and passing away before his partner could make the two-week round trip to Fresno for a physician. Whatever the cause of death, a better site for one's grave is hard to imagine, as the meadow is blessed with a sweeping panorama of the granite cathedral. Aspens and pines dot the meadow, and columbine, delphinium, daisy, Mexican hat, penstemon, pennyroyal, and shooting star are among the species of flower that grace the surroundings.

tered lodgepoles cling tenuously to the sparse soil around the lake, affording little protection to the exposed campsites on sandy flats near the north shore. The view down Deadman Canyon is quite dramatic.
END OF SIDE TRIP

Follow the gentle trail in Upper Ranger Meadow through sagebrush, grasses, sedges and wildflowers. The grade increases as you progress up the canyon and draw near the creek, which is lined with low-growing willows and clumps of flowers. As you approach the headwall, the climb becomes more pronounced and a series of switchbacks leads you up the rocky slope. After crossing the creek, the trail veers southwest to ascend a talus-and-boulder-filled cirque on an interminable set of switchbacks. Finally, the goal comes into view and you zigzag up dirt trail to Elizabeth Pass (11,370´±), 9.4 miles from Roaring River.

Although the 2100-foot ascent is now behind you, perhaps a more difficult challenge awaits as you begin the 3300-foot knee-wrenching descent to the Tamarack Lake Trail junction. Although recently constructed switchbacks wind up the north side of Elizabeth Pass, the south side has a very poor trail that seemingly hasn't been

and past another drift fence to the lip of Upper Ranger Meadow (9210´±). Just off the trail to the right, in a grove of pines are two good campsites, 6.1 miles from Roaring River.

[O] **CROSS-COUNTRY ROUTE TO BIG BIRD LAKE:** From the campsites in Upper Ranger Meadow, cross the main channel of the creek and climb up the steep hillside, staying well to the left of the deep cleft of the outlet stream from Big Bird Lake. Portions of a boot-beaten path may be evident, but if not, the route is straightforward, although quite steep. Work your way up to a bench overlooking the lake and several small ponds to the north. From there the route drops easily to the lakeshore. Big Bird Lake (9765´) is long and narrow, cradled in a U-shaped alpine cirque below the crest of the Kings-Kaweah Divide. A few wind-bat-

ELIZABETH PASS

Elizabeth Pass was once known as Turtle Pass, named after a rock about 4 feet long near the east side, which bears a striking resemblance to a turtle. In 1905 author Stewart Edward White, along with his wife and another man, traveled up Deadman Canyon, crossed the Kings-Kaweah Divide at the pass, and descended steep cliffs to Lone Pine Meadow. Their adventure was originally retold in *Outing* magazine, and later in White's book, *The Pass*. The name of the pass was subsequently changed to Elizabeth in honor of White's wife.

maintained since the General Sherman tree was a sapling. Much of the trail encounters eroded gullies and washed-out sections, more reminiscent of a popular cross-country route than a bona fide trail. Numerous cairns and ducks aid your descent, and the general route down the glacier-scoured trough is fairly obvious, even if the actual trail isn't always clear. Initially you're cheered by views of Moose and Lost lakes from just below the pass, and later by a profusion of wildflowers on the more hospitable slopes below. Farther down, as trail conditions improve, vistas of Lion Rock, Mt. Stewart, and Eagle Scout Peak issue a siren call luring backpackers up trails to the mountainous terrain surrounding Tamarack and Hamilton lakes. At 2.7 miles from the pass and 12.1 miles from Roaring River, after more switchbacks, the descent eases at the Tamarack Lake junction (8180′±).

SIDE TRIP TO TAMARACK LAKE: Head east from the Tamarack Lake junction across a boulder field to the ford of Lonely Lake's outlet. Just beyond the stream, a use-trail leads to campsites. Soon the grade of the trail increases as you climb above a scenic stair-step falls to sloping Lone Pine Meadow, backdropped regally by Lion

Rock and Mt. Stewart, as well as a bounty of unnamed towers and ramparts along the canyon rim. Continue the climb, initially through a tangle of ferns, grasses, and flowers, followed by the drier vegetation of manzanita and sagebrush. You reach the pleasant surroundings of Tamarack Meadow and stroll amid wildflowers to the far end, where you'll find a triple-branched crossing of Tamarack Creek. A short climb up a lodgepole-covered hill leads to Tamarack Lake, 1.8 miles from the junction, nestled into an impressive rock amphitheater topped by Mt. Stewart and Lion Rock. Plenty of campsites are scattered around the secluded lake (no fires). Brook trout will tantalize anglers. **END OF SIDE TRIP**

From the Tamarack Lake junction, you make a short, mild descent to another junction with your route, the Over the Hill Trail, and a trail connecting with the High Sierra Trail. Veer right, taking the Over the Hill Trail, and begin a stiff climb up the hillside. Where the slope is open you have incredible views east, initially of the rugged terrain surrounding Lone Pine Creek canyon; later on, past an intervening stretch of forest, you have similarly dramatic vistas up the Hamilton Creek drainage. The grade eases as you traverse around the brow of

Ranger Lake and Twin Peaks

the slope through lush vegetation, and then descend amid thickening fir forest. After 2.1 miles, you reach a signed T-junction with the High Sierra Trail. The ranger station and Bearpaw High Sierra Camp lie approximately 200 yards to the left (east), while the lateral trail to the Bearpaw Meadow backpackers camp is about the same distance to the right (west).

On the next leg of your journey, you'll follow the famed High Sierra Trail (HST). Begin by making a switchbacking descent through a forest of sugar pines and firs to a bridged crossing of Buck Creek. You ascend the mostly open slope of Buck Canyon and then bend around to a twin-branched tributary with nice campsites complete with a bear box. Beyond, a long, rolling traverse leads across the north slope of the Middle Fork Kaweah River canyon, crossing several refreshing brooks along the way. Through periodic gaps in the forest, you have excellent views of the canyon and Little Blue Dome, Sugarbowl Dome, and Castle Rocks. At 4.6 miles from Bearpaw Meadow, you reach the Sevenmile Hill Trail junction.

From the junction, climb steeply up the Sevenmile Hill Trail for half a mile through thick stands of white fir and incense cedar to Mehrten Creek. Cross the creek and continue the unrelenting ascent, weaving your way uphill through Jeffrey pines and manzanita, and crossing two more invigorating branches of the creek. As the trail bends back to the west, the grade eases, and you make an ascending traverse back over the creek and some rills to a series of switchbacks that lead up to the Alta Trail, 2.1 miles and 1300 feet from the HST. Campsites at Merhten Meadow are just a short quarter of a mile descent east of the junction.

Turn west at the junction and follow the Alta Trail down a series of short switchbacks to a spring-fed rivulet. Proceed across the south-facing open hillside, enjoying views of the Middle Fork Kaweah River canyon along the way. One mile from the junction, you reach a T-junction at Panther Gap (8520′±).

Leave the Alta Trail at Panther Gap by heading north on a short, moderate descent into the Wolverton Creek drainage. As you reach the valley floor, you proceed past meadows, lush foliage, and wildflower-lined tributaries, following the creek northwest downstream. Nearly a mile from Panther Gap, you encounter a junction with the Lakes Trail.

Follow the Lakes Trail for 1.6 miles, continuing roughly parallel to Wolverton Creek, first northwest and then west on a mild-to-moderate descent to a pair of T-junctions. From the first junction a trail heads southeast to circle Long Meadow, while from the second junction a path heads south to the Wolverton trailhead parking area. You continue straight ahead (west) at both junctions, following signs marked LODGEPOLE. As the descending trail bends south, you hear the roar of Wolverton Creek and come to an old roadbed, half a mile from the junctions. Turn right and follow the road 1.25 miles to the parking area at Lodgepole.

O This trip offers options for returning to trailheads other than Lodgepole. If the shuttle-bus system is operational, or if you can arrange for someone to pick you up, you can travel west on the HST from Bearpaw Meadow to any of a variety of trailheads in Giant Forest. To a return to Crescent Meadow via the HST to Crescent Meadow (11 miles), reverse the description in Trips 30 and 32. A fine network of trails makes added excursions to a variety of scenic destinations quite possible. If time allows, perhaps the most coveted trip extension would be a visit to Hamilton Lakes and Nine Lakes Basin (see Trip 32).

R **PERMITS:** Wilderness permit required for overnight stays. (Quota: 30 per day)

CAMPFIRES: Not permitted at Twin Lakes, Tamarack Lake, or Bearpaw Meadow.

CAMPING: Restricted to designated sites at Bearpaw Meadow.

TRIP **48**

Wuksachi Trail

Ⓜ ⬈ **DH**

DISTANCE: 1.5 miles to Twin Lakes Trail

ELEVATION: 7025/6890/7230, +220'/-430'

SEASON: Late June to mid-October

USE: Light

MAP: *Lodgepole* (trail not shown on map)

INTRODUCTION: A newly constructed trail with a pair of impressive bridges over Clover and Silliman creeks takes hikers on a secluded forest walk between Wuksachi Village and the Twin Lakes Trail. What little traffic the trail receives is usually from guests of the village out for a stroll, but backpackers headed up the Twin Lakes Trail can save a few hundred feet of elevation gain by starting at the Wuksachi trailhead rather than Lodgepole. An easy, mostly downhill, 3-mile extension to this hike, connecting Wuksachi with Lodgepole, makes a good day hike, but requires a shuttle. See Trip 46 for other feasible trips via the connection with the Twin Lakes Trail.

DIRECTIONS TO THE TRAILHEAD: Leave the Generals Highway 1.5 miles north of the Lodgepole turnoff and turn north toward Wuksachi Village. Follow the road past the village center to the last parking area, in an undeveloped section of the village. The trailhead is at the far end of the parking area.

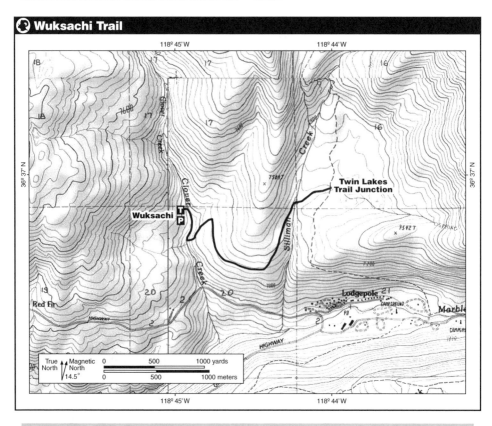

DESCRIPTION: A small sign marked TWIN LAKES 7.3, LODGEPOLE 3.1 is all that marks the trailhead. You head into a moderate cover of fir forest, quickly reaching a set of three switchbacks that take you downhill to a bridge across Clover Creek, which flows through a rocky gorge into a series of pools. A ways beyond the bridge, another set of switchbacks leads up the forested slope. You make an arcing traverse across the hillside into drier vegetation, where Jeffrey pine and manzanita enter the mix. The forest thins enough to allow a momentary view across the Lodgepole area to Wolverton Ridge. You curve into the Silliman Creek drainage and cross the stream at another newly constructed bridge. Silliman Creek is the domestic water supply for Lodgepole, so swimming, camping, fishing, and picnicking are not allowed. You follow the gentle trail along a tributary stream that drains Willow Meadow to a junction with the Twin Lakes Trail, 1.5 miles from Lodgepole.

Introduction to Dorst Creek

The main attraction of this heavily wooded area is Dorst Creek Campground, where a handful of trails lead day hikers on wooded journeys through some of the quietest parts of the park. Covered mainly with red and white firs, this stretch of Sequoia National Park contains some excellent sequoia groves as well. The most easily accessed stand is the Lost Grove, straddling the Generals Highway 2.5 miles north of the campground. However, one of the best sequoia groves in Sequoia or Kings Canyon national park, the Muir Grove, is tucked away from the road down a serene 2-mile trail. Trees are not all that's to be found around Dorst Creek, as a 1.75-mile path takes hikers to a vista point atop Little Baldy.

The creek and campground were named for Joseph Haddox Dorst (1852–1916), captain of the 4th Calvary, who was the first superintendent of Sequoia National Park.

Circle Grove, Muir Grove Trail

Campgrounds

Campground	Fee	Elevation	Season	Restrooms	Running Water	Bear Boxes	Phone
DORST CREEK	$16	6800′	Memorial Day to Labor Day	Flush Toilets	Yes	Yes	Yes

ACCESS: *(Subject to winter closures)* The Dorst Creek area has straightforward access from the Generals Highway during spring, summer and fall. Snow may close the highway during winter between the Y-intersection with Highway 180 and the gate north of Wuksachi. Dorst Creek Campground is 28.9 miles from the Ash Mountain Entrance and 17.3 miles from the Y.

AMENITIES: The nearest services are at Lodgepole (8.1 miles) and Grant Grove (17.6 miles). The closest lodging is to the south at Wuksachi or to the north at Stony Creek Village, Montecito-Sequoia Resort, and Grant Grove.

RANGER STATION: Lodgepole or Grant Grove.

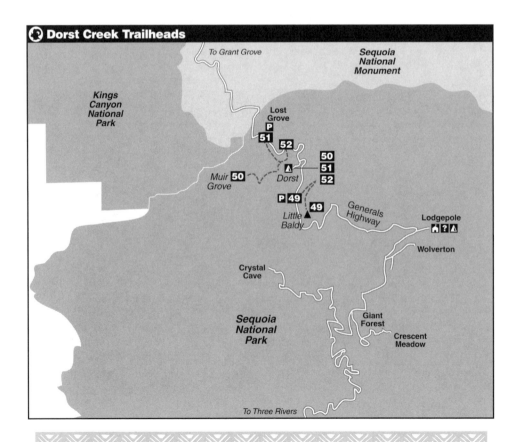

DORST CREEK TRAILHEADS

TRIP **49**

Little Baldy

Ⓜ ↗ DH

DISTANCE: 1.75 miles

ELEVATION: 7335/8044, +735´/-85´

SEASON: June to mid-October

USE: Moderate

MAP: *Giant Forest*

INTRODUCTION: Any excellent vista that requires less than a 4-mile hike should lure hikers who have the luxury of a couple of hours to spare. The moderate climb to the top of Little Baldy follows a well-graded

trail to arguably one of the western Sierra's supreme views. So expansive is the panorama that the Park Service used to maintain a fire lookout at the summit. Make sure you begin the hike with a full bottle of water, as none is available anywhere near the trail. In spite of this minor drawback, a few parties each year spend the night on top of Little Baldy, drawn by incomparable sunsets and fine stargazing.

DIRECTIONS TO THE TRAILHEAD: Follow the Generals Highway to Little Baldy Saddle, 6.6 miles north of the Lodgepole turnoff and 17 miles south of the Y-intersection with Highway 180. Park along the shoulder of the highway as space allows.

DESCRIPTION: Begin your journey by walking up the hillside through a light mixed forest, predominantly comprised of red fir with a smattering of Jeffrey pine. After

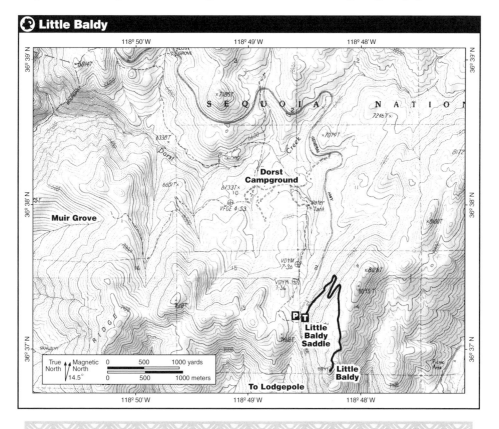

quickly reaching a pair of switchbacks, you proceed on a steady, moderate climb as the trail slices northeast across the steep hillside, roughly paralleling the highway below. As you climb, you have occasional glimpses of Big Baldy to the northwest through sporadic gaps in the forest. Directly in front are the craggy spires of Chimney Rock. Farther up the hillside, three more switchbacks lead to easier hiking along the ridgecrest. You follow the path through pockets of forest, manzanita, and oak, toward the rocky summit. A short, rocky climb leads to the top and the extraordinary view.

From the summit of Little Baldy, hikers are treated to a splendid vista of the Great Western Divide, plus Castle Rocks and the valley of Mineral King to the southeast. To the southwest is a rugged, remote portion of Sequoia National Park, where a once-prominent network of trails has mostly disappeared over the years, due to lack of maintenance and encroachment from the thick brush that is so common to the foothills.

DORST CREEK TRAILHEADS

TRIP 50

Muir Grove

Ⓜ ↗ DH

DISTANCE: 2.1 miles

ELEVATION: 6715/6800, +530′/-515′

SEASON: June through October

USE: Light

MAP: *Muir Grove*

INTRODUCTION: A rare gem, Muir Grove is tucked away from the hordes of tourists who frequent the more popular giant sequoia groves. The 1-mile drive from the Generals Highway through Dorst Campground and the 2-mile hike into the grove mean that diligent hikers can appreciate these massive trees in relative seclusion. If John Muir himself were alive to see any of the natural features that currently bear his name, he almost certainly would enjoy the peace and quiet in this grove of stately trees.

DIRECTIONS TO THE TRAILHEAD: Follow Generals Highway to the entrance into Dorst Campground, 17.3 miles southeast of the Y-junction with Highway 180 and 8 miles northwest of the Lodgepole turnoff. Proceed on the main access road through the campground 0.9 mile to the trailhead and continue along the road to the amphitheater parking lot.

DESCRIPTION: Begin your hike by walking back down the access road from the amphitheater parking lot to the start of the trail near a small metal sign marked MUIR GROVE TRAIL. Immediately, you cross a delightful tributary of Dorst Creek on a log bridge and then begin a mild descent to a signed trail junction. Turn sharply left at the junction and traverse around a hillside well above the main channel of Dorst

Creek to the crossing of another tributary stream, 0.6 mile from the trailhead.

A moderate ascent augmented by a pair of switchbacks follows, leading to the crest of a ridge and an exposed granite hump, where you have a fine view of Chimney Rock, Big Baldy, and the densely forested drainages of Stony and Dorst creeks. The confluence of these two streams, amid rugged and virtually inaccessible terrain, is the birthplace of the North Fork Kaweah River. Careful observation will reveal the crowns of giant sequoias protruding above the rest of the forest directly across the canyon. You proceed in and out of a mixed forest of firs, pines, and cedars on a slightly undulating traverse to a flower-lined stream, 1.5 miles from the trailhead.

Follow the trail on a mild ascent up to the top of the ridge, passing pockets of azalea and small groves of dogwood along the way. You reach the first of the Big Trees, a pair of burned remnants, and a massive sequoia that stands just off the trail.

A short distance farther is perhaps the highlight of the Muir Grove, a circle of 12 to 15 giant sequoias arranged in a nearly symmetrical pattern. Standing within this ring of Goliaths creates a reverent awe aptly fitting for such a grand cathedral. Short, faint paths lead away to other sequoias scattered about the grove, but the old trail that continued on to Skagway Grove, Hidden Spring, and the North Fork Kaweah River is overgrown and very hard to follow.

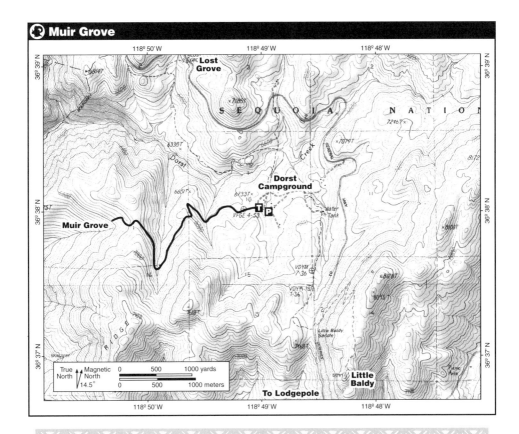

DORST CREEK TRAILHEADS

TRIP 51

Lost Grove to Dorst Campground

E / DH

DISTANCE: 2.3 miles

ELEVATION: 6645/6245/6665, +555'/-535'

SEASON: May to mid-October

USE: Light

MAP: *Muir Grove*

INTRODUCTION: This pleasant hike begins at Lost Grove, where hundreds of giant sequoias live within the grove's 50-plus acres. Unfortunately, the Lost Grove Trail visits only a fraction of the Big Trees, and quickly leaves the majesty of the stately monarchs to visit refreshing streams, rills, and verdant pocket meadows on the way to Dorst Campground.

Relatively quiet year-round, after Dorst Campground closes for the season in early September, this trip potentially offers a large dose of solitude, but requires nearly an extra mile of hiking up the access road to reach a vehicle-accessible location on Generals Highway at the closed entrance to the campground. For a fine extension to your trip, an unmarked path just before the campground provides a connection to the Muir Grove Trail.

No one seems to remember how this grove became lost in the first place, or how it was found again. Prior to the creation of

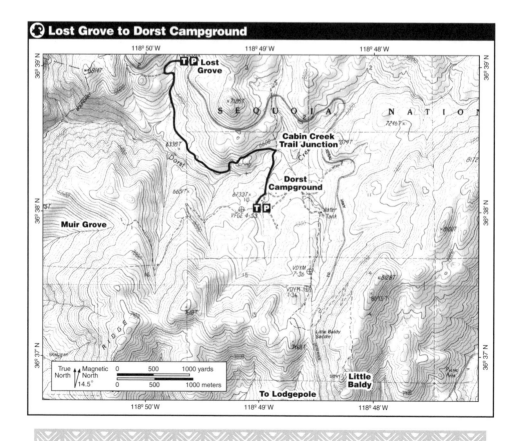

Mountain wildflowers

Roslyn Bullas

Kings Canyon National Park in 1940, Lost Grove housed the old entrance station to Sequoia National Park.

DIRECTIONS TO THE TRAILHEAD:

START: Follow Generals Highway to the Lost Grove parking area, 10.2 miles from Lodgepole and 14.7 miles from the Y-intersection with Highway 180.

END: Follow Generals Highway to the entrance into Dorst Campground, 8 miles from the Lodgepole turnoff and 17.3 miles from the Y-intersection with Highway 180. Proceed on the main access road through the campground approximately 0.8 mile, turn onto the Group Campground road, and drive to the trailhead parking area near the northeast end of parking area B.

DESCRIPTION: The signed trail begins below the south side of the highway, near the restroom building. First, zigzag steeply down the fern-carpeted hillside through mixed forest containing a nice collection of giant sequoias. You quickly cross a tiny tributary of Dorst Creek and, at 0.3 mile, reach an unsigned junction. The seldom-used trail to your right ends 0.5 mile to the west at the Generals Highway near the

park boundary. You continue downhill through more ferns and azaleas and come back alongside the tributary for a spell, before crossing a rivulet near a small pocket meadow. Soon, you cross a pair of tiny streamlets near the upper end of a thin band of meadow and, after a short while, leave the lush ground cover behind.

An ascending traverse through drier vegetation follows, which eventually leads to a junction with the Cabin Creek Trail at 2.0 miles. A short drop takes you to willow-lined Dorst Creek, which can be successfully crossed with the aid of boulders and logs. Use caution in early season, when the stream is at full force. Past the creek, climb up the slope and come above an appealing little tributary stream that you'll follow to the campground. A short moderate climb brings you to an unsigned junction with a path to the right, which wraps around the hill shown as *6733T* on the *Muir Grove* topo map. This trail, which doesn't appear on the 1993 map, connects to the Muir Grove Trail a quarter of a mile below the campground. From the junction, you continue the climb to Dorst Creek Campground.

DORST CREEK TRAILHEADS

TRIP **52**

Cabin Creek Trail

ⓔ **↗** **DH**

DISTANCE: 0.8 mile to Dorst Campground

ELEVATION: 6710/6545/6665, +165′/-120′

SEASON: May to mid-October

USE: Light

MAP: *Muir Grove*

INTRODUCTION: The short trail down Cabin Creek and on to Dorst Campground won't knock your socks off with stunning vistas, but for an easy stroll through a serene forest with few people it can't be beat. The route makes an excellent diversion if you're staying at the campground.

DIRECTIONS TO THE TRAILHEAD:

START: Follow Generals Highway to Cabin Creek, 9.1 miles from the Lodgepole turnoff and 14.1 from the Y-intersection with Highway 180. Park on the south shoulder to the west of the bridge as space allows.

END: Follow Generals Highway to the entrance into Dorst Campground, 8 miles from the Lodgepole turnoff and 17.3 miles from the Y-intersection with Highway 180. Proceed on the main access road through the campground approximately 0.8 mile, turn onto the Group Campground road, and drive to the trailhead parking area near the northeast end of parking area B.

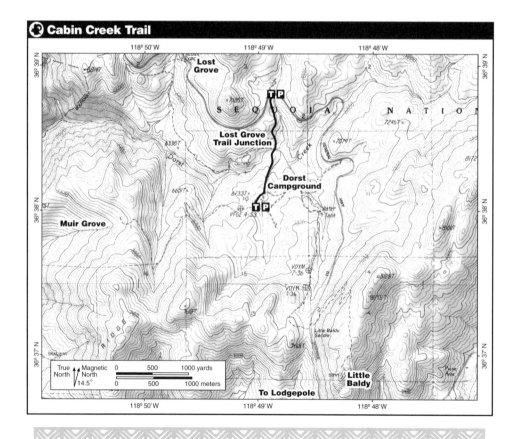

DESCRIPTION: Find the unmarked trail just below the turnout on the south shoulder, west of the bridge. Head downstream through light, mixed forest, following the course of Cabin Creek, which puts on a frothy display in early summer. Nearly a half mile from the road, you reach a junction with the Lost Grove Trail and make a brief descent to the low point of your journey at willow-lined Dorst Creek, where you'll find good pools for fishing or swimming.

An ascending traverse through drier vegetation follows, which eventually leads to a junction with the Cabin Creek Trail. A short drop takes you to willow-lined Dorst Creek, which can be successfully crossed with the aid of boulders and logs. Use caution in early season, when the stream is at full force. Past the creek, climb up the slope and come above an appealing little tributary stream that you'll follow to the campground. A short moderate climb brings you to an unsigned junction with a path to the right, which wraps around the hill shown as 6733T on the Muir Grove topo map. This trail, which doesn't appear on the 1993 map, connects to the Muir Grove Trail a quarter of a mile below the campground. From the junction, you continue the climb to Dorst Creek Campground.

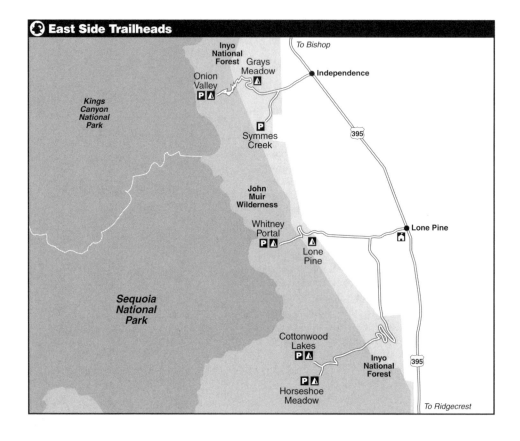

CHAPTER 5

East Side Trips

In sharp contrast to the gradually rising terrain on the west side of the Sierra, the east side rapidly catapults itself from the floor of Owens Valley, sharply upward toward the crest of the range. This massive wall of mountains can look like an impenetrable barrier to a wee, small individual staring upward thousands of feet from the western lip of the Great Basin to the spine of the Sierra. East side trails assume one of two approaches, either abandoning all possibility of crossing the range to follow raucous streams up the steep cleft of a dead-end canyon, or attacking the towering east face of the Sierra on a steep, protracted climb toward a handful of high passes where the crest dips to around 11,000 or 12,000 feet. No easy approach to the backcountry will be found from this side; the principal reward of an eastern approach is the shorter distance required to access the alpine heights of the High Sierra.

The high and rugged terrain on Sequoia National Park's east boundary has limited the number of trailheads to just four. Consequently, wilderness permit quotas tend to fill up very quickly. Hikers without an advanced reservation should try to begin their trip on a weekday rather than a weekend to allow themselves a better shot at securing a wilderness permit, especially if their sights are set on Mt. Whitney.

High Lake from the New Army Pass Trail

Introduction to Mt. Whitney Ranger District

The eastern escarpment of the Sierra Nevada spans the Mt. Whitney Ranger District and contains some of the region's most noteworthy scenery. The majestic east face of the Mt. Whitney group towers above the community of Lone Pine, more than 10,000 feet below. The Alabama Hills, near the base of the Mt. Whitney group, has been the location for filming a plethora of Hollywood movies. While this terrain is quite impressive when viewed from the window of a car or on the celluloid of a movie reel, the real splendor of the Mt. Whitney area is available only to those who venture into the backcountry via trail.

Certainly the majority of trail users focus on Mt. Whitney, as hundreds of hikers and backpackers leave Whitney Portal each day bound for the summit of the lower 48's highest peak. However, by concentrating only on the peak itself and ignoring the vast remaining terrain, these travelers miss out on some of the most impressive scenery in the High Sierra.

Other than the relatively gentle crossings at Cottonwood and New Army passes, at the extreme southern end, the nearly impenetrable wall of the Sierra crest within the Whitney district remains untarnished by any road. It is successfully surmounted by only five trails, two of which are unmaintained and have been virtually abandoned by the Forest and Park services. These 14,000-foot peaks lure not only backpackers, but mountaineers, technical climbers, and cross-country enthusiasts from all over the globe.

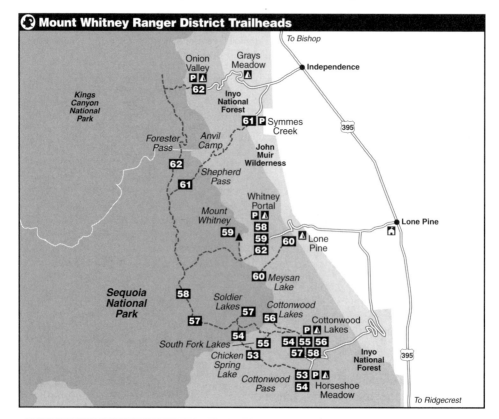

Mount Whitney Ranger District Trailheads

David Disbrow

Tarn at Trail Camp, Mt. Whitney Trail

West of the Whitney spine, a horseshoe-shaped ring of peaks incorporating the Sierra crest, Kings-Kern Divide, Great Western Divide, and Kaweah Peaks Ridge, defines some of the most remote and expansive backcountry in the Sierra. The deep gorge of the Kern River cleaves the middle of this arc, flowing through a lengthy, glacier-smoothed, Yosemite-like cleft on its way to the less restrictive terrain of the San Joaquin Valley. In the 6 miles between the summit of Mt. Whitney and the bottom of the Kern Trench, the elevation drops 7500 feet. This region is filled with myriad peaks, majestic canyons, wildflower-filled meadows, beautiful subalpine and alpine lakes, rushing streams, and gorgeous vistas that even the most discriminating wilderness traveler will enjoy.

ACCESS: The north-south thoroughfare of U.S. Highway 395 is the principal access route for all eastside trips. Secondary roads branch off the highway toward the trailheads.

AMENITIES: The small towns of Lone Pine and Independence provide basic services to travelers on U.S. 395 and recreationists visiting the eastern Sierra, offering motels, cafes, general stores, and gas stations. A very limited selection of outdoor equipment retailers sell mainly fishing and camping supplies.

The Whitney Portal Store and Café, located near the Whitney Portal trailhead, has been serving hikers, backpackers, climbers, and tourists for many years. Along with the typical cafe fare, which tastes really great after a stint in the wilderness, the store offers showers, souvenirs, and backcountry supplies, and the lowest price around for bear canisters.

SHUTTLE SERVICE: The following companies offer a trailhead shuttle service: Inyo-Mono Dial-A-Ride (800) 922-1930 or (760) 872-1901, Kountry Korners (877) 656-0756 or (760) 872-3951), and Sierra Express (760) 924-8294).

BUS SERVICE: Greyhound makes stops in both Lone Pine and Independence.

OUTFITTERS: The following pack stations operate trips into this region:

Mt. Whitney Pack Trains
PO Box 248
Bishop, CA 93515
(760) 872-8331
www.rockcreekpackstation.com

Cottonwood Pack Station
Star Route 1, Box 81-A
Independence, CA 93526
(760) 878-2015

Sequoia Kings Pack Trains
PO Box 209
Independence, CA 93526
(760) 387-2797 or (800) 962-0775
www.sequoiakingspacktrains.com/

RANGER STATION: The Inyo National Forest's Mt. Whitney Ranger Station is located in Lone Pine, on U.S. 395, south of the junction with the Whitney Portal Road. You can pick up reserved and walk-in wilderness permits during normal office hours, and purchase or rent bear canisters. A broad selection of books and maps is also for sale.

WILDERNESS PERMITS: Quotas are in effect between May 1 and November 1. While 60% of the quota is available by advance reservation, the remaining 40% is available on a first-come, first-served basis (no fee). A non-refundable, $5 per person fee is required for each member of your party for advance reservations. You can make reservations up to 6 months before your trip.

Campgrounds

Campground	Fee	Elevation	Season	Restrooms	Running Water	Bear Boxes	Phone
COTTONWOOD PASS (walk-in)	$6	10,000'	Late-May to mid-October	Vault Toilets	Yes	Yes	Yes
GOLDEN TROUT (walk-in)	$6	10000'	Late-May to mid-October	Vault Toilets	Yes	Yes	Yes
TUTTLE CREEK (BLM)	free	4000'	March to November	Vault Toilets	No	No	No
PORTAGEE JOE (Inyo Co.)	$10	3800'	Open All Year	Vault Toilets	Yes	No	Yes
LONE PINE	$12	6000'	Late April to mid-October	Pit Toilets	Yes	No	No
WHITNEY PORTAL	$14	8000'	Late-May to mid-October	Flush Toilets	Yes	Yes	Yes
WHITNEY TRAILHEAD (walk-in, 1-night limit)	$6	8300'	Late-May to mid-October	Flush Toilets	Yes	Yes	Yes
INDEPENDENCE CREEK (Inyo Co.)	$10	3800'	Open All Year	Flush Toilets	Yes	No	No
LOWER GRAYS MEADOW	$11	5200'	Mid-March to mid-October	Vault Toilets	Yes	No	Yes
UPPER GRAYS MEADOW	$11	5900'	Late May to November	Vault Toilets	Yes	No	No
ONION VALLEY	$11	9200'	Early June to early October	Vault Toilets	Yes	Yes	No
OAK CREEK	$11	5000'	Open All Year	Vault Toilets	Yes	No	No

For wilderness permits, call the reservation line at (760) 873-2483. You can also fax your application and fee at (760) 873-2484, or by regular mail to this address:

Inyo National Forest
Wilderness Permit Office
873 North Main Street
Bishop, CA 93514

You can pick up permits reserved in advance at the ranger station the day before departure.

For more information, visit the website at www.r5.fs.fed.us/inyo/.

MT. WHITNEY ZONE PERMITS: Different rules apply for permits to use the Mt. Whitney Trail. Both day hikers and backpackers must have a valid permit.

GOOD TO KNOW BEFORE YOU GO:

1. Both day hikers and backpackers must have a valid Whitney Zone permit for authorized travel on the Mt. Whitney Trail past Lone Pine Lake. These permits are in high demand, the majority distributed through a lottery. See the introduction to Trip 59 for more specific information.

2. The Onion Valley and Whitney Portal areas are notorious for bear activity and space in bear lockers is at a premium. As at all trailheads, don't leave any food or scented items in your vehicle while parked overnight at the trailheads. The authorities require backpackers on the Mt. Whitney Trail and on the Kearsarge Pass Trail west of Kearsarge Pass to carry bear canisters.

HORSESHOE MEADOW TRAILHEAD

TRIP 53

Chicken Spring Lake

Ⓜ ✒ DH / BP

DISTANCE: 4.1 miles one way

ELEVATION: 9935/11,245, +1400′/-90′

SEASON: Mid-July to mid-October

USE: Moderate

MAP: Cirque Peak

INTRODUCTION: Aside from the .75-mile switchbacking climb to Cottonwood Pass, the grade of this trip to Chicken Spring Lake is mild, providing backpackers and dayhikers with a relatively easy 4-mile trip to a scenic destination. Solitude is in short supply at picturesque lakes along the Pacific Crest Trail (PCT), especially those close to a trailhead, but Chicken Spring Lake at least offers more seclusion than the nearby Cottonwood Lakes. Note that this entire trip takes place outside the national park boundaries.

DIRECTIONS TO THE TRAILHEAD: In the heart of Lone Pine, turn west from U.S. 395 onto Whitney Portal Road and proceed 3 miles to the left turn onto Horseshoe Meadow Road. Head south for 18.5 miles, past the turnoff to the Cottonwood Pass trailhead, to the parking lot at the Horseshoe Meadow trailhead. Nearby you will find bathrooms, running water and a walk-in campground (one-night limit).

DESCRIPTION: The well-signed trail begins at an interpretive display board near the restrooms. You start walking on an easy grade on wide, sandy trail through scattered lodgepole and foxtail pines with very little ground cover. Shortly you cross the boundary of the Golden Trout Wilderness and encounter a junction with trails heading south to Trail Pass and north to the pack station. Continue straight ahead (west) from the junction, along the northern fringe of expansive Horseshoe Meadow. Although the grade is nearly level, traveling along sections of the well-used, horse-trod, sandy path is akin to trudging through beach sand. As the forest thickens, you come alongside and then cross a stream. On the far bank, a use-trail leads to a dilapidated cabin, where camping is prohibited. The trail quickly recrosses the stream, leaves Horseshoe Meadow behind, and begins a more moderate ascent. A series of switchbacks leads up a rock-strewn hillside adjacent to a willow-lined drainage. Eventually, the zigzagging path brings you to Cottonwood Pass (11,200′±), 3.4 miles from the trailhead. You have excellent views of Horseshoe Meadow below, backdropped nicely by the Panamint and Inyo mountains to the east and the southern extremity of the Great Western Divide to the west.

A short distance beyond the pass, you come to a junction with the PCT and the path to Big Whitney Meadow. Following signed directions to ROCK CREEK, turn right and follow the PCT on an easy half a mile traverse to Chicken Spring Lake's seasonal outlet. Leave the PCT and follow a use-trail upstream to the south shore of the lake (11,242′).

Tucked into a cirque bowl, the lake is nearly surrounded by rugged granite cliffs. The shoreline is dotted with foxtail pines, with several weather-beaten snags adding character to the postcard scene. You'll find several good campsites in patches of sand around a bay on the south side near the outlet and in the scattered trees above the west shore. A use-trail nearly encircles the open shoreline, providing access for anglers and swimmers.

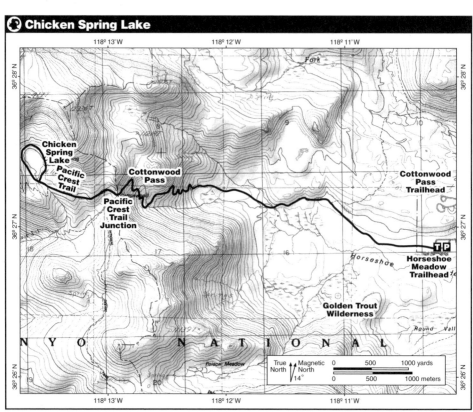

Chicken Spring Lake

O A visit to Chicken Spring Lake presents possibilities of side trips to Stokes Stringer Creek, Big Whitney Meadows, and Rocky Basin Lakes. A relatively straightforward loop heads over Siberian Pass from the west side of Big Whitney Meadow to a connect with the PCT, and then goes east toward Chicken Spring Lake.

R **PERMITS:** Wilderness permit required for overnight stays. (Quota: 40 per day)

CAMPFIRES: Not allowed at Chicken Spring Lake.

HORSESHOE MEADOW TRAILHEAD

TRIP **54**

Cottonwood Pass and New Army Pass Loop

Ⓜ ◯ BP

DISTANCE: 19 miles

ELEVATION: 9935/12,315/9935, +4115′/-4115′

SEASON: Mid-July to mid-October

USE: Moderate to heavy

MAPS: *Cirque Peak, Johnson Peak, Mt. Whitney*

TRAIL LOG:

4.1	Chicken Spring Lake
9.0	Rock Creek Trail Jct.
11.5	New Army Pass
12.5	High Lake
15.75	Cottonwood Lakes Trail Jct.

INTRODUCTION: Strong backpackers may be able to complete this loop in a weekend, but the sublime High Sierra terrain invites those with more time to enjoy the vistas, lakes, canyons, and flower-sprinkled meadows along the southeastern fringe of Sequoia National Park.

Anglers will enjoy fishing for golden trout in many of the lakes and streams along the way.

DIRECTIONS TO THE TRAILHEAD: In the heart of Lone Pine, turn west from U.S. 395 onto Whitney Portal Road and proceed 3 miles to the left turn onto Horseshoe Meadow Road. Head south for 18.5 miles, past the turnoff to the Cottonwood Pass trailhead, to the parking lot at the Horseshoe Meadow trailhead. Nearby you will find bathrooms, running water and a walk-in campground (one-night limit).

DESCRIPTION: The well-signed trail begins at a display board near the restrooms. You start walking on an easy grade, and shortly you cross the boundary of the Golden Trout Wilderness and encounter a junction with trails heading south to Trail Pass and north to the pack station. Continue straight ahead (west) from the junction, along the northern fringe of expansive Horseshoe Meadow. Travel along sections of the well-used, horse-trod, sandy path. As the forest thickens, you come alongside and then cross a stream. On the far bank, a use-trail leads to a dilapidated cabin, where camping is prohibited. The trail quickly recrosses the stream, leaves Horseshoe Meadow behind, and begins a more moderate ascent. A series of switchbacks leads up a rock-strewn hillside. Eventually, the zigzagging path brings you to Cottonwood Pass (11,200′±), 3.4 miles from the trailhead. You have excellent views of Horseshoe Meadow below and Inyo mountains to the east and the southern extremity of the Great Western Divide to the west.

A short distance beyond the pass, you come to a junction with the PCT and the path to Big Whitney Meadow. Following signed directions to ROCK CREEK, turn right and follow the PCT on an easy half a mile traverse to Chicken Spring Lake's seasonal outlet. Leave the PCT and follow a use-trail upstream to the south shore of the lake (11,242′).

Tucked into a cirque bowl, the lake is nearly surrounded by rugged granite cliffs. The shoreline is dotted with foxtail pines, with several weather-beaten snags adding character to the postcard scene. You'll find several good campsites in patches of sand around a bay on the south side near the outlet and in the scattered trees above the west shore. A use-trail nearly encircles the open shoreline, providing access for anglers 〰 and swimmers.

From Chicken Spring Lake, retrace your steps to the Pacific Crest Trail (PCT). Continue northbound on a moderate ascent to the crest of a ridge above the west side of the lake, where you have fine views of Big

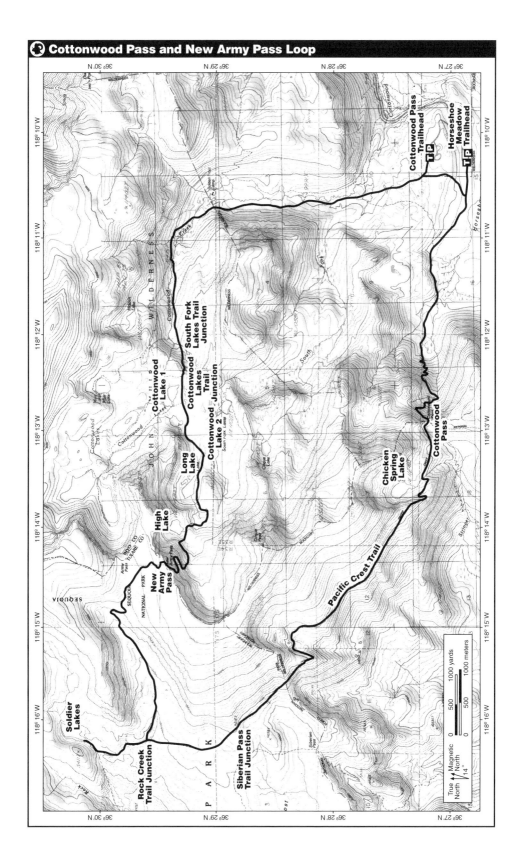

Cabin at Horseshoe Meadow, Cottonwood Lakes Trail

Whitney Meadow and the Great Western Divide. A mildly descending traverse on a sandy trail through scattered foxtail pine follows, eventually skirting a verdant meadow with a seasonal tarn. You wrap around the base of some cliffs and make a short climb to a vista point, where you have good views of Siberian Outpost, Mt. Kaweah and the Great Western Divide, as well as some of the craggy peaks near the Sierra crest above Rock Creek.

A short distance farther, you reach the boundary of Sequoia National Park, 7.5 miles from the trailhead, and continue the traverse across the lightly forested hillside to a junction. The lightly used Siberian Pass Trail heads south to the pass, the PCT continues west, and your path veers uphill to the right toward Rock Creek. Proceed northwest as the trail descends gently and then more steeply. At the 9-mile mark, you ford a meadow-lined tributary and quickly arrive at a junction with the New Army Pass Trail.

[O] **SIDE TRIP TO SOLDIER LAKES:** Instead of immediately heading east toward New Army Pass, continue northbound toward Soldier Lakes. You pass a thin strip of meadow to a signed lateral, which leads to pine-shaded campsites with a bear box on a low rise above the outlet from the lakes. A short distance farther, you boulder-hop the outlet and encounter another signed junction with the path to the lakes.

Follow the fringe of a thin band of flower-filled meadow through scattered pines to the southern tip of Lower Soldier Lake (10,805′±), three-quarters of a mile from the junction with the New Army Pass Trail. The boot-beaten path continues along the west edge of the lake. To reach the pine-shaded campsites, cross the outlet just below the lake via some well-placed rocks and logs and follow a faint path along the east shore. Dramatically framed by the towering walls of the Major General, Lower Soldier Lake reposes in a scenic cirque. Anglers should enjoy fishing for the resident golden trout. A short, steep cross-country jaunt from the north shore leads up the east side of the cirque to the secluded upper lake. Off-trail enthusiasts will discover that the Soldier Lakes are the

gateway to some of the southern Sierra's grandest scenery (such as that described in Trip 57). To continue the loop, retrace your steps back to the New Army Pass Trail.
END OF SIDE TRIP

From the junction, head east on a moderate climb through scattered lodgepole and foxtail pines, along the edge of a verdant, flower-bedecked meadow. As you continue upstream, the trees start to thin, and you emerge into a wide-open, boulder-dotted basin rimmed by rocky cliffs and ridges. After a lengthy, steady climb, you reach the pass, which is not at the low spot (Army Pass), but is 700 feet higher and 0.4 mile south. The new trail was built to avoid the old pass, which is buried by snow for much of the season and prone to rockfall. Eventually, you wind your way up to New Army Pass (12,315′±), 11.5 miles from the trailhead. Fine views of the Cottonwood Lakes and the Cottonwood Creek drainage invite you to linger at the pass while you catch your breath.

Descend rocky switchbacks from the pass to High Lake and then reverse the description in Trip 55 toward the Cottonwood Lakes trailhead. Before reaching the trailhead at the parking lot, watch for a signed Y-junction just before the wilderness boundary, where a path heads toward the pack station. Follow this trail through the pack station and continue south toward a junction with the New Army Pass Trail. From there, head east a short distance to the trailhead at the Horseshoe Meadow parking area.

[O] From Lower Soldier Lake, a faint use-trail leads knapsackers up the Rock Creek drainage to the unparalleled terrain of Miter Basin (see Trip 57).

Mountaineers may enjoy a straightforward class 1 ascent of Cirque Peak from New Army Pass.

[R] **PERMITS:** Wilderness permit required for overnight stays. (Quota: 40 per day)

CAMPFIRES: No fires at Chicken Spring Lake; no fires above 10,400 feet.

COTTONWOOD LAKES TRAILHEAD

TRIP **55**

New Army Pass Trail: South Fork, Cirque, Long, and High Lakes

E ✗ DH/BP

DISTANCE: 6.5 miles

ELEVATION: 10,040/11,483, +1650′/-215′

SEASON: Mid-July to early October

USE: Moderate to Heavy

MAP: *Cirque Peak*

TRAIL LOG:

3.25 New Army Pass Trail Jct.
4.33 South Fork Lakes Trail Jct.
5.75 Long Lake
6.5 High Lake

INTRODUCTION: Weekend backpackers enjoy a reasonably easy trip into a handful of scenic lakes along the New Army Pass and South Fork Lakes trails. Open, rock-strewn basins and grassy meadows permit fine views of the rugged eastern Sierra crest. Although the area is quite popular during the height of the season, Cirque Lake and some of the South Fork lakes receive relatively light use. Neighboring Cottonwood Lakes provide options for extending your visit beyond a weekend trip.

DIRECTIONS TO THE TRAILHEAD: In the heart of Lone Pine, turn west from U.S. 395 onto Whitney Portal Road and go 3 miles to the left turn onto Horseshoe Meadow Road. Proceed up this road 18 miles to a junction and turn right, following a sign for NEW ARMY PASS, COTTONWOOD LAKES. Pass the Cottonwood Lakes walk-in campground and continue to the Cottonwood Lakes trailhead parking area, 0.5 mile from the Horseshoe Meadow Road.

DESCRIPTION: The Cottonwood Lakes Trail begins auspiciously as a short, brick-lined path near the restroom building. Beyond the information signboard, you follow a gently graded, sandy trail slightly uphill, through widely scattered foxtail and lodgepole pines, where virtually no ground cover has taken root in the sandy soil. Soon you cross the Golden Trout Wilderness boundary, and then, quickly, you pass on your left a spur trail from the Cottonwood Lakes Pack Station. On an equally gentle descent you reach South Fork Cottonwood Creek, 1 mile from the trailhead, where some campsites appear on the far bank. The vegetation along the stream seems vibrantly green after the previous lack of plant life.

From the crossing, you climb gently through more scattered pines, soon meeting the main branch of Cottonwood Creek and following it up a broad valley for the next mile and a half. You leave the Golden Trout Wilderness and enter the John Muir Wilderness, beneath steep cliffs to your left and the wooden structures of the Golden Trout Camp across the meadow to your right.

Beyond the wilderness boundary, the trail curves west as you begin a more moderate climb up the narrowing canyon. Cross Cottonwood Creek on a beveled log, at 2.5 miles from the trailhead. A couple of campsites are near the crossing. In a light forest, you pass meadows lining the creek. Just after a crossing of a side stream, you reach the Y-junction between the Cottonwood Lakes Trail and New Army Pass Trail at 3.25 miles.

From the junction, veer left and quickly cross Cottonwood Creek. You climb moderately along the creek for a little over a mile to the junction with the South Fork

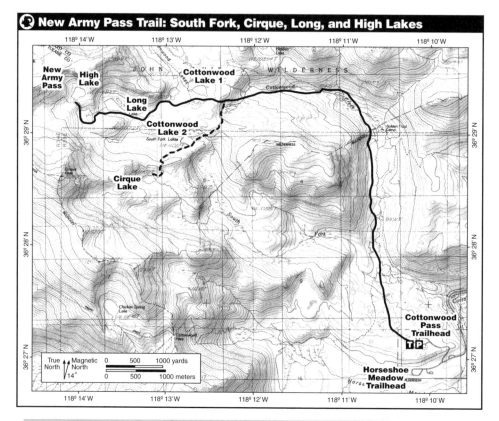

New Army Pass Trail: South Fork, Cirque, Long, and High Lakes

Lakes Trail, beside a large meadow 4.33 miles from the trailhead.

◻ **SIDE TRIP TO SOUTH FORK AND CIRQUE LAKES:** From the South Fork Lakes and New Army Pass trail junction, you head south along the edge of a sloping meadow lined with willows. Soon the trail bends southwest and you climb gently through scattered foxtail pines, followed by a brief descent to the crossing of the South Fork Cottonwood Creek. Beyond the creek, the trail cuts across a large meadow before reaching the easternmost South Fork Lake (11,200±). The roughly oval-shaped lake has a splendid backdrop of rocky ridges and craggy peaks. A few campsites appear on the hill above the southwest shore, near where the trail continues toward Cirque Lake.

To reach Cirque Lake (11,060±), you make a moderate climb through scattered foxtail pines to the top of a ridge. A short descent follows, which leads down to the northeast shore, 1.3 miles from the junction. Cirque Lake has a decidedly alpine feel at the base of steep cliffs below Cirque Peak. A few campsites are scattered around the sparsely forested shore, but seem more than adequate for the few adventurous souls who make it this far. **END OF SIDE TRIP**

Continue westbound from the South Fork Lakes and New Army Pass trail junction, climbing up a short hillside to another Y-junction. Keep heading west on the New Army Pass Trail, skirting the edge of the large meadow around Cottonwood Lake 1. Near the far end of the expansive meadow you pass Lake 2. Leaving the grassland and lakes behind, you make a short climb to a desolate area filled with large granite boulders. A few scattered pockets of pine are the only living things to gain a foothold in the sea of rocks. Eventually, you leave the desolate terrain behind as the mildly graded trail curves around a lightly forested hillside. Below, a meadow-lined, refreshing stream rushes down to the westernmost South Fork Lake (11,255±). A faint use-trail leads across the

stream to forested campsites between this lake and Long Lake above. A moderate climb leads up through thinning forest to the south shore of Long Lake (11,135´±), 5.75 miles from the trailhead. You'll find the best campsites beneath a stand of pines near the southeast shore, with a few less-protected sites above the north shore.

From the east shore of Long Lake the New Army Pass Trail begins a steeper traverse toward High Lake and the pass beyond. Through grasses, low-growing alpine vegetation, and widely scattered dwarf pines, you climb to timberline and then wind your way up rocky switchbacks to High Lake (11,510´±), 6.5 miles from the trailhead. The lake is set in a rocky, open bowl rimmed by steep cliffs. Campsites are extremely limited around the exposed lakeshore. For wide-ranging views, you can make the moderately graded, 1-mile climb from the lake up the long switchbacks to New Army Pass (12,340´) at the border of Sequoia National Park.

◻ Thanks to a network of trails and to open terrain that is easily traversed by cross-country travel, you can create a number of side trips to the lakes in Cottonwood Basin (see Trip 56). For a description of the continuation of the New Army Pass Trail to the Rock Creek area, see Trip 57.

Hopeful mountaineers can follow a strenuous but straightforward route from New Army Pass to the summit of Mt. Langley (14,042´), the southernmost 14,000-foot peak in the Sierra. Cirque Peak (12,900´) is also a non-technical climb, with a route from New Army Pass or from Cirque Lake.

ℝ **PERMITS:** Wilderness permit required for overnight stays. (Quota: 60 per day)

CAMPFIRES: Not allowed.

SPECIAL FISHING REGULATIONS: Catch-and-release at Cottonwood Lakes 1, 2, 3, and 4. All other lakes in the Cottonwood Lakes Basin are restricted to artificial lures or flies with barbless hooks; the limit is 5. Season is July 1 through October 31.

COTTONWOOD LAKES TRAILHEAD

TRIP **56**

Cottonwood Lakes

Ⓔ ↗ DH/BP

DISTANCE: 5.9 miles

ELEVATION: 10,040/11,160, +1450'/-295'

SEASON: Mid-July to early October

USE: Moderate to Heavy

MAPS: *Cirque Peak, Mt. Langley*

TRAIL LOG:

3.25 New Army Pass Trail Jct.
4.5 Muir Lake Trail Jct.
5.25 Lake 3
5.5 Lake 4
5.75 Lake 5

INTRODUCTION: Most of the journey to the Cottonwood Lakes is on a gently graded trail, with only 1.75 miles of the 4.5 miles of moderate climbing. The relatively easy trail, the outstanding scenery, and a notable golden-trout fishery combine to make the area a popular destination for hikers, backpackers, and anglers alike. However, solitude seekers should not despair, as the bounty of lakes disperses visitors around the basin. An extensive network of trails and straightforward cross-country routes makes for easy travel from one lake to another.

DIRECTIONS TO THE TRAILHEAD: In the heart of Lone Pine, turn west from U.S. 395 onto Whitney Portal Road and go 3 miles to the left turn onto Horseshoe Meadow Road. Proceed up this road 18 miles to a junction and turn right, following a sign for NEW ARMY PASS, COTTONWOOD LAKES. Pass the Cottonwood Lakes walk-in campground and continue to the Cottonwood Lakes trailhead parking area, 0.5 mile from the Horseshoe Meadow Road.

DESCRIPTION: The Cottonwood Lakes Trail begins auspiciously as a short, brick-lined path near the restroom building. Beyond the information signboard, you fol-

Junction, Cottonwood Lakes and New Army Pass trails

low a gently graded, sandy trail slightly uphill, and soon cross the Golden Trout Wilderness boundary, and then, quickly, you pass on your left a spur trail from the Cottonwood Lakes Pack Station. On an equally gentle descent you reach South Fork Cottonwood Creek, 1 mile from the trailhead, where some campsites appear on the far bank.

From the crossing, you climb gently through more scattered pines, soon meeting the main branch of Cottonwood Creek and following it up a broad valley for the next mile and a half. You leave the Golden Trout Wilderness and enter the John Muir Wilderness, beneath steep cliffs to your left and the wooden structures of the Golden Trout Camp across the meadow to your right.

Beyond the wilderness boundary, the trail curves west as you begin a more mod-erate climb up the narrowing canyon. Cross Cottonwood Creek on a beveled log, at 2.5 miles from the trailhead. A couple of camp-sites are near the crossing. In a light forest, you pass meadows lining the creek. Just after a crossing of a side stream, you reach the Y-junction between the Cottonwood Lakes Trail and New Army Pass Trail, at 3.25 miles.

From the junction, you veer right and continue up the Cottonwood Lakes Trail on a moderate climb through lodgepole-and-foxtail-pine forest. The ascent takes you well above the creek to a series of switchbacks. Through the trees you have periodic views up the canyon of Cirque Peak and the eastern Sierra crest. At 4.5 miles from the trailhead, you reach the signed junction with the Muir Lake Trail, at the eastern expanse of a large meadow and the lip of Cottonwood Lakes Basin.

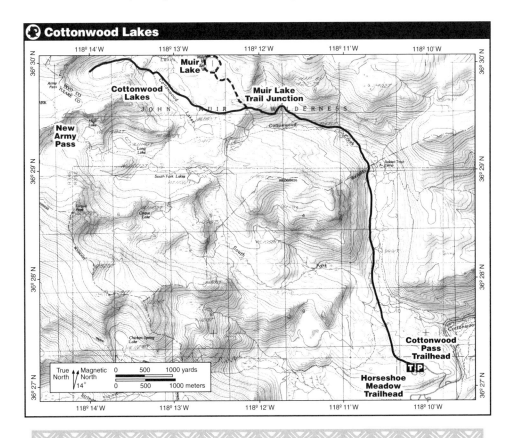

O SIDE TRIP TO MUIR LAKE: The beginning of the short trail to Muir Lake is a bit difficult to determine. The correct route from the junction is the faint path that skirts the northeast side of the meadow and then bends north to the lake, in spite of some indications that the trail heads northeast up the low hillside on your right (which is actually the beginning of a cross-country route to appropriately named Hidden Lake). Follow the trail around the meadows and then ascend north through pines and scattered boulders. Step over a flower-lined creeklet and continue to the lake. The path is hard to follow in places, but the lake is hard to miss, tucked into a horseshoe basin at the base of Peak 3913.

Muir Lake (11,010±) is quite scenic, with rugged cliffs surrounding the lakeshore and Mt. Langley as a backdrop. Judging by the condition of the trail, the lake seems to receive light use, in spite of very pleasant scenery and a choice of nice campsites nestled beneath scattered pines. **END OF SIDE TRIP**

From the Muir Lake junction, you continue west on a flat trail across the meadow, well to the right of Cottonwood Lake 1. The path soon bends northwest up a low, forested rise (where you'll find some campsites), and then crosses a stream and passes through grassy meadows dotted with boulders, clumps of willow, and widely scattered pines. The massive eastern wall of the Sierra crest dominates the surroundings. You pass a corrugated metal shed on your left and a small tarn to the right before reaching willow-rimmed Lake 3 (11,075'), 5.25 miles from the trailhead. Look for additional campsites on the forested rise between Lakes 3 and 4 to the left.

At the far end of Lake 3, you briefly skirt a meadow and then wind your way on an easy course through mostly open terrain to the northeastern shore of Lake 4 (11,110'), 5.5 miles from the trailhead. At an indistinct junction, a sign marked simply TRAIL denotes a faint path that follows the east shoreline on for nearly a mile to a junc-

tion with the New Army Pass Trail near Lake 1.

To reach Lake 5, at the terminus of the Cottonwood Lakes Trail, you must travel another quarter of a mile, first around the north shore of Lake 4 and then up a steep hillside to the lake. A short stream flows between the two large bodies of water in this basin, both of which are designated as Lake 5. Nestled in a rocky basin just below the crest, Lake 5 (11,160') is rimmed by cliffs and talus. Meadows surround the lake, with clumps of willows here and there, but very few trees grace the shore. Some campsites are around the lake, but better, more protected sites are below, on the rise between Lakes 3 and 4. While golden trout can be found in all the lakes in Cottonwood Basin, Lake 5 is the only one that is not catch-and-release.

O A network of trails connects just about every lake in and around the Cottonwood Lakes Basin, and short cross-country routes easily reach the rest. A straightforward, 1-mile cross-country route along the creek that flows into Lake 5 provides access to diminutive Lake 6 (11,600').

R **PERMITS:** Wilderness permit required for overnight stays. (Quota: 60 per day)

CAMPFIRES: Not allowed.

SPECIAL FISHING REGULATIONS: Catch-and-release at Cottonwood Lakes 1, 2, 3, and 4. All other lakes in the Cottonwood Lakes Basin are restricted to artificial lures or flies with barbless hooks; the limit is five. Season is July 1 through October 31.

COTTONWOOD LAKES TRAILHEAD

TRIP 57

Soldier Lakes and Rock Creek

Ⓜ ⟋ BP

DISTANCE: 14.6 miles to Rock Creek Crossing

ELEVATION: 10,040/12,315, +2555′/-445′

SEASON: Mid-July to mid-October

USE: Moderate

MAPS: *Cirque Peak, Johnson Peak*

TRAIL LOG:

6.5	High Lake
7.5	New Army Pass
10.5	Soldier Lake Jct.
14.6	Rock Creek Crossing

INTRODUCTION: Easy access and scenic surroundings in the Cottonwood Lakes Basin make the area one of the most popular weekend destinations on the east side of the southern Sierra. However, few adventurers have the time and energy necessary to continue across the divide at New Army Pass for an excursion into the exquisite backcountry of the Rock Creek drainage. The Rock Creek Trail leads those who tread it to meadows laden with wildflowers, quiet forests, and lovely subalpine lakes tucked into picturesque cirques. Trip 57 also provides the option of an off-trail excursion into Miter Basin, one of the most dramatic alpine basins in the High Sierra, where a bevy of pristine lakes reflect the summits of towering peaks.

DIRECTIONS TO THE TRAILHEAD: In the heart of Lone Pine, turn west from U.S. 395 onto Whitney Portal Road and go 3 miles to the left turn onto Horseshoe Meadow Road. Proceed up this road 18 miles to a junction and turn right, following a sign for NEW ARMY PASS, COTTONWOOD LAKES. Pass the Cottonwood Lakes walk-in campground and continue to the Cottonwood Lakes trailhead parking area, 0.5 mile from the Horseshoe Meadow Road.

DESCRIPTION: The Cottonwood Lakes Trail begins auspiciously as a short, brick-lined path near the restroom building. Beyond the information signboard, you follow a gently graded, sandy trail slightly uphill, and soon cross the Golden Trout Wilderness boundary, and then, quickly, you pass on your left a spur trail from the Cottonwood Lakes Pack Station. On an equally gentle descent you reach South Fork Cottonwood Creek, 1 mile from the trailhead, where some campsites appear on the far bank.

From the crossing, you climb gently through more scattered pines, soon meeting the main branch of Cottonwood Creek and following it up a broad valley for the next mile and a half. You leave the Golden Trout Wilderness and enter the John Muir Wilderness, beneath steep cliffs to your left and the wooden structures of the Golden Trout Camp across the meadow to your right.

Beyond the wilderness boundary, the trail curves west as you begin a more moderate climb up the narrowing canyon. At this time you cross Cottonwood Creek on a beveled log, at 2.5 miles from the trailhead. A couple of campsites are near the crossing. As you make your way through light forest, you pass meadows lining the creek. Just after a crossing of a side stream, you reach the Y-junction between the Cottonwood Lakes Trail and New Army Pass Trail, at 3.25 miles.

From the junction, veer left and quickly cross Cottonwood Creek. You climb moderately for a little over a mile to the junction with the South Fork Lakes Trail, beside a large meadow 4.33 miles from the trailhead.

Continue westbound from the South Fork Lakes and New Army Pass trail junction, climbing up to another Y-junction. Keep heading west on the New Army Pass

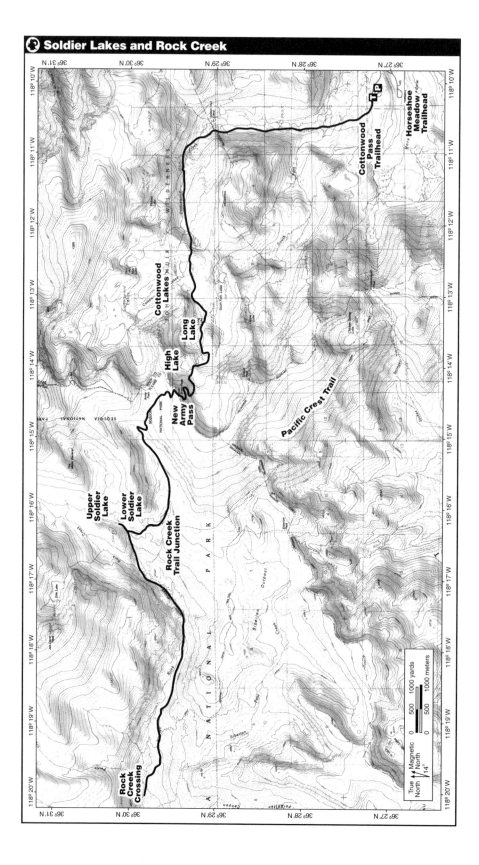

Trail. Near the far end of the expansive meadow you pass Lake 2. Leaving the grassland and lakes behind, you make a short climb to a desolate area filled with large granite boulders. Eventually, you leave the desolate terrain behind as the mildly graded trail curves around a lightly forested hillside. Below, a stream rushes down to the westernmost South Fork Lake (11,255±). A faint use-trail leads across the stream to forested campsites between this lake and Long Lake above. A moderate climb leads up the south shore of Long Lake (11,135′±), 5.75 miles from the trailhead. You'll find the best campsites beneath a stand of pines near the southeast shore, with a few less-protected sites above the north shore.

From the east shore of Long Lake the New Army Pass Trail begins a steeper traverse toward High Lake and the pass beyond. You climb to timberline and then wind your way up rocky switchbacks to High Lake (11,510′±), 6.5 miles from the trailhead. Campsites are extremely limited around the exposed lakeshore.

From High Lake, ascend rocky switchbacks to New Army Pass (12,315′), 7.5 miles from the trailhead. A moderate descent across barren slopes leads you from the pass to more hospitable terrain. You eventually meet and follow a tributary of Rock Creek downstream through boulder-sprinkled meadows rimmed by rocky cliffs and ridges. Stunted pines begin to appear and soon you're skirting flower-filled meadows through a scattered-to-light forest of lodgepole and foxtail pines. At 9.9 miles, you reach a junction with a lateral to the Pacific Crest Trail.

Veer right at the junction and travel past a thin strip of meadow to a signed lateral, which leads to pine-shaded campsites with a bear box on a low rise above the outlet from Soldier Lakes. A short distance farther, you boulder hop the outlet and encounter the signed junction with the Rock Creek Trail and the lateral to Soldier Lakes, 10.5 miles from the trailhead.

Head northeast toward Soldier Lakes and follow the edge of a narrow, flower-filled meadow through scattered pines to the southern tip of Lower Soldier Lake (10,805′±). The boot-beaten path continues along the west edge of the lake, but in order to reach the pine-shaded campsites you must cross the outlet just below the lake via some well-placed rocks and logs and follow a faint path along the east shore.

Dramatically framed by the towering walls of the Major General, Lower Soldier Lake reposes in a scenic cirque. Anglers should enjoy fishing for the resident golden trout. A short, steep, cross-country jaunt from the north shore leads up the east side of the cirque to the secluded upper lake. A supreme off-trail excursion follows the Rock Creek drainage to Miter Basin from the lower lake (see Options, below).

Back at the junction, you follow the tumbling outlet on a downstream journey through a thickening forest of lodgepole pines along the Rock Creek Trail. A short, steep descent down a narrow gully alongside a riotous section of creek passes a campsite just before the edge of a broad meadow. An obscure use-trail begins near the campsite and leads along the east side of Rock Creek toward Miter Basin. The path is fairly well defined to where the creek leaves the lower basin, but evaporates into a bona-fide cross-country route above (see Options, below).

A gently graded trail leads around the fringe of the meadow and fords the branch of Rock Creek that drains Sky Blue Lake. The trail then passes a large pond, beyond which are more campsites and a bear box in a grove of pines. At the far end of the meadow, you reenter lodgepole pine forest and pass through a drift fence as the moderate descent resumes and the trail veers away from the creek for a bit. Soon, you stroll alongside the stream again as it dances over slabs and cascades over boulders between meadow-and-willow-lined banks. Two miles from Lower Soldier Lake, you cross Rock Creek on a pair of logs and proceed downstream half a mile to another

Soldier Lake and the Major General from the PCT

picturesque meadow, with a number of lodgepole-shaded campsites along the edge. Beyond the meadow, a short, forested descent leads to the junction with the Pacific Crest Trail (PCT), 3.25 miles from the lake.

From the junction, a winding moderate descent along the PCT leads through alternating sections of forest and flower-and-fern-filled meadows, where the summit of massive Mt. Guyot can be seen looming to the west. As the descent continues, you pass the signed lateral leading to the Rock Creek Ranger Station and then stroll by some shady campsites. After yet another meadow, additional campsites (with a bear box) line the trail, and you arrive at the Rock Creek Crossing (9595´±), 4.1 miles from Lower Soldier Lake.

By utilizing the PCT, backpackers can create a loop trip over Cottonwood Pass and back to the Cottonwood Lakes trailhead (See Trip 54), as well as a number of interesting day hike possibilities.

For the continuing description northbound on the PCT, see Trip 58.

From Lower Soldier Lake, a faint use-trail steeply ascends the westernmost inlet

to open slopes below The Major General. From there, an exquisite cross-country route follows the Rock Creek drainage into the stunning amphitheater of Miter Basin, where iridescent lakes and a semicircle of rugged peaks create alpine scenery as dramatic as any in the High Sierra. A moderate off-trail route for a multi-day loop trip leads past Sky Blue Lake to Crabtree Pass (12,560´±) (class 2), down to a use-trail to Crabtree Lakes, and then on to a connection with the John Muir Trail. The route up Rock Creek may also be accessed via the use-trail that begins near the campsite at the east end of the meadow, 0.5 mile west of Lower Soldier Lake. The first mile ascends the forested hillside above Rock Creek to an undulating ridge of granite outcroppings, beyond which the routefinding becomes easier through open terrain. Mountaineers and technical climbers alike will find plenty of challenges on the peaks encircling the basin.

PERMITS: Wilderness permit required for overnight stays. (Quota: 60 per day)

CAMPFIRES: Not permitted in Cottonwood Lakes basin or above 10,400 feet).

TRIP **58**

Cottonwood Lakes to Whitney Portal

MS / BPx

DISTANCE: 35 miles

ELEVATION: 10,040/12,315/9595/
13,580/8360, +8070'/-9805'

SEASON: Mid-July to mid-October

USE: Moderate

MAPS: *Cirque Peak, Johnson Peak, Mt. Whitney, Mt. Langley*

TRAIL LOG:

6.5	High Lake
7.5	New Army Pass
10.5	Soldier Lake Jct.
14.6	Rock Creek Crossing
20.25	Lower Crabtree Meadow
21.5	John Muir Trail Jct.
25.75	Mt. Whitney Trail Jct.

INTRODUCTION: A multitude of peak baggers set their sights on Mt. Whitney each year, placing a high demand on the limited permits available for day hikers and backpackers who want to ascend the lower 48's highest summit. For parties with the luxury of extra days and the ability to arrange for a 28-mile shuttle between trailheads, this longer approach to the peak from the Cottonwood Lakes trailhead crosses some sublime High Sierra backcountry. Beautiful lakes, excellent vistas, tumbling creeks, flower-filled meadows, and quiet forests are all here in abundance. Although the areas around Whitney and around Cottonwood Lakes areas are usually crammed with people, solitude-seekers will reap rewards on the lightly used Rock Creek Trail and the somewhat-neglected stretch of the Pacific Crest Trail (PCT).

DIRECTIONS TO THE TRAILHEAD: Follow directions in Trip 55 to the Cottonwood Lakes trailhead.

DESCRIPTION: Follow directions in Trip 55 and Trip 57 to Rock Creek Crossing, 14.6 miles from the Cottonwood Lakes trailhead.

After fording Rock Creek, you begin a moderately steep, switchbacking climb on the PCT. The trail ascends the north wall of the canyon through a light forest of lodgepole pines. After about three-quarters of a mile, the grade eases as you climb toward the crossing of Guyot Creek (campsites). Before leaving the creek, make sure your water supply is sufficient for the 4.5-mile dry stretch of trail ahead. Nice views of Mt. Guyot and Joe Devil Peak accompany you as a mild section of trail leads to a steeper, boulder-filled climb through young pines to Guyot Pass (10,920'±), directly northeast of Mt. Guyot.

Beyond the pass, you make a moderate descent while enjoying excellent views of the Great Western Divide, Kern Canyon, Red Spur, and the Kaweah Peaks. Soon you encounter an easy trail across the wide expanse of the sandy basin known as Guyot Flat, where few plants are able to take root in the deep, sandy soils. Your fine views continue, with little vegetation to obscure them until you enter a light forest of foxtail pines beyond the north edge of the flat. For the next couple of miles, the trail makes an undulating traverse to the south lip of the canyon of Whitney Creek, where a steep, switchbacking descent drops you to the floor of the canyon. A gentle stroll over rocky terrain takes you to Lower Crabtree Meadow (10,320'±) and campsites with a bear box near the ford of Whitney Creek. Just beyond the creek is the junction between the PCT and your lateral to Mt. Whitney, 20.3 miles from the trailhead.

With constant views of Mt. Whitney's less dramatic west face, you make a gentle, half-mile ascent along the north bank of Whitney Creek to the lush environs of

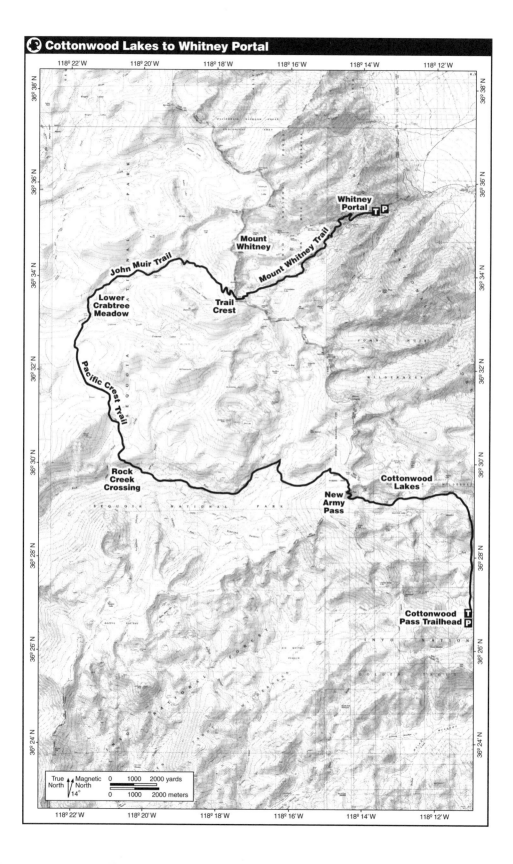

John Muir Trail

Mount
Whitney

Mount Whitney Trail

Whitney
Portal T P

Lower
Crabtree
Meadow

Trail
Crest

Pacific Crest Trail

Rock
Creek
Crossing

New
Army
Pass

Cottonwood
Lakes

Cottonwood
Pass Trailhead T P

True North | Magnetic North 14°
0   1000   2000 yards
0   1000   2000 meters

Cottonwood Lakes Basin on the Cottonwood Lakes Trail

Upper Crabtree Meadow. Near the far end of the meadow, just before the trail crosses the creek, the unmarked Crabtree Lakes Trail branches off to the east. Beyond the ford, you pass a lateral going to campsites with a bear box and the Crabtree Ranger Station before recrossing the creek to the north side. Shortly after the crossing, the lateral intersects the John Muir Trail (10,640′±), 1.2 miles from the PCT junction. More campsites can be found near the junction.

Now on the JMT, you ascend the relocated section of trail above the north bank of the creek, through a smattering of lodgepole and foxtail pines. Approximately half a mile from the junction, you climb past the last legal campsites below timberline and cross into the designated Whitney Zone just before reaching picturesque Timberline Lake. Although closed to camping for several decades, the lake is worthy of an extended rest stop, especially at a vantage point on the south shore, where the hulk of Mt. Whitney is reflected in the placid surface of the lake.

Beyond the lake, the steady ascent continues as you bid farewell to the trees and the creek and climb through an open basin laden with granite slabs and benches. You ascend over a flat-topped ridge to Guitar Lake (11,460′±), 3.5 miles from the PCT junction, where camping is still permitted in sandy pockets away from the meadow grass. Beyond the lake, a pair of tarns offers additional camping possibilities and the last reliable water near the trail before the stiff climb to Trail Crest.

As the climb intensifies, Hitchcock Lakes appear to the south, luring knapsackers to their remote location beneath the precipitous north face of Mt. Hitchcock. A series of long-legged switchbacks takes you up the steep west face of the Sierra crest on a steady 1500-foot climb to a junction with the Mt. Whitney Trail (13,560′±), 5.5 miles from the PCT junction. A typical summer day will see a plethora of backpacks reposing against the steep wall of rock near the junction, as backpackers jettison their backpacks for the final 2-mile push to the summit.

For a description of the 2-mile ascent from the junction to the summit of Mt. Whitney, see Trip 59.

From the junction, reverse the description in Trip 59 and hike 9 miles to the trailhead at Whitney Portal.

O Crabtree Lakes offer an excellent side trip for those with an extra day or two. A fairly well-defined trail from Upper Crabtree Meadow leads 2.75 miles to the upper lake. From there, a cross-country route heads east up the drainage to a climb over Crabtree Pass (12,560´±) that leads down into exquisite Miter Basin (see Trip 58).

O Peak baggers seeking less popular ascents than Mt. Whitney can make a straightforward, class 1 ascent of Mt. Guyot from Guyot Pass. The southwest and west slopes of Mt. Hitchcock are also rated class 1.

R **PERMITS:** Wilderness permit required for overnight stay. (Quota: 20 per day)

CAMPFIRES: No fires in Cottonwood Lakes Basin, within the Mt. Whitney Zone or above 10,400 feet.

CAMPING: No camping at Timberline Lake, Mirror Lake, or Trailside Meadow.

BEARS: Canisters required in Whitney Zone.

SANITATION: Outpost Camp and Trail Camp: use toilets for solid waste disposal only (do not urinate, as the toilets are easily overloaded with liquid). If toilets are unavailable, dispose of waste a minimum of 200 feet from water and bury it in soil at least 6˝ deep, or pack it out. Pack out all toilet paper and feminine hygiene products —do not burn.

WHITNEY PORTAL TRAILHEAD

TRIP 59

Mt. Whitney

Ⓢ ↗ DH / BP

DISTANCE: 10.5 miles

ELEVATION: 8361/14,494, +7830´/-1875´

SEASON: Mid-July to early October

USE: Heavy

MAP: *Mount Whitney*

TRAIL LOG:

2.75	Lone Pine Lake Jct.
3.75	Outpost Camp
4.5	Mirror Lake
5.75	Trailside Meadows
6.5	Trail Camp
8.6	Trail Crest
10.5	Mt. Whitney Summit

INTRODUCTION: Mt. Whitney is one of the most impressive mountains in North America. The classic, vertical east face presents a towering and dramatic alpine profile that rivals any in the American West. Not only is the view of the mountain exceptional, but the vista from the summit is even more extraordinary, a commensurate reward for the diligence required to reach the climax of the Sierra. To stand atop the 14,494-foot summit of Mt. Whitney is an unparalleled accomplishment.

To say that Mt. Whitney is a coveted ascent would be an understatement. So many people desire to climb the highest U.S. summit outside of Alaska that the Forest Service long ago implemented a strict quota system, but this attempt to stem the tide of hikers, backpackers, and climbers on the mountain has not been completely successful. Recently, a $15 per person fee was instituted for advance reservations, with the proceeds used for wilderness projects in the Inyo National Forest.

This small fee has done little to diminish the consistently large number of applications for permits.

See page 200 in the introduction to the Mt. Whitney Ranger District for information about how to reserve a permit for a trip in the Whitney Zone.

PLANNING YOUR CLIMB: Before submitting your application for the permit lottery, you must decide whether you want to attempt Mt. Whitney on a one-day ascent or on an overnight climb. The main advantage of the single-day option is that you don't have to carry a heavy backpack up the steep trail. However, to make the climb in one day, you must be in top condition and be prepared for a sustained and arduous effort at high altitude over a very long day. Contrarily, backpackers must become beasts of burden, trudging along the steep path, carting all the gear necessary for camping. In so doing, they have the advan-

tage of a more leisurely ascent and more time to acclimatize along the way. Either approach to climbing Mt. Whitney constitutes much more than a stroll in the park.

THE CLIMB: With permit in hand, the focus shifts to the actual climb, which has plenty of factors to consider. The high altitude, elevation gain, and distance all require that you be physically fit and well acclimatized. Spending at least one night at altitude prior to departure will aid in the acclimatization process. The walk-in backpackers' camp at Whitney Portal Trailhead (8350′) has 10 sites (one-night limit). The lower-elevation Whitney Portal and Lone Pine (5995′) campgrounds provide multiday camping options. The nearby Meysan Trail makes an excellent conditioning hike the day before the climb (see Trip 60). Once on the trail, stay well hydrated, eat plenty of high-energy foods, and continuously

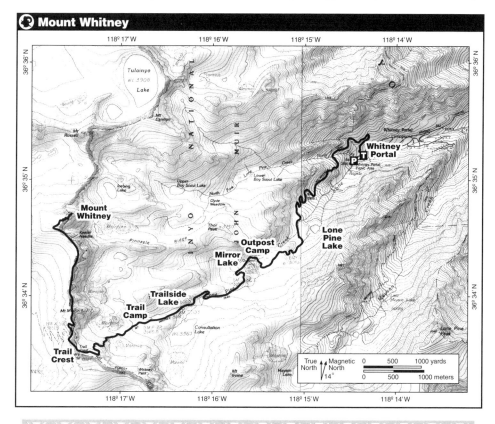

monitor your body for signs of altitude sickness.

Not only must you be prepared physically for this endeavor, but you should also be outfitted with the proper equipment. The intensity of the sun at this elevation necessitates the use of sunglasses, and the application and reapplication of sunblock. Be sure to take clothing that is suitable for the wide temperature fluctuations between the trailhead and the summit, and that will protect you from adverse weather, such as high winds, heavy rain, hail, and even snow. Afternoon thunderstorms are not uncommon; at the first signs of developing cumulonimbus thunderclouds you should beat a hasty retreat to lower elevations, particularly along the last 2-mile traverse to the summit, as there is virtually nowhere to hide from lightning strikes.

These warnings about overcrowding, permits, strenuous climbs, potential health problems, and adverse weather conditions might well lead you to conclude that you should avoid this area. However, they should not deter you, as the reward of climbing Mt. Whitney far outweighs the drawbacks.

MT. WILLIAMSON

What is the second highest peak in California? The right response is Mt. Williamson, at 14,375 feet, 5.5 miles north of Mt. Whitney—which nearly everyone correctly recognizes as not only the highest mountain in California, but in the continental United States as well. While Mt. Williamson languishes in relative obscurity, hundreds of pilgrims attempt to reach the summit of 14,494-foot Mt. Whitney via the 10.5-mile Mt. Whitney Trail virtually every summer day. If a mere 120 feet could be added to the height of Mt. Williamson, no doubt it would be the peak with the trail to the summit and the hundreds of devotees spread across its flanks.

DIRECTIONS TO THE TRAILHEAD: In the heart of Lone Pine, turn west from U.S. 395 onto Whitney Portal Road and drive 13 miles to the parking lots at Whitney Portal. Campgrounds, restrooms, and a small store with cafe are nearby.

DESCRIPTION: At the beginning of the Mt. Whitney Trail, an abundance of signs, placards, and display boards create quite a fanfare, which seems perversely suited to the most heavily regulated and popular backcountry route in the Sierra. After being bombarded with the multiple regulations and warnings, you pass a human waste receptacle, perhaps the most vivid reminder of the limitations of an alpine environment to sustain this level of human impact.

Away from the hoopla at the trailhead, the well-beaten path winds through a light forest of red firs, Jeffrey pines, and mountain mahogany, before curving up the hillside to the first major switchback. Now heading roughly east, across a chaparral-covered slope, you have a good view up the canyon of the falls on Lone Pine Creek. Soon you come to an unnamed tributary, lined by lush foliage, and then make a quarter-mile upward traverse across the hillside to the crossing of the North Fork. A steep mountaineer's route climbs this drainage to base camps at the alpine lakes below the east face of Whitney (see Options, below). Farther up the trail, 1 mile from Whitney Portal, you cross the John Muir Wilderness boundary.

A mostly shadeless, steady climb ensues, incorporating numerous switchbacks into the ascent. If the forecast is for hot weather, try to avoid this section of the climb during the heat of the day, as you will be exposed to the sun for much of the next 1.5 miles. Welcome relief comes in the form of lodgepole pines as you approach the ford of Lone Pine Creek. A short distance beyond the ford, you come to a junction with the short spur trail heading northeast to Lone Pine Lake, 2.75 miles from the trailhead.

The stone hut at the summit of Mt. Whitney

 SIDE TRIP TO LONE PINE LAKE: From the Mt. Whitney Trail junction follow the trail 200 yards through light forest down to the shore of Lone Pine Lake (9975′±). Perched at the edge of a steep drop, the roughly oval lake is blessed with fine views down the Lone Pine Creek canyon across the mostly treeless, boulder-strewn shore. With no permanent inlet, the lake depends on snowmelt. Anglers can test their luck on the rainbow and brook trout that inhabit the lake. A limited number of campsites are beneath foxtail pines near the trail above the southwest shore. **END OF SIDE TRIP**

From the Lone Pine Lake junction, you stroll through a rocky wash on a gentle grade through a light covering of pine and enter the Whitney Zone. Soon a steeper climb resumes on a series of switchbacks that lead up and over a rocky slope to a large, willow-lined meadow dotted with wildflowers. You follow a mildly graded path alongside the meadow to the far end and turn northwest to a crossing of Lone Pine Creek.

Just beyond the creek, in the shadow of a waterfall, is Outpost Camp (10,335′), 3.75 miles from the trailhead. In olden days, Outpost Camp bustled with activity during the summer months. A packer's wife rented tents and sold meals, while stock grazed in the meadows of Bighorn Park, named for the native sheep that once inhabited the area.

Although camping is possible at Lone Pine Lake (see the above Option), the sloping campsites surrounded by gravel and rock beneath widely scattered pines at Outpost Camp represent the first practical alternative for Whitney climbers. A composting toilet is located just a short way beyond the crossing of Mirror Creek. Make sure you properly store your food for protection against rodents as well as for possible bear encounters.

Leave the peaceful surroundings of Outpost Camp, cross Mirror Creek, and then make a steep climb via switchbacks alongside the wildflower-lined, tumbling stream. At the top of the climb you boulder hop back over the creek and pass through head-high willows to the southeast shore of Mirror Lake (10,640′), 4.5 miles from Whitney Portal. The lake is quite attractive, set in the deep cirque below the steep cliffs of Thor Peak. Anglers can try their luck on the brook trout rumored to reside here, but backpackers will have to continue up the trail to find camping, since the Forest Service banned it in 1972 because of severe overuse. While you can no longer stay here overnight, Mirror Lake does provide a fine haven for a rest stop or lunch break.

More switchbacks greet you on the ascent out of Mirror Lake's cirque basin. The stiff climb leads to the top of a ridge near timberline, where you resume a more southwesterly ascent. Soon the rugged east face of Mt. Whitney appears over Pinnacle Ridge. You climb moderately through boulders and rocky terrain, the rugged landscape occasionally interrupted by widely scattered wildflowers and small shrubs. A series of rock steps brings you closer to Lone Pine Creek, and eventually you cross the stream on a rock bridge. A ways beyond, an ascent takes you to beautiful Trailside Meadows (11,855′), 5.75 miles from the trailhead, where sparkling color from a profusion of shooting stars, paintbrush, and columbine accents the deepgreen meadow grass lining the creek.

Beyond the oasis of Trailside Meadows, you encounter a nearly endless sea of rock and a seemingly endless climb ahead. After you recross Lone Pine Creek, Consultation Lake comes into view to your left, flanked dramatically by Mts. Irvine and McAdie. You continue to climb steadily upward, around boulders and over rock steps. Just after a short stretch of gentle grade, a final climb takes you into Trail Camp (12,035′), 6.5 miles from Whitney Portal.

Although the camp itself is slightly circus-like, the Trail Camp setting, below the rugged east face of the Whitney massif, is spectacular. You'll find campsites, access to water from the nearby stream and tarns, and a three-hole toilet. To the north lies Wotan's Throne, with Pinnacle Ridge behind, while to the south 13,680-foot Mt.

TRAIL CAMP

On just about any summer day, Trail Camp assumes the atmosphere of an expedition base camp. While colorful tents flap in the breeze, expectant mountaineers sort and check equipment, others gaze at the route or check the skies for hints of the weather, and still others query returning summiteers about their climbs. This is definitely not the place for isolationists in search of a solitary wilderness experience. Plenty of developed campsites have been created over the years amid the near-barren terrain surrounding the camp, but don't expect any privacy. With 200 hikers and backpackers departing each day from Whitney Portal, the potential exists for 400 people to stay at or pass through Trail Camp on any particular day. Some backpackers seek campsites in slightly less-crowded areas around Consultation Lake, but usually without much relief from the perennial overpopulation.

McAdie and 13,770-foot Mt. Irvine form an amphitheater for the icy waters of Consultation Lake. Directly above the camp, 100 switchbacks climb the slope beneath the gap in the ridge known as Trail Crest. Many a prospective Whitney climber has experienced a restless night in the foreboding shadow of those switchbacks.

Leaving Trail Camp, you resume the hike along the Mt. Whitney Trail, on a mild path for a very brief time before the grade increases as you head for the first of the 100 switchbacks. You zigzag your way directly up the rocky slope above Trail Camp, noting ever-expanding views to the east (Mt. Whitney becomes hidden behind the Needles). Near the mid-point of the climb, you ascend the side of a rock wall where a seep may create icy conditions; old iron railings add a wary sense of safety. The interminable switchbacks continue as you head toward the crest. Be prepared for snow patches lingering through the summer below the pass. Eventually, you reach Trail Crest (13,580′), 8.5 miles from the trailhead, where staggering views of the Great Western Divide reign to the west, encompassing a broad expanse of Sequoia National Park. Directly below, in the barren basin, are the shimmering waters of the Hitchcock Lakes.

A short descent from Trail Crest leads to the junction with the John Muir Trail, where you begin the nearly 2-mile slog to the summit. A steady climb takes you along the west side of the ridge, where the trail periodically enters notches that provide acrophobic vistas straight down the east face. As you proceed up the rocky trail, sharp eyes will find the hut on the summit, built for research purposes by the Smithsonian Institute in 1909. Nearing the final slope, the grade increases, and multiple paths lead toward the top. Cairns may aid in finding a route, but the way from here is unmistakable — head for the highest point!

Soon the roof of the hut appears over the horizon above and you quickly reach the summit of Mt. Whitney (14,494′). The top of the peak is a broad, sloping plateau of jumbled slabs and boulders. Toward the edge of the plateau is the pit toilet, not only the highest waste receptacle in the lower 48, but perhaps the one with the grandest view as well. Mark your accomplishment by signing the summit register near the hut.

Any adjective used to describe the incredible vista from the summit of Mt. Whitney is grossly inadequate. Suffice to say, the view from the highest point in the lower 48 is a complete 360-degree panorama, with each bearing of the compass holding something extraordinary to discover — a just reward for the toil necessary to achieve such a lofty goal.

○ The nearby Meysan Trail provides a nice hike, especially good for summit-bound hikers who need to acclimatize before the big climb (see Trip 60).

○ From near the 1-mile point on the Mt. Whitney Trail, an interesting but strenuous hike follows the mountaineer's trail up the North Fork Lone Pine Creek to Boy Scout and Iceberg lakes, nestled in scenic alpine basins beneath the impressive east face of Mt. Whitney (Whitney Zone permit required for travel past Lower Boy Scout Lake). From Iceberg Lake, a class 2 cross-country route proceeds over the crest at Whitney-Russell Pass (13,040′) west to Arctic Lake and on to a connection with the Muir Trail at Guitar Lake.

Whitney hikers with the necessary off-trail skills can vary their return from the summit by descending the north slope of Mt. Whitney to Whitney-Russell Pass and then following the North Fork route back to the trail.

R **PERMITS:** Whitney Zone: All hikers and backpackers must possess a valid Forest Service wilderness permit for each group. $15 per person fee for advance reservations. (Permits are not required for day hikes to Lone Pine Lake on the Mt. Whitney Trail, or to Lower Boy Scout Lake on the North Fork Lone Pine Creek route.) (Quota: 130 day hikers per day/60 overnight per day)

CAMPFIRES: No

CAMPING: No camping at Mirror Lake or Trailside Meadow.

BEARS: Canisters required.

SANITATION: Outpost Camp and Trail Camp: use toilets for solid waste disposal only (do not urinate, as the toilets are easily overloaded with liquid). If toilets are unavailable, dispose of waste a minimum of 200 feet from water and bury it in soil at least 6 inches deep, or pack it out. Pack out all toilet paper and feminine hygiene products — do not burn.

NORTH FORK LONE PINE CREEK: All human waste, toilet paper, and feminine hygiene products should be packed out and disposed of in the receptacle near the trailhead.

TRIP **60**

Meysan Trail

MS ↗ DH / BP

DISTANCE: 4.5 miles to Meysan Lake

ELEVATION: 7890/11,625, +3860′/-310′

SEASON: Mid-July to early October

USE: Light

MAPS: *Mt. Langley*

INTRODUCTION: What a difference a mile makes! Each summer day hundreds trudge their way along the Mt. Whitney Trail toward the highest point in the continental U.S., but in a canyon just 1 mile to the south, only a few will be found hiking along the Meysan Trail. Although the rewards may not be as prestigious as an ascent of Whitney, the scenery and the relative solitude found in the canyon of Meysan Creek are not without their own appeal. As an added bonus, since this trail lies outside the Whitney Zone, a one-day permit is not required for dayhikers as it is for the Mt. Whitney Trail. Upon reaching Meysan Lake, however, visitors may feel as though they had completed the equivalent of a Whitney climb, as the trail is a steady uphill grind, gaining nearly 4000 feet in 4.5 miles.

For those peak baggers awaiting their turn at Whitney, the hike up the Meysan Trail is an excellent way to acclimatize before the big climb. The hike, coupled with an overnight stay at Whitney Portal, may greatly aid the acclimatization process.

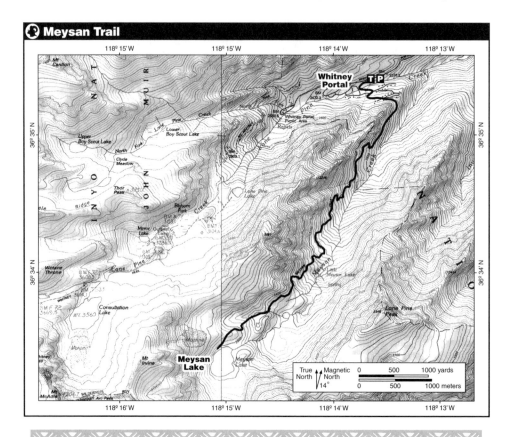

DIRECTIONS TO THE TRAILHEAD: In the heart of Lone Pine, turn west from U.S. 395 onto Whitney Portal Road and drive 13 miles to the parking lots at Whitney Portal. Campgrounds, restrooms, and a small store with cafe are nearby.

DESCRIPTION: To begin the hike you must descend the old service road from the Whitney Portal Road to the Whitney Portal Campground. Following a series of signs, go left on the campground loop road and then across Lone Pine Creek to an intersection. Turn left again, and pass a couple of summer homes, continuing to the official trailhead on your right. On a single-track trail you make a steep climb up the hillside, the severe grade possibly producing second thoughts about the wisdom of hiking this trail. Fortunately, the grade eases as you approach another road, along which a short walk leads past more summer homes to the resumption of trail.

Having left the last vestiges of civilization behind, you resume a more moderate climb across a dry hillside dotted with red firs, pinyon pines, Jeffrey pines, and mountain mahogany. Soon you reach the canyon of Meysan Creek and curve southwest, climbing moderately up the steep hillside, well above the level of the creek. You encounter the first of many switchbacks, where you have nice views northeast of the Alabama Hills and Owens Valley. Near the 1.5-mile mark, you cross into the John Muir Wilderness.

Continue to climb up the canyon via switchbacks. As you draw slightly closer to the creek, you catch glimpses of a pretty cascade that glides down a rock slab into a delightful pool below. More switchbacks lead to even better views farther up the canyon, including another cascade dropping down the headwall of the lake-filled basin above. Scattered foxtail pines greet you just before you reach a grassy meadow, approximately 3.5 miles from the parking area. A sign directs traffic to Grass Lake straight ahead, and Camp Lake and Meysan Lake to the right.

Beyond the junction, ducks periodically mark the faint trail as you make the final climb to Meysan Lake. Follow the route around the large meadow encircling Camp Lake and then up a grassy couloir. Where the slope ahead becomes steeper, veer southwest and climb over rock slabs to a gap above the lake. A short descent leads to the northeast shore, 4.5 miles from the parking area. Small pockets of flower-filled meadow dot the otherwise rocky shore of Meysan Lake (11,480±). The dramatic headwall formed by Mts. Irvine and Mallory backdrops the lake. Backpackers may want to consider more inviting campsites below, near Camp Lake.

O Once within the steep canyon of Meysan Creek, there's virtually no place to go. However, mountaineer-types can take advantage of class 2 routes up Lone Pine Peak and Mt. Mallory.

R **PERMITS:** Wilderness permit required for overnight stays. (Quota: 15 per day)
   CAMPFIRES: No
   BIGHORN SHEEP AREA: Dogs and domestic sheep are prohibited.

SYMMES CREEK TRAILHEAD

TRIP 61

Shepherd Pass Trail

Ⓢ ⟋ BP

DISTANCE: 12.5 miles to John Muir Trail (JMT)

ELEVATION: 6310/12,050/10,890, +6785′/-2205′

SEASON: Mid-July to mid-October

USE: Light

MAPS: *Mt. Williamson, Mt. Brewer*

TRAIL LOG:

7.0	Anvil Camp
9.0	Shepherd Pass
12.5	John Muir Trail Jct.

INTRODUCTION: The Shepherd Pass Trail is not for the weak or timid, but for those who don't mind a low elevation start, hot temperatures, and carrying extra water, it is the gateway into incredible backcountry, without the hordes so prevalent on nearby trails.

Beginning almost on the floor of Owens Valley, the trail is steep and hot with little shade or water in the first 7 miles. However, diligent backpackers in good shape will be well rewarded for their efforts. Unlike sister trails over Baxter, Sawmill, and Taboose passes, this route has benefited from some recent trail maintenance and the tread remains in reasonable shape.

The initial climb follows two typical east side Sierra canyons that slice into the rugged eastern escarpment. Beyond the pinyon-sagebrush zone of the lower canyons, travelers climb into subalpine and alpine terrain on the way to the pass and to Sequoia National Park. At the higher elevations, visitors are treated to dramatic mountain scenery, lush meadowlands, and the possibility of extra excursions to beau-

tiful lake-dotted basins. Cross-country enthusiasts and mountaineers will enjoy the wide-ranging alternate routes accessible from this trail.

DIRECTIONS TO THE TRAILHEAD: From U.S. 395 in the town of Independence, turn west onto Market Street, following signs for Onion Valley. At 4.4 miles from U.S. 395, leave the paved Onion Valley Road and turn left onto Foothill Road, heading south on a well-traveled dirt road marked 13S08. Stay on the main road for 2.6 miles to a junction, where you turn left on the signed road to the hikers' trailhead (equestrian parking is a short distance up the right-hand branch) and immediately cross Symmes Creek. Continue on this road (13S07) for half a mile to another signed junction and turn right. Proceed southwest, taking the right-hand fork at two junctions, and travel 1.6 miles to the Symmes Creek parking area, which has a screened pit toilet and room for about a dozen cars.

DESCRIPTION: Through vegetation typical of the eastside pinyon-sagebrush zone, you follow sandy tread near the edge of the riparian zone along the south bank of Symmes Creek into the narrowing canyon. Just past a junction with the stock trail, but before the first ford of the creek, a set of signs provides information on the Bighorn Sheep Zoological Area and Sequoia National Park. After two more quick fords, you cross the signed John Muir Wilderness boundary and proceed up the deep cleft of the canyon to the beginning of a long switchbacking climb up the south wall. Before leaving Symmes Creek, make sure you fill your water containers, as the upcoming climb is steep and hot, and most of the water sources between here and Shepherd Creek are dry by midsummer.

The 1.75-mile winding climb gains 2000 feet from the canyon floor to the crest of the ridge above. Initially, the scattered pinyon pine and mountain mahogany offer next to no shade from the blistering eastern Sierra sun, and there is little hope of more as only a sprinkling of red firs and western

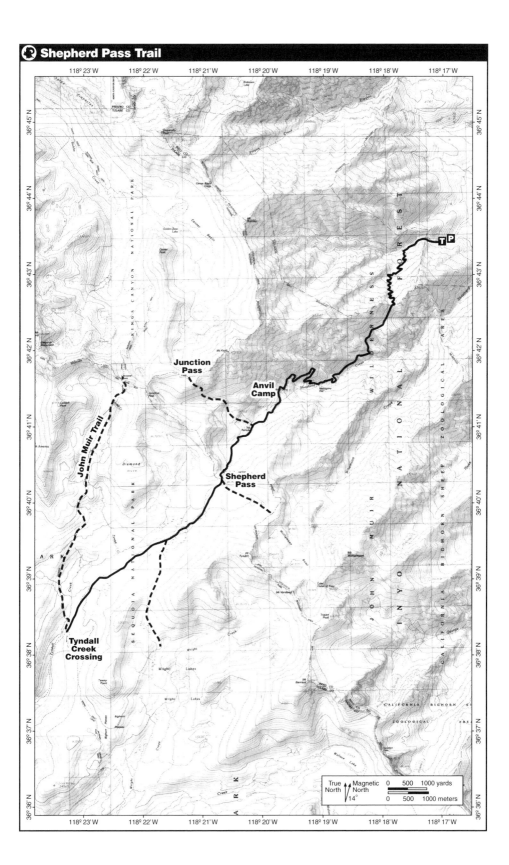

Junction
Pass

Anvil
Camp

Shepherd
Pass

John Muir Trail

Tyndall
Creek
Crossing

T P

True
North

Magnetic
North

14°

0   500   1000 yards

0   500   1000 meters

white pines join the mix higher up the slope. In the midst of the incessant climb, you reach a small pinyon-shaded flat with a campsite near a seasonal stream. Early season backpackers could make a first-night's camp here, but the trickling brook dries up quickly after snowmelt. Away from the flat, you continue the switchbacking ascent to the ridgecrest, from where you have a nice view of Mt. Williamson and the deep cleft of Shepherd Creek.

A welcome stretch of easier trail leads you to a couple of sub-ridges and then on a generally descending traverse across the steep hillside high above the deep gash of Shepherd Creek. Although the easy hiking is welcome, the loss of some of that hard-won elevation gain is a bit discouraging in light of the climb ahead. The brief respite ends at a seasonal stream, as a moderate climb resumes, leading a half mile to a perennial tributary that drains down the slopes below Mt. Keith, 4.6 miles from the trailhead, the first reliable source of water since Symmes Creek. The trail leads up and around the hillside to a switchback, where you have a fine view of a waterfall on the stream you just crossed. From there, you pass marginal campsites at Mahogany Flat (which isn't much of a flat), well above Shepherd Creek, and follow long-legged switchbacks on a climb up the manzanita-and-mahogany-covered slopes of the north wall of the canyon, into talus.

Eventually, a light forest of pines heralds the approach to Anvil Camp (shown incorrectly on the 1994 *Mt. Williamson* quad). A short distance beyond the crossing of a tiny brook and a NO FIRES sign, a bounty of campsites just prior to the crossing of Shepherd Creek signals your arrival at Anvil Camp (10,300′±), 7 miles and nearly 4000 vertical feet from the trailhead. Since the camp has the only quality campsites in the first 7 miles of trail, it receives a fair share of use, even though the trail is not heavily traveled. A number of level sites nestle beneath young foxtail pines, near the willow-lined creek.

After a well-earned rest at Anvil Camp, you cross Shepherd Creek and resume the ascent, leaving the pines behind to climb around a boulder-covered hillside to the Pothole, a willow-carpeted depression at the convergence of a number of watercourses. Beyond a small rivulet, a short, steep climb leads up a hillside dotted with stunted whitebark pines, passing a couple of poor campsites on the way to the crossing of a more substantial stream. The route then passes through treeless, boulder-strewn, morainal debris with diminishing patches of alpine flora.

Proceeding up the deep, rocky gorge, you reach the base of the headwall below the Sierra crest and begin the final climb to the top. The slope above often holds patches of snow well into the summer. You follow a series of switchbacks that zigzag across the headwall to the climax at Shepherd Pass (12,050′±). The pass is 9 miles from the trailhead, where a fine view of the Kaweah Peaks awaits and signs mark the boundary of Sequoia National Park.

Just over the pass, a large tarn provides an exposed alpine basecamp, with views into Williamson Bowl (area closed July 15–December 15). For climbs of Mt. Tyndall, see Options, below.

Gentler terrain greets you on this side of the pass, as the sandy trail follows a mild descent through the boulder-strewn meadows of the broad vale. With constant views of the Great Western Divide, you descend steadily along Tyndall Creek, hopping across numerous tributaries along the way. Clumps of lodgepole pines start to appear

THE CENTER BASIN TRAIL

Before completion of the John Muir Trail over Forester Pass in 1932, the Center Basin Trail over Junction Pass was the maintained route of the JMT. Nowadays it is a bona-fide cross-country route between Golden Bear Lake and the Shepherd Pass Trail, as only traces of the old path still exist.

View west from Shepherd Pass

as you enter more hospitable elevations, where the trail curves toward a connection with the John Muir Trail. At 12.5 miles from the trailhead, you reach the well-signed junction with the JMT. You'll find campsites near the junction, as well as farther south on the trail to the Tyndall Creek Ranger Station and along the JMT near the crossing of the stream that drains a series of small, unnamed tarns.

The connection with the JMT provides numerous possibilities for further wanderings (see Trip 62).

O **CENTER BASIN/JUNCTION PASS ROUTE:** A potential multi-day, semi-loop route follows the JMT northbound over Forester Pass to the Center Basin Trail and then cross-country over Junction Pass; it returns to the Shepherd Pass Trail near The Pothole.

From the Shepherd Pass junction, 12.5 miles from the Symmes Creek trailhead, head north on the JMT to the junction with the Center Basin Trail (10,600′±), 4.5 miles north of Forester Pass (see Trip 62 for a description of this segment of the JMT). The junction is at a camp area (with a bear box) just beyond the ford of Center Basin Creek. Turn east at the junction and follow the Center Basin Trail on a moderately

steep climb up the hillside, making your way across a flower-lined tributary, and around marshy sections of the stream to Golden Bear Lake (11,170′±).

A fair number of seldom-used, pine-shaded campsites can be found on the north shore of this picturesque lake. Above the lake, the gently ascending route passes through some near-idyllic flower gardens before a more pronounced climb through talus-covered terrain delivers you to the first of a pair of alpine tarns (3592), where you can find good campsites.

Pass the lake on the west side and climb toward the ridge to the west and above the second tarn. From there, make an ascending arc to the east over to the flat saddle of Junction Pass (13,085′±), 0.4 mile northeast of Junction Peak (the pass is incorrectly labeled on the 1994 *Mt. Williamson* quad).

Few traces of the old trail remain on the south side of the pass as you make the steep, rocky descent toward the Shepherd Pass Trail. Initially, the route heads south down steep talus, before veering east to follow a stream down the valley. After about a mile, where the stream bends sharply toward The Pothole, you descend a steep slope to the west of a beautiful subalpine meadow and then meet the trail beyond.

WRIGHT LAKES ROUTE: About 1.5 miles west of Shepherd Pass, leave the trail and head south toward a prominent saddle, 0.7 mile northeast of peak *3755*. From the saddle, a straightforward descent leads into the heart of the Wright Lakes basin, where a bevy of remote lakes repose in a broad meadow-covered basin. The highest lake in the chain (*3645*) is particularly stunning, backdropped by the rugged Sierra crest between Mts. Tyndall and Versteeg, and the fishing is reported to be quite good.

WILLIAMSON BOWL: Most of this area is closed to summertime travel as part of the California Bighorn Sheep Zoological Preserve, but a view into the barren Williamson Bowl and a chance to spy some bighorn sheep is worth the minor effort. If your visit is between December 15 and July 15, you can drop from the crest into the bowl. From Shepherd Pass, work your way southeast about a mile to a broad gap in the crest above the westernmost lake in the bowl. From the crest, you have an excellent view nearly straight down into the austere, lake-dotted basin.

CLIMBS: Mountaineers have plenty of potential conquests to consider. From the vicinity of Shepherd Pass, the northwest ridge of Mt. Tyndall is class 2, as is the south face of Mt. Keith. A moderate class 3 route up Junction Peak follows the southeast ridge from the pass.

A stay in Center Basin provides a number of interesting diversions. The east face of Center Peak and the west face of Mt. Bradley are both rated class 2, while technical climbers will enjoy the challenges of the five Center Basin Crags.

PERMITS: Wilderness permit required for overnight stays. (Quota: 15 per day)

CAMPFIRES: No fires within 1000 feet of Anvil Camp, or above 10,400 feet.

BIGHORN SHEEP AREA: Dogs and domestic sheep are prohibited.

JOHN MUIR TRAIL

TRIP **62**

John Muir Trail: Mt. Whitney Trail to Kearsarge Pass Trail

M / BPx

DISTANCE: 27.5 miles

ELEVATION: 13,580/10,405/13,070/9535/ 10,870, +5935'/-8660'

SEASON: Late July to early October

USE: High

MAPS: *Mount Whitney, Mt. Kaweah, Mt. Brewer, Mt. Williamson, Mt. Clarence King*

TRAIL LOG:

0.0	Mt. Whitney Trail Jct.
5.7	PCT Jct.
9.5	Wallace Creek/ High Sierra Trail Jct.
13.0	Frog Ponds
13.75	Tyndall Creek Trail Jct.
14.0	Shepherd Pass Trail Jct./ Tyndall Creek Ford
18.5	Forester Pass
23.0	Center Basin Trail Jct.
26.0	Vidette Meadow/ Bubbs Creek Trail Jct.
27.5	Kearsarge Pass Trail Jct.

INTRODUCTION: Without a doubt, you'll see some of the most impressive High Sierra scenery there is on this 27.5-mile stretch of the 220-mile John Muir Trail (JMT). The trail begins in Yosemite Valley and ends at the 14,494-foot summit of Mt. Whitney. Usual access is on the east side of the range from Whitney Portal via the very popular Mt. Whitney Trail. Consequently, required wilderness permits are at an extremely high premium, fought over by summiteers and

JMT through-hikers alike. A limited number of permits and an overwhelming number of applications have resulted in an advance reservation lottery, which leaves many a hopeful backpacker holding the bag. Lucky winners have not only the privilege of attempting a climb to the summit of Whitney, but also of traveling to the less popular backcountry beyond. However, don't expect too much solitude and serenity, as the JMT is not exactly a forgotten trail. Fortunately, by wandering just slightly off this backcountry freeway, travelers can find wilderness nooks and crannies that offer a modicum of peace and quiet.

If your party is fortunate enough to begin this trip from Whitney Portal, don't miss the highlight of the 2-mile ascent of Mt. Whitney from the junction with the Mt. Whitney Trail near Trail Crest (see Trip 59), where sane backpackers drop their packs at the junction before their final ascent. Beyond this junction, most of the hordes are left behind. The JMT passes a couple of excellent opportunities for off-trail excursions up Wallace and Wright creeks, makes a protracted climb to lofty Forester Pass, and follows delightful Bubbs Creek before reaching the Kearsarge Pass Trail.

DIRECTIONS TO THE TRAILHEAD:

START: In the heart of Lone Pine, turn west from U.S. 395 onto Whitney Portal Road and drive 13 miles to the parking lots at Whitney Portal. Campgrounds, restrooms, and a small store with cafe are nearby.

END: From U.S. 395 in the town of Independence, turn west onto Market Street, following signs for Onion Valley. Travel 12.5 miles along the steep, winding Onion Valley road to the parking area at Onion Valley. Do not leave food overnight in vehicles, as Onion Valley is a favorite target of bears. A campground, restrooms and running water are available near the trailhead.

DESCRIPTION: At the beginning of the Mt. Whitney Trail, an abundance of signs, plac-

ards, and display boards create quite a fanfare, which seems perversely suited to the most heavily regulated and popular backcountry route in the Sierra.

Away from the hoopla at the trailhead, the well-beaten path winds through a light forest before curving up the hillside to the first major switchback. Heading roughly east, soon you come to an unnamed tributary, and then make a quarter-mile upward traverse across the hillside to the crossing of the North Fork. A steep mountaineer's route climbs this drainage to base camps at the alpine lakes below the east face of Whitney. Farther up the trail, 1 mile from Whitney Portal, you cross the John Muir Wilderness boundary.

A steady climb ensues, incorporating numerous switchbacks into the ascent. Try to avoid this section of the climb during the heat of the day, as you will be exposed to the sun for much of the next 1.5 miles. Welcome relief comes as you approach the ford of Lone Pine Creek. A short distance beyond the ford, you come to a junction with the short spur trail heading northeast to Lone Pine Lake, 2.75 miles from the trailhead.

From the Lone Pine Lake junction, you stroll through a light covering of pine and enter the Whitney Zone. Soon a steeper climb resumes on a series of switchbacks that lead up and over a rocky slope to a large meadow. You follow a mildly graded path alongside the meadow to the far end and turn northwest to a crossing of Lone Pine Creek.

Just beyond the creek, in the shadow of a waterfall, is Outpost Camp (10,335′), 3.75 miles from the trailhead.

Although camping is possible at Lone Pine Lake, the sloping campsites surrounded by gravel and rock at Outpost Camp represent the first practical alternative for Whitney climbers.

Leave the peaceful surroundings of Outpost Camp, cross Mirror Creek, and then make a steep climb via switchbacks alongside the stream. At the top of the climb you boulder hop back over the creek

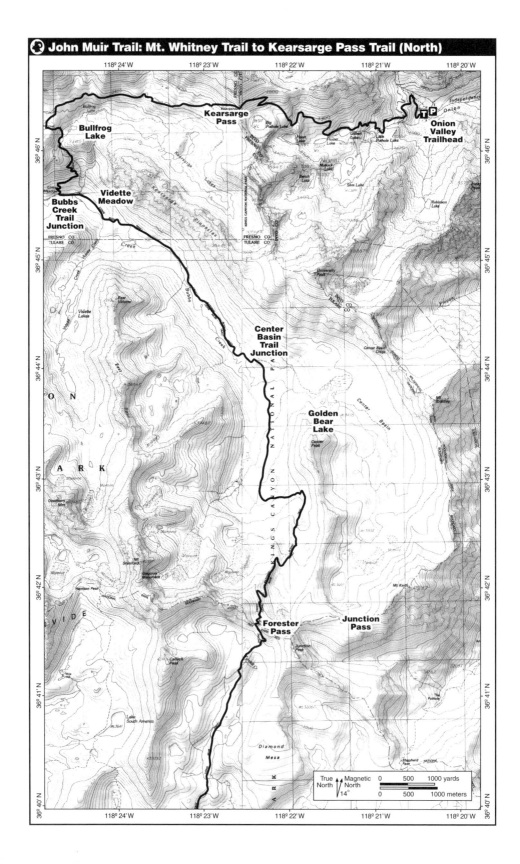

Kearsarge Pass

Bullfrog Lake

Onion Valley Trailhead

Vidette Meadow

Bubbs Creek Trail Junction

Center Basin Trail Junction

Golden Bear Lake

Forester Pass

Junction Pass

KINGS CANYON NATIONAL PARK

True North / Magnetic North 14°

0 500 1000 yards

0 500 1000 meters

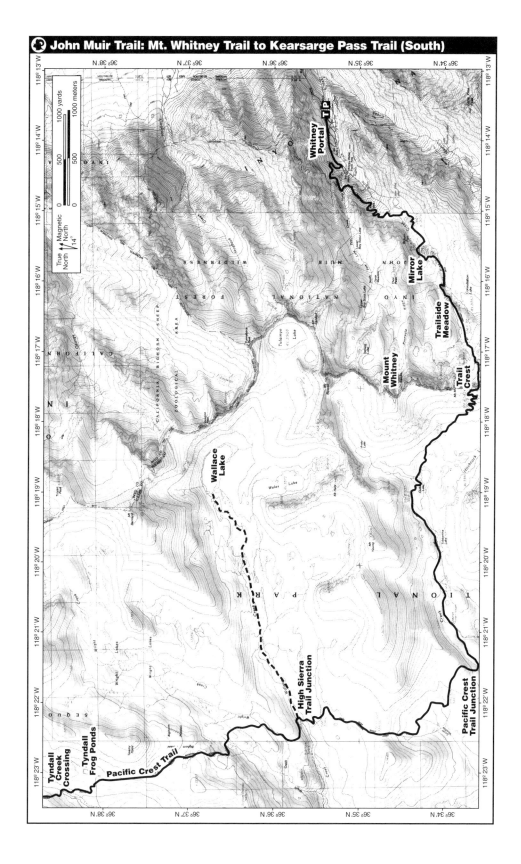

and pass through head-high willows to the southeast shore of Mirror Lake (10,640´), 4.5 miles from Whitney Portal. While you can no longer stay here overnight, Mirror Lake does provide a fine haven for a rest stop or lunch break.

More switchbacks greet you on the ascent out of Mirror Lake's cirque basin. The stiff climb leads to the top of a ridge near timberline, where you resume a more southwesterly ascent. Soon the rugged east face of Mt. Whitney appears over Pinnacle Ridge. You climb moderately through boulders and rocky terrain. A series of rock steps brings you closer to Lone Pine Creek, and eventually you cross the stream on a rock bridge. A ways beyond, an ascent takes you to Trailside Meadows (11,855´), 5.75 miles from the trailhead.

Beyond the oasis of Trailside Meadows, you encounter a nearly endless sea of rock and a seemingly endless climb ahead. After you recross Lone Pine Creek, Consultation Lake comes into view to your left, flanked by Mts. Irvine and McAdie. You continue to climb steadily upward, around boulders and over rock steps. Just after a short stretch of gentle grade, a final climb takes you into Trail Camp (12,035´), 6.5 miles from Whitney Portal.

Directly above the camp, 100 switchbacks climb the slope beneath the gap in the ridge known as Trail Crest. Leaving Trail Camp, you resume the hike along the Mt. Whitney Trail, on a mild path for a very brief time before the grade increases as you head for the first of the 100 switchbacks. You zigzag your way directly up the rocky slope above Trail Camp, noting ever-expanding views to the east (Mt. Whitney becomes hidden behind the Needles). Near the mid-point of the climb, you ascend the side of a rock wall where a seep may create icy conditions; old iron railings add a wary sense of safety. The interminable switchbacks continue as you head toward the crest. Be prepared for snow patches lingering through the summer below the pass. Eventually, you reach Trail Crest (13,580´), 8.5 miles from the trailhead. Just beyond

Trail Crest is the junction between the John Muir and Mt. Whitney trais, 8.6 miles from Whitney Portal.

From the junction, you descend a series of switchbacks, where you have a constant view of the shimmering Hitchcock Lakes below, backdropped nicely by the impressive northeast wall of Mt. Hitchcock. Beyond the switchbacks, a moderate descent leads to a bench with a pair of small lakelets and some overused, exposed campsites. (You'll find better spots off-trail at Hitchcock Lakes.) You continue to Guitar Lake (11,480´±), where the grade eases momentarily and more overused campsites appear. Once again, superior campsites reside away from the lake, along the outlet from Arctic Lake or on rises above the south shore of the lake.

After crossing the outlet from Arctic Lake, you make a mile-long, moderately steep descent on rocky trail through a sparse cover of lodgepoles to Timberline Lake, which is closed to camping, but offers a nice reflection of Mt. Whitney from the southwest shore. You pass a lovely meadow, drop into the valley of Whitney Creek, and encounter the junction (10,640´±) with the Crabtree Meadow lateral, from which a connecting path leads to the Crabtree Ranger Station. Good campsites (with a bear box) can be found along this trail on either side of the ford of Whitney Creek, a short distance from the junction. From the junction, continue west on the JMT away from Whitney Creek through a smattering of foxtail pine to a junction with the Pacific Crest Trail (PCT) (10,680´±), 5.7 miles from the junction with the Mt. Whitney Trail.

Turn north at the junction and climb over a rise to the ford of a seasonal stream. Skirt Sandy Meadow, stepping across many small brooks, and then make a steady climb through lodgepole pines to a saddle (10,963´). Beyond the saddle, you make a gentle descent across the west shoulder of Mt. Young to a field of boulders where the grade eases momentarily. On a moderate descent, you head down a rocky hillside,

Mt. Tyndall, near the JMT

enjoying excellent views of the Sierra Crest and the Kings-Kern Divide. Stepping across numerous brooks along the way, you drop into a stream canyon. At the bottom of the descent, 3.7 miles from the PCT/JMT junction, you encounter the wide ford of Wallace Creek (10,403´), which can be difficult in the early season. Just beyond the creek are numerous campsites (with a bear box) and a well-signed junction. The High Sierra Trail meets the JMT here, and an unmaintained path heads upstream to the east along Wallace Creek, providing knapsackers with a route to scenic Wallace and Wales lakes (see Options below).

Away from the junction, you ascend a boulder-strewn hillside through a light forest of lodgepole pines on a sustained climb out of the canyon of Wallace Creek. Before reaching Wright Creek, you pass a few forested campsites. A moderate climb after the crossing follows the course of the creek briefly, before a steeper ascent leads into

the open for a grand view of the Wright Lakes basin backdropped nicely by Mts. Tyndall, Versteeg, and Barnard. Soon, you climb back into scattered lodgepoles intermixed with foxtail pines on a route to the broad, barren expanse of the Bighorn Plateau. Across the sandy flat, you have an impressive panorama of the Great Western Divide, from Red Spur in the south to the Kings-Kern Divide in the north. A tarn just west of the trail provides a nice photogenic touch.

At the far edge of the plateau, scattered foxtail pines greet you once more, on a mild descent across the western slope of Tawny Point. At 3.8 miles from the High Sierra Trail junction, you hop across a tributary of Tyndall Creek, the outlet from a trio of lakelets known as Tyndall Frog Ponds. Near the trail are good campsites with a bear box, and more secluded sites away from the trail can be found closer to the ponds, where swimming should be pleasant by mid-summer. A winding three-quarter-mile descent through a moderate cover of a lodgepole forest takes you to a junction with the Tyndall Creek Trail, which leads down to the seasonal ranger cabin and campsites along the creek.

A quarter-mile climb from the Tyndall Creek junction brings you to the Shepherd Pass Trail and the daunting ford of Tyndall Creek just beyond, where campsites with a bear box can be found on the far bank. The ascent continues, leading quickly to a junction with a trail toward Lake South America, 5.1 miles from the High Sierra Trail junction. A tarn to the west of the trail provides secluded campsites.

On a mild-to-moderate climb, you proceed up the JMT past timberline, through open terrain with excellent views of the upper Tyndall Creek basin. You pass lovely tarns and step across trickling streams along the way to the base of the headwall below Forester Pass. As with many of the High Sierra passes, a viable route over the wall ahead seems unlikely, until you begin the switchbacking climb that zigzags up the face. The trail is something of an engineering marvel, literally blasted and cut out of the vertical rock wall—portions of the trail are definitely not for acrophobes. You finally reach the narrow gap in the Kings-Kern Divide, at Forester Pass (13,180′), on the boundary between Sequoia and Kings Canyon parks, 9.4 miles from the High Sierra Trail junction at Wallace Creek. Expansive views from the pass take in myriad peaks to the north and south.

After the precipitous terrain on the south side of the pass, the descent of the north side is a piece of cake, on a smooth, sandy trail that switchbacks down to the top of a rock rib above the tarn in the head of the canyon. You follow the path to the end of the rib, enjoying the excellent views along the way. An angling descent leads to a crossing of Bubbs Creek just below the tarn. From the crossing, you have a grand alpine view of the tarn backdropped by Junction Peak.

You continue the winding, rocky descent, fording the creek a couple more times and following the course of the stream as it bends west and descends into more hospitable terrain. In a grove of pines, just beyond a no fires sign, you pass a couple of poor campsites, tiered down the steep slope. More switchbacks lead you into a light forest of scattered lodgepole and whitebark pines, past small pockets of verdant, wildflower-dotted meadows, and through clumps of willow to the ford of Center Basin Creek. Past the ford, you encounter campsites with a bear box and the unsigned junction with the Center Basin Trail (10,675′), 4.5 miles from Forester Pass. A side trip to Golden Bear Lake is well worth the extra time and effort (see Trip 61).

In and out of scattered-to-light lodgepole forest, you continue the descent on the JMT, following the tumbling course of Bubbs Creek, sandwiched between the towering pinnacle of East Vidette to the west and the rugged spine of the Kearsarge Pinnacles to the east. Along the way, you hop across a number of tributary streams. Eventually, you pass through a wire fence

to reach Upper Vidette Meadow and a number of overused campsites reposing under pines next to the creek. Beyond the camp at an unsigned Y-junction, the left branch of a use-trail leads down to a large packer's camp alongside the stream. A ways farther is the ever-popular Vidette Meadow Camp (with bear boxes) that caters to JMT through-hikers and backpackers bound for the Rae Lakes Loop from Cedar Grove. After a pair of stream crossings, you come to the junction with the Bubbs Creek Trail (9530′±) to Cedar Grove, 7.7 miles from Forester Pass.

From the junction, you follow a moderate, switchbacking climb up the north wall of Bubbs Creek canyon. Views to your right of the Kearsarge Pinnacles are quite dramatic, but don't neglect the views behind you of the Videttes and Deerhorn Mountain. After a pair of creek crossings, you come to a junction with the Bullfrog Lake Trail (the original Kearsarge Pass Trail), which provides an alternate route to Kearsarge Pass past Bullfrog and Kearsarge Lakes (see *Kings Canyon National Park: A Complete Hiker's Guide*). Picturesque Bullfrog Lake, 0.4 mile east of the JMT, has been closed to camping for several decades due to severe overuse, and the Kearsarge Lakes have a one-night limit.

A series of short switchbacks lead over a lightly forested rise to a broad sandy flat and a multi-signed junction, 1.5 miles from the Bubbs Creek Trail. The Kearsarge Pass Trail heads east from this junction for 7 miles to the Onion Valley trailhead (see *Kings Canyon National Park: A Complete Hiker's Guide*) and the JMT continues north (this 0.2-mile section is not shown on the *Mt. Clarence King* quad). The Charlotte Lake Trail heads northwest for three-quarters of a mile to the lake, which has a one-night camping limit.

◻ **WALLACE LAKE CROSS-COUNTRY ROUTE:** Although the path to Wallace Lake is unmaintained and indistinct in parts, by cross-country standards the route is fairly straightforward. From the JMT, a use-trail follows the north bank of Wallace Creek on a mild ascent through a light-to-moderate cover of lodgepole pines. Near the meadow at the confluence of Wallace Creek and the outlet from Wales Lake, the route crosses to the south side of Wallace Creek, fords the outlet from Wales Lake, and continues upstream to some timberline camps, approximately a half mile below the lake. From there, proceed along the south bank of the main branch to Wallace Lake (11,473′), 3.6 miles from the JMT. Anglers should find the good-sized golden trout an adequate challenge. Less-visited Wales Lake is a short off-trail jaunt from Wallace Lake.

O **WRIGHT LAKES CROSS-COUNTRY ROUTE:** The wide-open Wright Lakes basin provides easy off-trail travel. Leave the Muir Trail where it bends away from Wright Creek and continue upstream through lodgepole pines following the course of the creek. Soon, you break out of the trees and enter the wide-open, lake-dotted basin. In early and mid-season the meadows may be quite boggy, fed by a plethora of springs and rivulets. The highest lake requires a short but steep climb up the brush-and-rock-filled slope, but will reward the diligent hiker with good views and fishing. More adventurous souls can continue toward Tulainyo Lake.

O **CENTER BASIN:** Center Basin provides another option for seeing some awesome mountain scenery (see Trip 61).

O **SOME WORTHWHILE CLIMBS:** The obvious first choice for climbing along this section is the 2-mile trail from the Mt. Whitney junction to the summit of the highest peak in the continental U.S. (see Trip 59).

From Wallace Creek, the southwest slope of Mt. Barnard is class 1. From the upper lake of the Wright Lakes group, the southwest slopes of Mts. Versteeg and Tyndall are both class 2.

Before you reach Forester Pass, a class 2 route up Caltech Peak follows the southeast slope. From the pass, a moderate class 3 climb of Junction Peak can be made via the west ridge. North of the pass, the east ridge of East Vidette is a fine class 3 ascent.

R **PERMITS:** Wilderness permit required for overnight stays. (Quota: 60 per day) See Trip 59 for special Whitney Zone regulations.

CAMPFIRES: Not allowed above 11,200 feet, in the Whitney Zone, within 1200 feet of Tyndall Creek Frog Ponds, within 1200 feet of the crossing of Tyndall Creek, or above 10,800 feet along Wallace and Wright creeks.

CAMPING: No camping at Timberline Lake, Mirror Lake, or Trailside Meadow.

BEARS: Canisters required in Whitney Zone.

SANITATION: Outpost Camp and Trail Camp: use toilets for solid waste disposal only (do not urinate, as the toilets are easily overloaded with liquid). If toilets are unavailable, dispose of waste a minimum of 200 feet from water and bury it in soil at least 6 inches deep, or pack it out. Pack out all toilet paper and feminine hygiene products—do not burn.

Appendices

APPENDIX ▌

Backpacks Features Chart

Note: Time of year headings represent the average point in the season when trails become snow free. Times may very from year to year depending on variables, such as the amount of snow that fell in the previous winter and how fast that snow melts in the spring.

Backpacks Features – West Side							
Best Time / Trip	**Route**	**Ratings 1 – 10**			**Length in**		**Elevation**
		Scenery	**Solitude**	**Difficulty**	**Days**	**Miles**	**Gain/Loss**
MARCH							
24. Colony Mill Road	➚	6	10	Ⓜ	2	8	+5170/-1085
LATE-MAY							
2. Garfield-Hockett Trail	➚	7	9	Ⓜ	2–4	10	+6115/-1175
32. Bearpaw Meadow	➚	7	5	Ⓜ	2–3	11	+4085/-3155
JUNE							
5. Atwell-Hockett Trail	➚	7	9	Ⓜ	2–4	10	+3690/-1785
MID-JUNE							
44. Lakes Trail	◖	9	4	Ⓜ	2–3	6	+2795/-535
LATE-JUNE							
32. Hamilton Lakes	➚	9	6	Ⓜ	3–4	14	+5730/-4215
46. Twin Lakes	➚	7	5	Ⓜ	2–3	7	+3030/-285
EARLY JULY							
8. Mosquito Lakes	➚	8	7	Ⓜ/X	2–3	5	+2135/-375
9. Eagle Lake	➚	8	5	Ⓜ	2	3	+2285/-55
10. White Chief Canyon	➚	8	6	Ⓢ	2–3	4	+2360/-150
12. Franklin Lakes	➚	8	3	Ⓜ	2–3	6	+2910/-465
17. Redwood & Bearpaw Meadows	➚	7	8	Ⓜ	2–3	13	+4360/-4340
41. Mehrten & Alta Meadows	➚	8	5	Ⓜ	2–3	6	+2600/-570

Best Time/Trip	Route	Scenery	Solitude	Difficulty	Days	Miles	Elevation Gain/Loss
MID-JULY							
13. Franklin & Sawtooth Passes Loop	↻	9	5	(S)	3–5	28	+9250/-9250
14. Crystal Lakes	↗	8	7	(MS)	2–3	4	+3675/-500
16. Little 5 & Big 5 Lakes Loop	↻	9	8	(MS)	3–5	27	+9930/-9930
32. Nine Lakes Basin	↗	10	7	(M)	3–5	18	+7270/-3390
33. High Sierra Trail	↗	10	8	(MS)	8–14	69	+18475/16835
47. Kings-Kaweah Divides Loop	↻	9	9	(M)	5–9	52	+14100/-14100

Backpacks Features – East Side

Best Time/Trip	Route	Scenery	Solitude	Difficulty	Days	Miles	Elevation Gain/Loss
MID-JULY							
53. Chicken Springs Lake	↗	8	5	(M)	2	4	+1400/-90
54. Cottonwood & New Army Loop	↻	8	7	(M)	2–4	19	+4115/-4115
55. New Army Pass Trail	↗	8	5	(E)	2	7	+1650/-215
56. Cottonwood Lakes	↗	7	3	(E)	2–3	6	+1450/-295
57. Soldier Lakes & Rock Creek	↗	8	8	(M)	2–4	15	+2555/-445
58. Cottonwood Lakes to Whitney Portal	↗	9	5	(MS)	3–5	35	+8070/-9805
59. Mt. Whitney	↗	10	1	(MS)	2–3	11	+7830/-1875
60. Meysan Lake	↗	7	8	(MS)	2	5	+3860/-310
61. Shepherd Pass Trail	↗	8	8	(S)	2–3	13	+6785/-2205
62. JMT-Whitney to Kearsarge	↗	10	4	(MS)	3–5	28+16	+5935/-8660

APPENDIX **II**

Day Hikes Features Chart

Note: Time of year headings represent the average point in the season when trails become snow free. Times may very from year to year depending on variables, such as the amount of snow that fell in the previous winter and how fast that snow melts in the spring.

Day Hikes Features – West Side						
Best Time / Trip	**Route**	**Ratings 1 – 10**			**Length in Miles**	**Elevation Gain/Loss**
		Scenery	**Solitude**	**Difficulty**		
ALL YEAR						
1. Putnam & Snowslide Canyons	↗	6	9	Ⓜ	3.25	+2540
3. Ladybug Camp	↗	5	9	Ⓜ	1.75	+900/-115
18. Potwisha Pictograph Loop	↻	5	6	Ⓔ	0.5	+205/-205
19. Marble Falls	↗	6	6	Ⓜ	3.25	+1750/-295
20. Hospital Rock to Potwisha	↗	6	8	Ⓔ	2.4	+345/-935
21. Paradise Creek Trail	↗	6	8	Ⓜ	2.3	+975/-280
22. Hospital Rock to Panther Creek	↗	6	8	Ⓜ	2.75	+1325/-670
23. North Fork Trail	↗	5	9	Ⓜ	4.2	+1454/-555
MARCH						
24. Colony Mill Road	↗	6	10	Ⓜ	8	+5170/-1085
EARLY-APRIL						
45. Tokopah Falls	↗	8	3	Ⓔ	2	+700/-100
LATE APRIL						
30. High Sierra Trail to Panther Creek	↗	7	5	Ⓜ	2.7	+850/-800
EARLY MAY TO MID-MAY						
26. Colony Mill Ranger Station	↗	6	10	Ⓜ	2	+865/-245

Best Time / Trip	Route	Ratings 1–10 Scenery	Solitude	Difficulty	Days	Length in Miles	Elevation Gain/Loss
28. Bobcat Point Loop	↻	7	8	**E**		1.25	+255/-255
31. Giant Forest East Loop	↻	8	7	**M**		14	+2370/-2370
35. Sunset Rock	↗	6	3	**E**		0.8	+215/-115
36. Big Trees Trail	↻	7	1	**E**		1.3	negligible
37. Hazelwood Nature Trail	↻	7	2	**E**		0.5	negligible
38. Congress Trail	↻	8	1	**E**		2	+550/-550
39. Trail of the Sequoias	↻	8	6	**M**		6.1	+1770/-1770
40. Circle Meadow Loop	↻	8	6	**E**		3.8	+740/-740
51. Lost Grove to Dorst Campground	↗	6	6	**E**		2.3	+555/-535
52. Cabin Creek Trail	↗	5	8	**E**		0.8	+165/-120
LATE MAY							
2. Garfield-Hockett Trail	↗	5	10	**M**		5	+4150/-200
4. East Fork Grove	↗	5	9	**M**		2.5	+525/-820
7. Cold Springs Trail	↗↗	6	6	**E**		1.2	+350/-20
34. Moro Rock Loop	↻	8	5	**M**		4.4	+1475/-1475
EARLY JUNE							
25. Marble Fork Bridge to Sunset Rock	↗	5	9	**M**		2.4	+1350/-100
27. Huckleberry Meadows Loop	↻	6	6	**E**		3.75	+840/-840
29. Crescent and Log Meadows Loop	↻	7	5	**E**		2.2	+435/-435
49. Little Baldy	↗	7	4	**M**		1.75	+820/-110
50. Muir Grove	↗	8	7	**M**		2.1	+670/-585
MID-JUNE							
6. Paradise Peak	↗	7	9	**MS**		5.5	+3450/-610
44. Lakes Trail	↻	9	4	**M**		5.75	+2795/535

Best Time / Trip	Route	Ratings 1–10 Scenery	Solitude	Difficulty	Days	Length in Miles	Elevation Gain/Loss
LATE JUNE							
46. Twin Lakes	↗	7	5	Ⓜ		6.75	+3030/-285
48. Wuksachi Trail	↗	5	8	Ⓜ		1.5	+220/-430
EARLY-JULY							
8. Mosquito Lakes	↗	8	7	Ⓜ/X		3.5/1.5	+2135/-375
9. Eagle Lake	↗	8	5	Ⓜ		3.25	+2285/-55
10. White Chief Canyon	↗	8	7	Ⓢ		3.75	+2360/-150
12. Franklin Lakes	↗	8	3	Ⓜ		5.5	+2910/-465
41. Mehrten and Alta Meadows	↗	8	5	Ⓜ		5.9	+2600/-570
42. Alta Peak	↗	10	6	Ⓢ		6.7	+4265/-330
43. Panther Gap Loop	↺	8	5	Ⓜ		7	+1720/-1720
MID-JULY							
11. Farewell Gap	↗	8	7	ⓂⓈ		5.5	+3320/-455
14. Crystal Lakes	↗	8	7	ⓂⓈ		3.75	+3675/-500
15. Monarch Lakes	↗	7	5	Ⓜ		3.25	+2740/-200

Dayhikes Features – East Side

Best Time / Trip	Route	Ratings 1–10 Scenery	Solitude	Difficulty	Length in Miles	Elevation Gain/Loss
MID-JULY						
53. Chicken Springs Lake	↗	8	5	Ⓜ	4.1	1400/-90
54. New Army Pass Trail	↗	8	5	Ⓔ	6.5	+1650/-215
55. Cottonwood Lakes	↗	7	3	Ⓔ	5.9	+1450/-295
59. Mt. Whitney	↗	10	1	Ⓢ	10.5	+7830/-1875
60. Meysan Trail	↗	7	8	ⓂⓈ	4.5	+3860/-310

Appendix

Highest Sierra Nevada Peaks and
Largest Giant Sequoias in Sequoia and Kings Canyon

Highest Peaks in the Sierra Nevada					
Rank			Elevation		
CA	Sierra	Name	Feet	Meters	USGS 7.5 min. map
1.	1.	Mt. Whitney	14,494	4418	Mount Whitney
2.	2.	Mt. Williamson	14,375	4382	Mt. Williamson
4.	3.	North Palisade	14,242	4334	North Palisade
6.	4.	Mt. Sill	14,153	4314	North Palisade
7.	5.	Mt. Russell	14,086	4293	Mount Whitney
8.	6.	Split Mountain	14,058	4285	Split Mtn.
9.	7.	Middle Palisade	14,040	4279	Split Mtn.
10.	8.	Mt. Langley	14,028	4275	Mt. Langley
11.	9.	Mt. Tyndall	14,018	4273	Mt. Williamson
12.	10.	Mt. Muir	14,009	4270	Mount Whitney
13.	11.	Thunderbolt Peak	14,003	4268	North Palisade

Several "points" in the Sierra are higher than some of the mountains listed above, but are not considered to be actual peaks. Among these sub-peaks are Keeler Needle (14,272), Starlight Peak (14,220), West Horn of Mt. Williamson (14,160), East Horn of Mt. Williamson (14,125), and Polemonium Peak (14,000).

Largest Giant Sequoias in Sequoia and Kings Canyon

Rank CA	Seq/Kings	Name	Volume (cu ft)	Height (ft)	Circumference (ft)	Location
1.	1.	General Sherman	52,508	274.9	102.6	Giant Forest
2.	2.	Washington	47,850	254.7	101.1	Giant Forest
3.	3.	General Grant	46,608	268.1	107.6	Grant Grove
4.	4.	President	45,148	240.9	93.0	Giant Forest
5.	5.	Lincoln	44,471	255.8	98.3	Giant Forest
8.	6.	Boole	42,472	268.8	113.0	Converse Basin
9.	7.	Franklin	41,280	223.8	94.8	Giant Forest
10.	8.	King Arthur	40,656	270.3	104.2	Garfield Grove
11.	9.	Monroe	40,104	247.8	91.3	Giant Forest
12.	10.	Robert E. Lee	40,102	254.7	88.3	Grant Grove
13.	11.	John Adams	38,956	250.6	83.3	Giant Forest
14.	12.	Ishi Giant	38,156	248.1	105.1	Kennedy Grove
15.	13.	Unnamed	37,295	243.8	93.0	Giant Forest
17.	14.	Unnamed	36,292	239.4	75.5	Giant Forest
18.	15.	Unnamed	36,228	281.5	95.1	Giant Forest
21.	16.	Pershing	35,855	246.0	91.2	Giant Forest
22.	17.	Diamond	35,292	286.0	95.3	Atwell Grove
24.	18.	Roosevelt	35,013	260.0	80.0	Redwood Mtn.
26.	19.	(AD)	34,706	242.4	99.0	Atwell Grove
27.	20.	Hart	34,407	277.9	75.3	Redwood Mtn.
29.	21.	Chief Sequoyah	33,608	228.2	90.4	Giant Forest

APPENDIX **IV**

The Bear Facts and Other Animal Concerns

Bears

The last grizzly bear in the Sierra Nevada was shot near Horse Corral Meadows in the early 1900s. Since then, the common American black bear has been the only species of bear in the range. Despite their name, black bears range in color from jet black to cinnamon. They are very quick and agile animals, and often quite large— mature males can weigh as much as 300 pounds. Black bears are active both day and night, and have highly developed senses of smell. Usually found on the west slope of the Sierra, between 5000 and 8500 feet, black bears occasionally travel to higher elevations. Although they are considered omnivores, black bears subsist mainly on vegetation and typically are not aggressive animals, especially toward humans. Bears who have not become familiar with humans tend to be shy and retiring, avoiding contact at virtually any cost. However, black bears that grow accustomed to human food and garbage through our carelessness can become destructive and potentially dangerous animals.

Once bears discover food or garbage from coolers, cars, or backpacks, it is extremely hard to recondition them. Bears that frequent developed campgrounds tend to be the boldest and potentially most dangerous ones. Relocating such animals to backcountry areas has not proven effective, as bears generally find their way back to civilization, or become highly aggressive toward recreationists. "Problem bears" eventually have to be destroyed.

Despite a reputation for being stupid animals, bears have figured out ways to render our attempts at deceiving them useless. The standard way to protect food from bears in the backcountry was the counter-balance method of hanging food, but this method no longer works. Nowadays, if you attempt to protect your cache by hanging a stuff sack full of food from a tree limb a bear may climb the tree to snap the cord, simply break the branch, or dive-bomb the sack; or a mother bear will send a cub up the tree to the same end. The counter-balance method had drawbacks from the beginning for campers near or above timberline, where the trees are either too small or absent entirely. Several years ago the park managers for Yosemite and Sequoia/Kings Canyon, along with the surrounding forest managers, embarked on a plan to help minimize encounters between bears and backcountry users. Popular backcountry campsites provide bear-proof lockers; bear-proof canisters are required in the most heavily used areas and strongly encouraged elsewhere. Hopefully, this plan will help break the association between humans and food by making it impossible for the bears to obtain human food that is stored in lockers and canisters. The plan requires the cooperation of all who use the backcountry and park campsites. It is the responsibility of park visitors to store food so that it is inaccessible to bears and to deposit garbage in the appropriate receptacles, so that bears do not become accustomed to food and garbage and thus to prevent the destruction that might result. The canisters add a couple of pounds to backpackers' loads, but that burden is offset by the security the canisters provide. The presence of bears needn't discourage anyone from hiking or backpacking in the Sierra.

The following guidelines should enhance your experience and help protect the bears.

CAMPGROUNDS

- Leave extra or unnecessary food and scented items at home.
- Store all food, food containers, and scented items in bear lockers and latch them securely.

Locations of Backcountry Bear Lockers (subject to change)

Sequoia	Kings Canyon

Sequoia

Hockett Plateau *(1)*
Hockett Meadow *(1)*
South Fork Meadow/Rock Camp *(1)*
Hidden Camp/Lower South Fork
  Meadow *(1)*
Upper Camp/South Fork Pasture *(2)*
Kern Canyon *(1)*
Lower Funston Meadow *(1)*
Upper Funston Meadow *(2)*
Kern Hot Springs *(2)*
Junction Meadow *(1)*
Little Five Lakes/Cliff
  Creek/Chagoopa *(1)*
Moraine Lake *(1)*
Cliff Creek/Timber Gap Junction *(1)*
Pinto Lake *(1)*
Big Five Lakes *(1)*
Big Arroyo Crossing *(1)*
Lost Canyon/Big Five Junction *(1)*
Lodgepole Backcountry *(1)*
HST-Mehrten Creek *(1)*
HST-9 Mile Creek Crossing *(1)*
Bearpaw Meadow *(4)*
Upper Hamilton Lake *(3)*
Emerald Lake *(2)*
Pear Lake *(2)*
Clover Creek *(1)*
JO Pass/Twin Lakes Junction *(1)*
Twin Lakes *(2)*
HST-Buck Creek Crossing *(1)*
Rock Creek *(1)*
PCT-Lower Rock Creek Crossing *(1)*
Lower Rock Creek Lake *(1)*
Lower Soldier Lake *(1)*
Tyndall/Crabtree Area *(1)*
JMT-Tyndall Creek *(1)*
Tyndall Creek Frog Ponds *(1)*
JMT-Wallace Creek *(1)*
Lower Crabtree Meadow *(1)*
Crabtree Ranger Station *(1)*
Mineral King *(1)*
Monarch Lake *(2)*
Franklin Lake *(3)*

Kings Canyon

Bubbs Creek Area *(1)*
Sphinx Creek *(2)*
Charlotte Creek *(1)*
Junction Meadow (lower) *(1)*
Junction Meadow (East Creek) *(1)*
East Lake *(1)*
Vidette Meadow *(2)*
JMT (9900´±) *(1)*
JMT/Center Basin Junction *(1)*
Charlotte & Kearsarge Lakes *(1)*
Charlotte Lake *(1)*
Kearsarge Lakes *(1)*
Copper Creek *(1)*
Lower Tent Meadow *(1)*
Lewis Creek *(1)*
Frypan Meadow *(1)*
Sugarloaf Valley/Roaring River *(1)*
Ranger Lake *(1)*
Seville Lake *(1)*
Lost Lake *(1)*
Sugarloaf Meadow *(1)*
Roaring River Ranger Station *(1)*
Comanche Meadow *(1)*
Woods Creek *(1)*
Lower Paradise Valley *(1)*
Middle Paradise Valley *(1)*
Upper Paradise Valley *(1)*
JMT-Woods Creek Crossing *(1)*
Arrowhead Lake *(1)*
Lower Rae Lake *(1)*
Upper Rae Lake *(1)*

- Dispose of all trash in bear-proof garbage cans or dumpsters.
- Do not leave food out at an unattended campsite.

BACKCOUNTRY

- Don't leave your pack unattended while on the trail.
- Once in camp, empty your pack and open all flaps and pockets.
- Keep all food, trash, and scented items in a bear-proof locker or canister.
- Pack out all trash.

EVERYWHERE

- Don't allow bears to approach your food—make noise, wave your arms, throw rocks. Be bold, but keep a safe distance and use good judgment.
- If a bear gets into your food, you are responsible for cleaning up the mess.
- Never attempt to retrieve food from a bear.
- Never approach a bear, especially a cub.
- Report any incidents or injuries to the appropriate agency.

TRAILS THAT REQUIRE USE OF BEAR CANISTERS

- Mt. Whitney Trail (Trip 59) (Inyo National Forest)
- Kearsarge Pass Trail (east of Kearsarge Pass) (Trip 62) (Inyo National Forest)
- Bishop Pass Trail (including Dusy & Palisade Basins) (Kings Canyon National Park)

Other Animal Concerns

COUGARS: The chances of seeing a cougar, or mountain lion, in the backcountry are extremely small, as cougars are typically shy and avoid human contact at nearly all costs. It is more likely that one has seen you, especially if you've hiked much in the western foothills. Unlike black bears, mountain lions are strictly carnivorous. Mule deer is the main staple of their diet; when hunting for venison is poor, they sup-

plement with smaller animals. A typical lion is estimated to kill 36 deer per year, and the health of the deer population is directly linked to the predatory nature of these cats as they thin the herd of its weaker members. In the unlikely event of an encounter with one of these big cats, keep in mind the following guidelines:

- Never hike alone, especially in the foothills.
- If you encounter a cat, don't run, as they might mistake you for prey.
- Make yourself appear as large as possible—don't crouch or try to hide.
- Hold your ground or back away slowly while facing the cat.
- Don't leave small children unattended; pick them up if a cat approaches.
- If the lion seems aggressive, make noise, wave your arms, and throw rocks.
- If the animal attacks, fight back.
- Report any encounters to a ranger as soon as possible.

MARMOTS: These fuzzy, chirping rodents hardly seem threatening to humans. However, members of their clan have been known to wreak havoc on cars at Mineral King by chewing on engine parts such as rubber hoses, wires, and even radiators. Many a vehicle has been disabled in spring and early summer, leaving drivers stranded until they can arrange for repairs or for a long, arduous tow to Three Rivers. If you plan on visiting Mineral King during spring or early summer, check with park rangers about the best places to leave your car and what measures to take to minimize this potential hazard. By midsummer, their curious cravings for engine parts seem to disappear.

Marmots in other areas of the park, particularly near popular campsites, have been known to chew through backpacking equipment in search of a treat. Store your food in bear lockers and hang your belongings from a tree when leaving your campsite unattended for any length of time.

RATTLESNAKES: Although rattlesnakes are common to the foothills community on the west side of the Sierra and the pinyon-sagebrush zone on the east side, human encounters with them are relatively rare. Actual bites are even more infrequent, and are almost never fatal in adults. While rattlers live in a wide range of environments, pay special attention when hiking along streams and creeks below 6000 feet. These reptiles seek sun when the air temperature is cold and retreat to shade in hot weather; they are typically nocturnal for most of the summer hiking season. Rattlers are not aggressive and will seek an escape route unless cornered. If you happen upon one, quickly back away. If bitten, seek medical attention.

TICKS: Ticks are most common in the lower elevations of the foothills zone; their numbers are highest in spring, especially after wet winters. Ticks are rarely a problem at higher elevations in the southern Sierra during the normal hiking season.

These blood-sucking pests would be just another nuisance if they weren't also carriers of Lyme disease and Rocky Mountain spotted fever. Although rare in the southern Sierra, these tick-born conditions can be serious if not treated by antibiotics. If you have been bitten by at tick, watch for flu-like symptoms, headache, rash, fever, or joint pain, and consult your physician if you develop any of these symptoms.

Myths, old wives tales, and urban legends abound about how to remove ticks. The medically accepted method advises using a pair of tweezers to get a good hold on the pest, and then applying gentle traction to back the tick out of the flesh. Check the wound to make sure the head hasn't been left behind. After removal of the whole tick, thoroughly wash the wound with soap and water, and apply of an antibiotic ointment. Monitor your health for the next several days afterward to detect any symptoms of serious illness. Prevention is the best medicine, so observe the following measures when traveling in tick country:

- Use an effective insect repellent on skin and clothing and apply liberally.
- Wear long-sleeved shirts and tuck pant legs into socks.
- Inspect your entire body for bites at least once each day while in the backcountry.
- Check clothing thoroughly for any loose ticks.

MOSQUITOES: While not a major health concern, pesky mosquitoes can ruin a peaceful day in the mountains. Fortunately, the mosquito cycle in the Sierra Nevada builds for a short time in early summer, peaks for about two weeks, and then steadily diminishes; the peak varies from year to year, yet usually coincides with the climax of wildflower season.

Mosquitoes seem to prefer some humans over others. For those people who mosquitoes do find attractive, supposed deterrents are the modern era's snake oil, from sleeping beneath a pyramid, ingesting a boatload of vitamin B, bathing in a vat of hand lotion, lighting aroma-therapy candles, or emitting a high-pierced electronic shriek heard only by bugs and aliens. Although the only sure-fire protection against the ubiquitous mosquito is to stay home, which isn't much of an alternative, the following suggestions might help you enjoy the backcountry during the perpetual buzz of peak mosquito season.

- Use an insect repellent with DEET as the active ingredient and reapply often.
- Wear a long-sleeved shirt and long pants.
- Wear a mosquito head net for extreme conditions.
- Select a mildly wind-prone campsite away from wet or marshy areas.
- Don't forget your tent.

Minimum Impact Stock Regulations

While "no trace" camping is standard practice in the wilderness, you can also minimize your impact on the land and help to preserve wilderness access privileges by properly caring for your stock animals. Everyone in your party should be familiar with the following guidelines and regulations for wilderness stock use. You will receive a copy of these regulations when you pick up your wilderness permit.

PLANNING YOUR TRIP

• The *Forage Area Guide* describes the designated forage areas and grazing regulations. It is available through the Wilderness Office. Use it to select areas where your stock can graze with minimum impact. An on-line copy of the *Forage Area Guide* will be available in the future.

• Opening dates have been established to protect meadows from stock impacts while they are wet and soft. Grazing is not permitted prior to these dates.

• Take only as many animals as necessary to make your trip successful. Use lightweight, compact equipment to minimize the number of pack animals you'll need. Maximum number of stock allowed per party is 20. Some areas have lower limits.

ON THE TRAIL

• Stock are restricted to maintained trails in most areas. You may travel up to half a mile from trails to reach a campsite. Off-trail stock use is permitted only in certain areas—see the *Forage Area Guide*.

• Shortcutting trails and switchbacks is prohibited. Reduce impacts by riding in the center of the trail. Avoiding sandy, muddy or rocky spots by riding off-trail causes additional damage to the trail. Ride over, not around, water bars, causeways, and riprap. Move trail obstacles instead of skirting them. Double-rope (put a lead rope around both sides of the animal ahead) string animals that habitually walk off-trail. Notify a ranger of obstacles or problems.

• Use tact and courtesy with hikers when asking for the right-of-way. Ask hikers to step off the trail on the downhill side in plain view and to remain still until stock have passed.

• Dead stock must be moved at least 300′ from trails, campsites and water within 72 hours. If any of your stock dies in the backcountry, notify a ranger as soon as possible for help in properly disposing of the animal.

IN CAMP

• Stock should be confined as little as possible. Restless, restrained animals trample vegetation, paw up tree roots and debark trees.

• However, stock must be restrained at all times prior to the grazing opening dates and in areas closed to grazing. Carry substitute feed (processed hay pellets, cubes or weed-free hay) in these areas. Use nosebags or lay feed out on a tarp, not on the ground.

• When confinement is necessary, use existing hitch rails or a hitch line with "tree-saver" straps between two trees or rocks on a flat, hard, non-vegetated site at least 100′ away from the trail, water and camp. Hobble animals that paw excessively.

• Tie animals to trees only when packing or unpacking stock. Never tie to a tree smaller than 6 inches in diameter.

• Water stock downstream and well away from campsites. Avoid fragile stream banks and lakeshores.

GRAZING

- Be sure that forage and water near your camp can support the needs of your stock. Avoid places that have already been heavily grazed, and don't stay too long in one area. Overgrazing weakens grasses, allows weeds to grow, leaves nothing for the next party, and ruins the beauty of the meadows. Some areas have length-of-stay limits; check the *Forage Area Guide* or grazing regulations.

- Drift fences have been provided in many areas to help hold stock. When turning your stock loose to graze, examine the terrain to predict where they'll go. Use bells only on lead animals. Hobbles may be used, but will become less effective with time. Picketing and portable electric fences are permitted as long as they are moved frequently enough to prevent trampling and overgrazing. If you use these methods, try restraining only enough animals to keep the rest from straying. To minimize risk of injury, introduce stock to hobbles, picketing, and electric fences at home, before entering the wilderness.

- Your stock will be easier to catch if they are trained beforehand to expect grain.

LEAVING CAMP

- Carry a rake to fill in pawed-up areas and scatter all manure piles when you leave camp. Remove all manure from within 100′ of the campsite to reduce odors and insect problems, and to maintain the appearance of the site.

- Pack out everything you packed in! Leave nothing behind!

AFTER YOUR TRIP

- The Park Service welcomes your comments on the condition of the wilderness and your wilderness experience.

- Effective management of stock use requires accurate data on patterns of use. Please return the Stock Use Reporting Card (available from the Wilderness Office or wherever you obtain your wilderness permit) to the nearest ranger station, or mail it to:

Wilderness Office
Sequoia & Kings Canyon
National Parks
Three Rivers, CA 93271
(559) 565-3761

APPENDIX **VI**

Nonprofit Organizations

Sequoia Natural History Association

The Sequoia Natural History Association is a non profit organization dedicated to the enhancement of visitor experiences in Sequoia and Kings Canyon national parks. The SNHA is committed to promoting awareness of the parks through educational programs, publications, and financial support. The SNHA participates in the following activities:

- Operation of the park's visitor center bookstores
- Operation of the Sequoia Field Institute and Beetle Rock Education Center
- Free and low-cost school programs
- Publication of the Sequoia and Kings Canyon National Parks newspaper
- Tours of Crystal Cave
- Operation of the Pear Lake Ski Hut
- Purchasing supplies for ranger programs
- Financing active protection of black bears
- Field seminar courses
- Funding visitor center and trail exhibits
- Information staff at visitor centers
- Publishing books and maps of the parks
- Funding scientific research within the parks

MEMBERSHIP CATEGORIES

Individual	$25/year
Family	$30/year
Supporter	$50/year
Business	$150/year
Sponsor	$500/year
John Muir Circle	$1000/year

MEMBERSHIP BENEFITS

- 15% discount on mail order and visitor center purchases
- 50% off ticket price for Crystal Cave tours
- 20% discount at Pear Lake Ski Hut
- Discounts on field seminars
- Special members only sales
- Discounts on books and maps at many other national park visitor centers
- Low-cost internet access
- Membership newsletter
- Seasonal copies of the park visitors guide
- Invitation to members' annual picnic

SNHA
HCR 89—Box 10
Three Rivers, CA 93271-9792
(559) 565-3759
(559) 565-3728 (fax)
snha@sequoiahistory.org (email)
www.sequoiahistory.org

The Sequoia Fund

The Sequoia Fund is the primary non profit fundraising organization for Sequoia and Kings Canyon national parks and Devils Postpile National Monument. Their mission is to support projects that enhance the restoration, conservation, and enjoyment of these parks. The fund has raised over $500,000 for park projects, including the Beetle Rock Environmental Education Center and the Bradley Meadow Interpretive Loop Trail.

The Sequoia Fund
PO Box 3047
Visalia, CA 93278-3047
(559) 739-1668
(559) 739-1680 (fax)
savethetrees@sequoiafund.org (email)
www.sequoiafund.org

APPENDIX

List of Abbreviations

List of Abbreviations	
CCC	Civilian Conservation Corps
DNPS	Delaware North Park Services
FS	Forest Service
GSNM	Giant Sequoia National Monument
HST	High Sierra Trail
INF	Inyo National Forest
JMT	John Muir Trail
KCNP	Kings Canyon National Park
KCPS	Kings Canyon Park Services Co.
NPS	National Park Service
PCT	Pacific Crest Trail
quad(s)	quadrangle (usually refers to 7.5 minute USGS maps)
RD	Ranger District
S&KCNP	Sequoia and Kings Canyon national parks
SNHA	Sequoia Natural History Association
SNP	Sequoia National Park
USFS	United States Forest Service
USGS	United States Geological Survey

APPENDIX

Quick Guide to Frequently Called Numbers and Websites

General	
Campground Reservations (NPS)	(800) 365-2267
Campground Reservations (USFS)	(877) 444-6777
Caltrans (Road Conditions)	(800) 427-7623
The Map Center	(510) 841-MAPS (6277)
Wilderness Press	(800) 443-7227

Inyo National Forest	
Information	(760) 873-2400
Mt. Whitney RD	(760) 876-6200
White Mountain RD	(760) 873-2500
Wilderness Permits	(760) 873-2483; Fax (760) 873-2484

Lodging	
DNPS	(888) 252-5757
Kings Canyon Lodge	(866) KCANYON (522-6966)
KCPS	(559) 335-5500
Montecito-Sequoia Lodge	(800) 227-9900
Silver City Resort	(559) 561-3223 or (805) 528-2730 (winter)

Sequoia & Kings Canyon national parks	
Information	(559) 565-3341
Wilderness Permits	(559) 565-3708; Fax (559) 565-4239
The Sequoia Fund	(559) 739-1668; Fax (559) 739-1680
Sequoia Natural History Assoc.	(559) 565-3759; Fax (559) 565-3728
Sequoia National Forest Information	(559) 338-2251
Hume Lake RD	(559) 338-2251

Sierra National Forest	
Information	(559) 855-5360
Pineridge RD	(559) 855-5360
USGS	(800) ASK-USGS (275-8747)
Field Station	(559) 565-3171

Websites	
Caltrans (road conditions)	www.dot.ca.gov/hq/roadinfo/
Inyo National Forest	www.fs.fed.us/r5/inyo/
Lodging (DNPS)	www.visitsequoia.com
Lodging (KCPS)	www.sequoia-kingscayon.com
Montecito-Sequoia Lodge	www.montecitosequoia.com
Sequoia & Kings Canyon national parks	http://nps.gov/seki/
The Sequoia Fund	www.sequoiafund.org
Sequoia National Forest	www.fs.fed.us/r5/sequoia/
Sequoia Natural History Assoc.	www.sequoiahistory.org
Sierra National Forest	www.fs.fed.us/r5/sierra/
Silver City Resort	www.silvercityresort.com
USGS	www.usgs.gov/
Wilderness Permits (INF)	www.fs.fed.us/r5/inyo/passespermits/index.html
Wilderness Press	www.wildernesspress.com

Bibliography and Suggested Reading

Arnot, Phil. 1996. *High Sierra, John Muir's Range of Light*. San Carlos, CA: Wide World Publishing/Tetra.

Backhurst, Paul, Editor. 2001. *Backpacking California*. Berkeley, CA: Wilderness Press.

Browning, Peter. 1991. *Place Names of the Sierra Nevada*. Berkeley, CA: Wilderness Press.

Cutter, Ralph. 1991. *Sierra Trout Guide*. Portland, OR: Frank Amato Publications.

Dilslayer, Larry M. and William C. Tweed. 1990. *Challenge of the Big Trees*. Three Rivers, CA: Sequoia Natural History Association.

Farquhar, Francis P. 1965. *History of the Sierra Nevada*. Berkeley, CA: University of California Press.

Felzer, Ron. 1992. *High Sierra Hiking Guide: Mineral King*. 3rd Ed. Berkeley, CA: Wilderness Press.

Horn, Elizabeth L. 1998. *Sierra Nevada Wildflowers*. Missoula, MT: Mountain Press Publishing Co.

Jackson, Louise A. 1988. Buelah, *A Biography of the Mineral King Valley of California*. Tucson, AZ: Westernlore Press.

Jenkins, J.C. and Ruby Johnson Jenkins. 1992. *Exploring the Southern Sierra: East Side,* 3rd Ed. Berkeley, CA: Wilderness Press.

Jenkins, J.C. and Ruby Johnson Jenkins. 1995. *Exploring the Southern Sierra: West Side,* 3rd Ed. Berkeley, CA: Wilderness Press.

Johnston, Verna R. 1994. *California Forests and Woodlands, A Natural History.* Berkeley, CA: University of California Press.

Johnston, Verna R. 1998. *Sierra Nevada, The Naturalist's Companion*, Revised Edition. Berkeley, CA: University of California Press.

Krist, John. 1993. *50 Best Short Hikes in Yosemite and Sequoia/Kings Canyon*. Berkeley, CA: Wilderness Press.

Moore, James G. 2000. *Exploring the Highest Sierra*. Stanford, CA: Stanford University Press.

Morey, Kathy. 2002. *Hot Showers, Soft Beds, and Dayhikes in the Sierra Nevada,* 2nd Ed. Berkeley, CA: Wilderness Press.

Petrides, George A. and Olivia Petrides. 1998. *Western Trees*. New York: Houghton Mifflin.

Robinson, John W. and Andy Selters. 1986. *High Sierra Hiking Guide: Mt. Goddard.* 3rd Ed. Berkeley, CA: Wilderness Press.

Robinson, John W. 1974. *High Sierra Hiking Guide: Mt. Pinchot.* Berkeley, CA: Wilderness Press.

Roper, Steve. 1976. *The Climber's Guide to the High Sierra.* San Francisco, CA: Sierra Club Books.

Roper, Steve. 1997. *Sierra High Route, Traversing Timberline Country.* Seattle, WA: The Mountaineers.

Schaffer, Jeffrey P., Ben Schifrin, Thomas Winnett and Ruby Johnson Jenkins. 2002. *Pacific Crest Trail.* Berkeley, CA: Wilderness Press.

Secor, R.J. 1992. *The High Sierra, Peaks, Passes, and Trails.* Seattle, WA: The Mountaineers.

Selters, Andy. 1987. *High Sierra Hiking Guide: Triple Divide Peak,* 2nd Ed. Berkeley, CA: Wilderness Press.

Smith, Genny, Ed. 2000. *Sierra East, Edge of the Great Basin.* Berkeley, CA: University of California Press.

Sorensen, Steve. 1991. *Day Hiking Sequoia,* 2nd Ed. Three Rivers, CA: Fuyu Press.

Spring, Vicky. 1995. *100 Hikes in California's Central Sierra & Coast Range.* Seattle, WA: The Mountaineers.

Stone, Robert. 2000. *Day Hikes in Sequoia and Kings Canyon National Parks.* Red Lodge, MT: Day Hike Books, Inc.

Strong, Douglas H. 2000. *From Pioneers to Preservationists, A Brief History of Sequoia and Kings Canyon National Parks.* Three Rivers, CA: Sequoia Natural History Association.

Tweed, William. 1986. *Beneath the Giants, A Guide to the Moro Rock-Crescent Meadow Road of Sequoia National Park.* Three Rivers, CA: Sequoia Natural History Association.

Tweed, William.1986. *Kaweah Remembered.* Three Rivers, CA: Sequoia Natural History Association.

Weeden, Norman F. 1996. *A Sierra Nevada Flora,* 4th Ed. Berkeley, CA: Wilderness Press.

Whitney, Stephen. 1979. *A Sierra Club Naturalist's Guide.* San Francisco, CA: Sierra Club.

Winnett, Thomas with Melanie Findling. 1994. *Backpacking Basics,* 4th Ed. Berkeley, CA: Wilderness Press.

Winnett, Thomas and Kathy Morey. 1998. *Guide to the John Muir Trail.* Berkeley, CA: Wilderness Press.

Winnett, Thomas. 2001. *Hikers Guide to the High Sierra: Mt. Whitney.* 3rd Ed. Berkeley, CA: Wilderness Press.

Winnett, Thomas, Jason Winnett, Kathy Morey and Lyn Haber. 2001. *Sierra South, 100 Backcountry Trips in California's Sierra,* 7th Ed. Berkeley, CA: Wilderness Press.

Wuerthner, George. 1993. *California's Sierra Nevada.* Helena, MT: American & World Geographic Publishing.

INDEX

About the Author

Mike was raised in the suburbs of east Portland, Oregon, in the shadow of Mt. Hood (whenever the cloudy Pacific Northwest skies cleared enough to allow such things as shadows). His mother never learned to drive, so walking was a way of life for her, as it was for her young son in tow. As a teenager with access to a car, Mike took advantage of his new mobility to explore further afield, and began hiking, backpacking, and climbing in the Cascades of Oregon and Washington. He continued these interests as a young adult with a group of buddies from Seattle Pacific University. After acquiring a BA from SPU, he married his wife, Robin, and settled down in Seattle for a couple of years while continuing his outdoor pursuits.

Mike and his wife soon left the greenery of the Pacific Northwest to relocate to the high desert of Reno, Nevada. The mountains lured Mike first to the Tahoe Sierra, and later down the thoroughfare of U.S. 395 to the east side of the High Sierra. The aesthetic beauty of the Sierra, combined with the typically sunny California skies, opened the door to many fine adventures. However, his forays were not limited to the Sierra, as over the years several extended trips led him away from Reno to numerous wild areas across the West.

In the early 1990s, Mike left his last "real" job with an engineering firm, and began writing about the places he had visited. His first project for Wilderness Press was an update and expansion of Luther Linkhart's classic guide, *The Trinity Alps*, which became a third edition in 1994 (now an updated fourth edition). *Nevada Wilderness Areas and Great Basin National Park* appeared in 1997, followed by the *Snowshoe Trails* series (Tahoe in 1998, Yosemite in 1999, and California in 2001). Mike was also a contributor to *Backpacking California*, published in 2001. In addition to his work with Wilderness Press, he has written articles for *Sunset*, *Backpacker*, and the *Reno Gazette-Journal*. As a part-time instructor, Mike passes on his accrued outdoor wisdom to students in hiking, backpacking and snowshoeing classes at Truckee Meadows Community College.

Current projects include, *Afoot and Afield in Reno and Lake Tahoe*, *Backpacking Nevada*, and *50 Best Short Hikes in Nevada*.

Mike continues to live in Reno with Robin and their two boys, David and Stephen, along with their yellow lab, Barkley.